In The Shadow Of The Wizard

Rainbow

1975-1976

Jerry Bloom

WP
WYMER
PUBLISHING
Bedford, England

First published in Great Britain in 2020
by Wymer Publishing
www.wymerpublishing.co.uk
Tel: 01234 326691
Wymer Publishing is a trading name of Wymer (UK) Ltd

ISBN: 978-1-912782-41-3

Every effort has been made to trace the copyright holders of the
photographs in this book but some were unreachable. We would
be grateful if the photographers concerned would contact us.

Design by 1016 Sarpsborg
Printed by Imago Group.

A catalogue record for this book is available from the British Library.

This hardback is a limited edition of 1,000.

Copies one through two hundred and fifty include a memorabilia pack.
(The first fifty copies with an additional A3 advertising poster as illustrated on page 14)

ROLL OF HONOUR

Wymer Publishing duly acknowledges the following people who all put their faith in this publication by pre-ordering it:

Michael Abram
Mario Abud
Allen Alberg
Mike Albero
Arjen Alkemade
Martin Ambrose
Cristian Ambrosio
Kjell Andersson
Chuck Aragon
Victor Arduini
Etsuko Azuma
Jan Backenroth
Steve Baker
Mike Basic
Michael Bauer
Matt Beaman
Ritchie Bee
John Bell
Dean Bennett
Michael Bennett
Michael Berg
Fabio Betti
Peter Biks
Michael Bimonte
Robert Blake
Nils Boothe
Tim Bootsman
Jamie Bow
Samuel Bowman
Patrick Brandts
Jeff BreisHeim
David M. Brinley
Marlin Brown
Mark Brown
Stuart Brown
Douglas Brown
Andrew Brown
Lester Bruzik
Jörgen Bryngnäs
Dennis Butchek
Cedric Cabrera
Stephen Capp
Shane Carroll
Joel Casso
Massimiliano Cervetti
Cherdchai Chaivaivid
Paul Champelovier
Mariia Chernysh
Wesley Chu
Sergio Cianca
Dominic Ciliberto
Andy Clark
Bob Clements
Steve Clouting
Lawrence Cochran
Laurence Cohen
Bruce Collie
Andy Copping
Ralf Cordes
Mark Craig
Guy Creswell
László Cselőtei
Dougie Currie
Bjørn Dalvang
Olaf Dausch
Francesc de Anta Montardit
Kees de Leeuw
Jeffrey DeMaso
Jason Dickinson
Kevin Dixon
Konrad Doerflinger
Alvaro Dominguez
Igor Duerloo
Neil Duncan
Mark Durbin
David Edwards
Brad Erb
Scott Ewings
Martin Ferguson
Nick Finlinson
Andy Fitzsimmons
Paul Flecklin
Andrew Flux
Gary Flye
Michael Fodorán
Sven Forsell
Chris Frankum
Sam Friedman
Alan Frizzell
John Gac
George Galanis
Mike Galway
Friedrich Geller
Patryk Generalczyk
Christian Gerken
Michael Giammanco
Adrian Gilliatt-Wall
Michael Gilling
Nicolas "Minstrel at Home" Gobet
Frank Gomez
Marco Gonzales
Heinz Gottwald
Hilton Gowar
Mark Anthony Gregory
Patrick Griffiths
Urban Gustafsson
Jason Guttridge
Bodo Guyet
Robin Haddon
Howard Haider
Martin Halsall
John Handy
Jeff Hano
Andrew Hardman
Ryan Harmon
Greg Harrop
Marcel Hartenberg
Jacob Hastedt
John Hatchard
Thomas Healy
Michael Hernandez
Palle Hichmann
Daniel Hidalgo
Yoshihiro Higuchi
Jez Hindle
Andrew Howard
Karl-Heinz Huenecke
David Hughes
Paul Hughes
Steve Hunt
Thomas Inman
Dan Irwin
Michael Jacobs
Andrew James
Marc Janssen
Ib Jensen
Knut Morten Johansen
Jay John
Frank Johow
David Jones
Richard Jones
Kenneth Jorgensen
Manu Juanes
Andrew Kahn
Peter Kannapin
Steve Karlsson
Kazuyasu Kawakami
Dimitris Kazantzis
Zoran Kepcija
Michael Kicker
Kenny Kincaid
Thomas Klapper
Krzysztof Korczak
Vladimiras Kovaliovas
Bernt Kuepper
Arkady Kurin
Todd Ladner
Phil Lageat
Johannes Lampert
Torbjörn Larsson
Mats Larsson
Richard Lawson
Jeff Lemas
Tuomo Leskinen
Felix Lethmate
Mats Leven
David Lewins
Søren Lindberg
Steven Lobmeier
Wout Lodder
Fabio Loli
Mario Lucchi
Roland Lutz
Tomohiro Makihara
Raul Mateos
Neil Maughan
Dmitry Mayorov
Dennis McDonnell
Cuyler McGinley
Craig McGovern
Ronnie McGowan
Chris McMillan
Michael Meissner
Gene Merriman
Vincent Messina
Stephen Miguelez
Roberto Mijat
Glen Miller
Yoshito Mimasu
Tim Mitchell
Kevin Moore
Roy Morley
Chris Morrison
Giles Morrison
Mark Morrissey
Hisayuki Nagase
Steve Nej
Slava Nekrasov
Adrian Nightingale
Mark Nolde
Tom Noles
Andy Nordlander
Martin Oberg
James Osinski
Naoki Otsuka
Philip Ouimet
Kyle Parrish
Lee Parsons
Wayne Pashley
Mark Pearce
Martti Pesso
Nick Peters
Jürgen Piskorowski
Graham Pope
Alex Pritsker
Alexander Pronyakin
Paul Puljiz
Anton Rakovskiy
Fabio Ramponi
Ritchie Randall
Trevor Rangitsch
Peter Raschk
Per Rasmussen
Kevin Re LoVullo
Jochen Reh
Carlos Fernandez Rodríguez
Héctor Rodríguez Huerta
Jacques Rolfo
Karin Rummler
Matti Ruotsala
Moray Russell
Heiko M. Rust
John Saathoff
Miguel Angel Marin Sanchez
Pauline Sandell
Enrico Scalco
Michael Schmid
Andree Schneider
CJ Scioscia
Rod Sein
Richard Selby
Nathan Sensicall
Giuseppe Serrao
Frank Sheppard
Daniel Shumac
Kevyn Silverman
Terence Singerline
Gert Skjødt
Callum Smail
Gary Smith
Arthur Smith
David Smith
Craig Smith
Matthew Smith
Stian Smith Hansen
Thomas Sobiech
Erling Solem
Paul Spiering
Anthony Spina
Andreas Spitznagel
Joe St. Laurent
Neil Stanley
Jan Atle Steinsland
Kenneth Stewart
Denis St-Germain
Michael Stickney
Jacqueline Stokes
Charlotte Stone
Martin Strohbeck
Johan Stromqvist
Joe Stump
Joachim Stumpf
Anthony Sudworth
Hans-Ulrich Surburg
Michael Swift
Chris Temby
Daniel Tepper
Konstantinos Theodorakakos
Paul Thompson
Calum Trail
Andrea Turrell
Nick Tyminski
Jeannette Ullmann-Lopez
Rob van der Loo
Johan van Enk
Israel Vega
Alex Veil
Eddy Vermieren
Stephan Waldhart
Kevin Walkley
Allan Watkins
Peter Weber
Andreas Weigelt
Martin Weirauch
Mark Welch
Kiah West
Winfried Wieland
Markus Winterhalter
Brian Wismer
Dylan Anthony Wix of Delaware US
Hagen Wolf
David Wolk
Scott A. Wood
Brian Worth
Paul Wren
William Wrenn
Stephen Wunrow
Joseph Yaple
Hiroko Yono
Paul Zagaglioni
Jean Pascal Zanders
Kevin Zimka
Mark Zyk

CONTENTS

Preface

When Ritchie Blackmore made the decision to quit Deep Purple in order to pursue a direction with more personal control, he did so at a point where Deep Purple's success was at an all time high. The continued touring and album releases had delivered riches that most people can only dream of, but few rarely attain.

But if on the face of it, the decision would appear to most people to be financially questionable, the income stream from the Deep Purple catalogue was still substantial and would remain so. Just two years after leaving Purple, the mechanical royalties for the Deep Purple back catalogue for that financial year (1977) amounted to three quarters of a million. Equivalent today to a figure in excess of £4.6million. Whilst it has to be factored in that this is before tax; and divided amongst all the appropriate musicians and managers; add to that publishing royalties as well as performance fees and record sales attained with Rainbow, and it's clear to see that Blackmore had no reason to fear pursuing a new direction. Indeed, he was forthright about his financial situation when speaking to the *Los Angeles Times*, later that year: "I've made plenty of money so I didn't want to go on in a situation I disliked. I wanted to get out before I got too bitter."

In fact, all the panic and concern came from within the Deep Purple organisation. In February 1975, accountant Bill Reid relayed to the management a conversation he'd had with Ritchie in a letter in which he said, "*during my talk with Ritchie I asked him what his attitude was towards the future of Deep Purple on the assumption that the Ritchie and Ronnie single and album would be successful. As always Ritchie was honest from which it emerged that he felt he could only fulfil his obligation to Deep Purple until the end of this year, difficult though this would be as he would be required inevitably to tour in order to promote record sales. It follows that someone to replace Ritchie will have to be found, an extremely difficult if not impossible task — or both Deep Purple (Overseas) Ltd. and Hec Enterprises Ltd. will be in breach of their contracts with Warner Bros. and EMI/Interton as neither company would be able to produce the remaining Deep Purple albums under the contract. Whether or not Ritchie will change his mind as events emerge remains to be seen, but the task of the management is to consider all the implications, of which at this point in time I do not think anyone other than those to whom this letter is going is aware — with the possible exception of Bruce who has probably worked it out for himself.*"

As it turned out, Ritchie brought his decision forward after the last show in Paris on 7th April 1975. The following month, the first Deep Purple UK compilation album *24 Carat Purple* was released, consisting entirely of tracks from the classic MKII line-up. By July, even though his replacement Tommy Bolin was in place, it was announced that another album made up of recordings from Ritchie's last shows with the band was to be released (it eventually materialised in November the following year). It was suggestive of a lack of confidence in Deep Purple's future without him.

Also by the time that Blackmore quit Purple, the management team had invested in numerous projects, most of which Blackmore stood to share from. For example, a company called Soundacre Ltd. had been set up, investing money from the band's earnings in order to build and sell villas in Spain. A complex web of companies had been created, as well as bank accounts all around the world where the vast sums they were earning were deposited.

Not all investments bore fruit however. Such as an aborted film project that £70,000 was invested into (equivalent to more than £400,000 today) — (see my book, *Deep Purple A Matter of Fact* for more on that story).

From the outset, Purple's touring in America — without doubt their biggest market — had been arranged in conjunction with the American Talent International Agency. The company's Vice President was Bruce Payne. As America proved to be the band's biggest market, Deep Purple paid substantial commissions to the agency.

By 1974 Deep Purple (Overseas) Ltd. invested in a new company Thames Talent with Payne as its sole president. This meant that Deep Purple (Overseas) Ltd. would receive 50% of profits as well as a considerable saving in agency fees. As well as arranging Purple's tours and subsequently Rainbow's, Thames Talent was also arranging US tours for numerous other artists including Nazareth, Be Bop Deluxe and Thin Lizzy. Sadly, Thames Talent's income was far outweighed by expenses and Purple's investment was on shaky ground as it looked for a time as if Thames Talent could go into administration.

How much interest Blackmore took in the financial side of things is undetermined and in keeping with most musicians and creative people, they generally focus on their art and leave the other stuff to management. So, whilst money was flying around left, right and centre, Blackmore had clearly become disillusioned with Purple.

Even though he had been instrumental in instigating change that saw him rejuvenated for *Burn*, his restlessness had got the better of him by the time that the follow-up *Stormbringer* was made in 1974. In interviews at the time, Blackmore also confessed to taking his eye off the ball as his marriage to Babs had broken down and divorce proceedings were in place.

Amidst this background emerged Blackmore's new band. For some fans, musically Rainbow eclipsed Purple — at least in that first period of the band with Ronnie James Dio on vocals and Cozy Powell on drums — certainly a musical tour de force; the live performances during that period were exceptional.

Since I wrote my full Blackmore biography *Black Knight*, fifteen years ago, access to management documents written at the time that I previously was unaware of has allowed additional information to be added, as well as correcting the chronology of some events.

This book explores the start of Rainbow in 1975 when Blackmore recorded his "solo" album before setting off on his last tour with Purple, through to the end of the following year, by which time in his career he had left an indelible mark on the music scene with a band for the second time.

1975

RITCHIE BLACKMORE'S
R-A-I-N-B-O-W
Including the forthcoming single
"Man On The Silver Mountain" OYR 103
RITCHIE BLACKMORE'S RAINBOW
Oyster Records
Marketed by EMI Records
Album OYA 2001
Cassette TC-OYA 2001
Cartidge 8X-OYA 2001

1.
It's Only Been An Hour: Ritchie Blackmore's Rainbow

"My favourite rock track on the album is 'Sixteenth Century Greensleeves'. It was written by Robin Hood of Sherwood Forest. I went to the door one night and there was an arrow in the door holding a piece of paper, and it had this song written on it. There was a note attached reading, 'Please record this song or I'll shoot you'."

There's a case to be had for suggesting that Rainbow's roots can be traced back to 1972. Some might even say 1971 when Blackmore went into the studio for what are referred to as the "Baby Face" sessions with Ian Paice plus Phil Lynott of Thin Lizzy. It showed there was an indication that Blackmore was already getting restless in Deep Purple but 1972 was the year that Ritchie first met Ronnie James Dio.

During Deep Purple's second American tour of that year, Ritchie was struck down with hepatitis, necessitating the postponement of the remaining tour dates as well as three gigs planned for Japan in May.

Raymond D'addario, then a roadie for a small-time American band called Elf recalled, "We'd done an album and it was a really funny story because the guy who was booking Purple at the time was Ronnie's manager Bruce Payne and he set up an audition in New York City with Columbia Records for Elf so we were going to do that. In the meantime Purple had come over to do a tour and Ritchie got hepatitis and went back to England to get healthy and they got Randy California – played one or two gigs and they said 'nah forget it, we're knocking it on the head until Ritchie's healthy again.' So Roger and Ian Paice come to New York City and Bruce brings them to the audition and they go 'whoa that band's great.' Bruce said, 'you wanna produce them?' So three weeks later in Warren, Georgia, Bruce is having Ian Paice and Roger Glover produce the band and a month later we were back touring with Purple. We did a lot of touring with them. That's how he got really familiar with Ronnie. You could tell Ritchie liked Ronnie's voice. When I first started working for them Gillan was still in the band and it was around the time when Ian and Ritchie weren't speaking."

Blackmore talked about his first encounters with Elf in an interview with Steve Rosen in June 1975: "It started first of all with Roger Glover and Ian Paice who had produced Elf. I never heard the LP but Roger and Ian both said how good the band were. Elf were signed to Purple Records and then we met them on the tour in America and they used to support us a lot on the American tours. We got to be friendly and I noticed in particular the singer. It was his style and the way he was singing."

Elf started supporting Purple that summer during a US tour of the East Coast although the band's debut album wasn't released until December. The tour was also pivotal in Blackmore's love life. At Purple's show at Gaelic Park in the Bronx, New York City on 31st August he met a young operatically trained vocalist Judith Feinstein, who was trying her luck with pop music under the stage name of Shoshana. She recalled in an interview in 2017: "One of my first bands, a very good band was called Uncas named after the *Last Of The Mohicans*. We played Jefferson Airplane, The Doors, Grand Funk, Cold Blood, Moody Blues, Yes, The Beatles. Everything from the era of the sixties and early seventies. The drummer and I loved Deep Purple and would attend many concerts one of which (the Bronx) is where I met Ritchie. I especially admired Jon Lord's playing. I had studied classical piano since age nine and I knew that Jon Lord was classically trained, which is what drew me to Deep Purple, to begin with. I loved the sound and energy of Deep Purple."

Ritchie and Judith at his apartment in California

Ritchie jamming with Judith's band at the Gladiator Club, Providence, December 1974

Judith Feinstein, otherwise known as Shoshana at Ritchie's House in Camberley, Surrey in 1974

Despite being married, Blackmore appeared to be immediately besotted with Feinstein. "I was standing outside waiting for the band to play. I had black hair down to my waist, a scarf tied around my breasts and a long flowing skirt on. I looked like a very exotic Gypsy. Ritchie came up to me immediately as he was perusing the audience and invited me backstage. That is when it began... our romance. We communicated through the mail and phone calls. When we met, we had an immediate connection that I was rather surprised about because I considered Ritchie to be a rather dark brooding type of guy (he was) but I must have brought something out in him that was vulnerable and more gentle."

Young, and naïve, Judith claims she was loyal to Blackmore despite what she saw as his insecurities and suspicious nature. Whilst they kept in touch, Blackmore had to continue touring and recording but they met again on 23rd May 1973 when Purple played at the Civic Centre, in Providence, Rhode Island. Blackmore arranged for her to be taken to the show in a limo and afterwards she spent the evening back at his hotel suite. In the morning Ritchie broke the news to her that he was married. Feeling angry and hurt, Judith left and told him she never wanted to see him again.

Fast forward to April 1974 and Deep Purple is back in the States, touring with the new line-up in promotion of the *Burn* album. In the intervening time Feinstein had moved from the North East to Los

Angeles and with a friend had decided to go to the California Jam — confident that she would be able to get her and her friend in through her past connection. Having somehow bypassed security, the next obstacle was a ten-foot fence which she climbed over to get onto the tarmac on the road leading to the venue. By some quirk of fate, just as she had grounded on the other side, a black limo was heading towards her. It stops. Unbelievably, Ritchie opened the door, as surprised as she was. "He greets me with, 'well hello,' or something like that, but before he could say another word I replied, 'Hello Richard (I never called him Ritchie, he was Richard to me) it's me, Judith. (Richard always called me Judith never Shoshana) I want to apologise to you for being such a bitch last time we were together.' He wondered how I suddenly reappeared in front of him and he asked, 'Where in the world did you come from?' with a big smile on his face and simply said, 'get in'."

Judith spent the rest of the time with Ritchie, watching the show from the wings and after his explosive finale, they were quickly whisked out of the county. "We had to fly via helicopter. Well, this is exciting — a bit like MI6, *James Bond* style. Next moment we are at the Beverly Wilshire Hotel and off I go with Richard into his suite," she recalled.

After the tour concluded with two further gigs, Ritchie had his assistant Ian Broad drive him to Judith's apartment where he spent the next few days together with her, including his twenty-ninth birthday on 14th April. With a UK tour starting on the 18th, Ritchie had to leave and asked her to go back to England with him. With his wife Babs having stayed in Los Angeles, Blackmore and Feinstein lived together for a short while in Blackmore's house in Camberley in Surrey.

Of her own admission Feinstein accepts that they were both headstrong and independent and frequently clashed — even about music theory. She recalls that they would argue about many things including who the all-time best composer was! Ritchie was adamant it was Bach, with whom he had become particularly enamoured and whose music he would frequently play on his guitar at home.

According to her memory he talked about leaving Deep Purple and starting a new project with his mind set on Bad Company's Paul Rodgers. Whilst clearly that had been the case before Coverdale had joined Purple, was he really considering Rodgers again for what would become Rainbow? Judith also suggested he could use a female vocalist such as herself, but Ritchie told her he believed a woman's voice wasn't powerful enough to front a rock band. She also recalls that Blackmore expressed his interest in doing a renaissance project and he was becoming quite proficient on the cello.

1974 also saw Elf becoming more embroiled into the Deep Purple machine, having signed to both Purple's record label and publishing company for what would be their second album, *Carolina County Ball*, produced by Roger Glover in England. The first album had not been released in Europe apart from the Netherlands. *Carolina County Ball* gave Elf added exposure throughout Europe and was released in April to coincide with their support slot on Purple's April/May UK tour.

This second album also saw a change of line-up, with Craig Gruber brought in on bass — Dio had played the bass on the first album. There was also a change of guitarist with Steve Edwards replacing Dio's cousin Dave Feinstein. All of the songs on the album were joint compositions by Dio and keyboard player Mickey Lee Soule.

Although information is sketchy, it's possible that during those first few months of 1974 that Elf spent in the UK, the first seeds of what became Rainbow were planted. As mentioned elsewhere in this tome, there is documentation from within the Purple organisation that mentions a Blackmore and Dio recording session at Gillan's Kingsway Recorders. In his interview with Steve Rosen the following year, Blackmore said, "We got to be friends and then Ronnie was in a lot of sessions in England. I listened to this single called 'Black Sheep Of The Family' and I asked Purple if they wanted to do it on the next LP and they said they didn't want to do anybody else's songs. I really wanted to do this song. I said to Ronnie when I got him around one night and I got him drunk, 'Do you fancy doing it?' and he said, 'Yeah, I might sing it.' He got the song off in about a half an hour. Then we went into the studio and we put it down. It sounded great and that was what started it." This suggests a session before *Stormbringer* was recorded in August. Following the *Burn* tour Purple largely had a couple of months break and it is possible that Blackmore and Dio did something around this time.

1974 concluded for Deep Purple with another huge American tour in November and December, with Judith travelling with Ritchie, his marriage by now, irreconcilable. For this tour Purple had two support acts, the ever-dependable Elf and the emerging English, Birmingham based Electric Light Orchestra. Ritchie soon approached ELO cellist Hugh McDowell to discuss the instrument as the now sadly deceased musician relayed to the author in 2005: "It must have been the first concert we supported them on that tour. After the concert he started talking about how he liked the cello, and how he liked things like Pachelbel's Canon, the whole style of it. I suggested I could show him a couple of lessons or at least give him ideas. At some point during the tour we found a little town and he had a bit of a go. Being very musical, with a great ear it all went very well. I don't think we did a huge amount on the actual tour but sometime after that tour we got together a few times and I gave him a couple of lessons. It might have been at his old house in the Hollywood Hills. It might have been Babs' house at that point. I seem to remember going up there a couple of times and gave him lessons. He was always interested in baroque music."

Ritchie was still fixated with doing his own version of Quatermass' 'Black Sheep Of The Family' and decided to record it as a solo single. During the tour, he found time to go into a studio with Ronnie Dio to lay down the track. D'addario recalls that, "in Minneapolis there were a couple of days off and he took Elf into a studio and they recorded a couple of tracks. It was more like a test for Ronnie before he left the band."

The previous gig had been in Cleveland and when interviewed in 2009 about this time, Craig Gruber can be forgiven for recalling the event as having taken place in Cleveland, although it was definitely in Minneapolis: "I remember we were in Cleveland, Ohio when Colin, our road manager said, 'Quick, get in the car. We're going to the studio today.' And I said, 'What are you fucking talking about? We're playing tonight.' He said, 'No. We've booked time in the studio. We've only got about four hours and we've got to get back to get a sound check. Ritchie and Ronnie have written a song and we're going to go in and record it.' What? So anyway, so we jump in the car."

"We went to this kind of shitty, crummy studio, downtown Cleveland, and Ritchie comes in, starts playing this riff. All right — he's smiling, he's kind of really super friendly, and it's really out of character for him. Ronnie said, 'We wrote this song, Craig. It's called 'Sixteenth Century Greensleeves', which is one Ritchie and I had been working on. And we're just going to put it out as a single, and it's going to be on Ritchie's solo album,' and I went, 'Wow, that's fucking amazing. We're going to back Ritchie Blackmore.' We knocked it out in about an hour. It came out great. There's some really cool stuff in it."

Lyrically, Dio was interested in the same historical periods that Ritchie was now being drawn to and it didn't take long for the pair to discover a musical chemistry. Having done some work on the songs in Minneapolis, Hugh McDowell remembers that Ritchie also asked him to help out with the recordings a few days later on 12th December. "We were around the Florida area in Tampa. I remember he'd got these two-inch master multi track tapes and Ronnie Dio came along. It was a day off on the tour and I put down some cello tracks. We spent a few hours there doing that. The impression I got was that he loved the instrument and the sonorities of it, a basic attraction in that sense. I think it was very much a personal interest."

In January 1975, Elf travelled to London, where they recorded their third album *Trying To Burn The Sun* at Kingsway Recorders, once again with Roger Glover producing. The band by now had an additional member in percussionist Mark Nauseef — like the rest of the band, Nauseef also hailed from Cortland, New York.

In the same month, Deep Purple performed a one-off show in Australia, after which Ritchie took the opportunity to lay down an album's worth of material with Ronnie. With Ritchie now living in Oxnard in California, he requested that Rob Cooksey — a roadie who had now gravitated to part of the management team — book seven days of studio time at the Record Plant in Los Angeles, commencing on 13th February with the view to completing an album.

When news of this reached accountant Bill Reid, he wrote a letter to Deep Purple's solicitor Richard Bagehot explaining the tax implications if Ritchie went ahead with his plans. Already concerned that the session in Minneapolis would result in worldwide royalties being taxed in America, more importantly, advice from their US representatives suggested that retrospective royalties could be taxed at US rates as well.

Once this was explained to Ritchie he wasted no time in changing his mind about recording in Los Angeles and instead took the opportunity to use Musicland Studios in Munich. Deep Purple had already provisionally booked the studio for their own use but had postponed recording of the follow-up to *Stormbringer* until after the European tour was completed.

The session at Musicland was booked to run from Thursday 20th February through to Sunday 9th March. As Musicland was in the basement of the Arabellahaus Hotel, it provided the suitable residency that was required whilst working on the album.

Ritchie decided that aside from Ronnie — his new songwriting partner — it made sense to use the other Elf members, keyboard player Mickey Lee Soule, drummer Gary Driscoll and bassist Craig Gruber, although initially Soule was against doing it: "At that time Ritchie wanted to do a solo project and it was only really going to be a couple of songs in the beginning but then he decided that he wanted to do a whole album so he asked our band to play on the album for him and we did that. So, it was actually Ritchie's band but he sort of took the whole band Elf along. I was actually the only one that didn't want to do it (laughs). We had spent quite a long time slowly working our way up the ladder and we had a couple of albums out and the record company that we had at the time was just getting ready to sink some time and energy into us. We had a couple of full page ads in *Rolling Stone* and you know, everybody saw the Rainbow thing as instant success or instant money but I kind of looked at it like, 'Well, we have been trying so long and so hard to do this on our own and we are very close now.' And to be honest, it was the music, I mean, Rainbow and Ritchie's music is pretty much guitar music and I am a keyboard player."

Mickey Lee Soule was clearly looking at things from a personal perspective as he was a major part of Elf. "I wrote half of the songs with Ronnie, we wrote the songs and pretty much gave direction to the band so it was a nice feeling to see a little bit of success come from that and then it kind of went away as soon as we formed Rainbow. It was pretty much dead at that point. As soon as Blackmore wanted to form the band as a "band" as opposed to just a solo project then I was outvoted. Everyone else wanted to do it and I didn't so I went along with it and that is how the first Rainbow happened but it didn't last too long in that form."

With Bruce Payne managing Elf, it was agreed with Deep Purple's management that Ronnie would have a 20% share of record sale royalties, but the other three did the album on a session basis. It was also agreed that, should the record be successful, and a second album was made, that Ronnie would receive a greater share on it.

But in general the situation wasn't one that sat comfortably with Deep Purple (Overseas) Ltd. Although they had known and worked with Payne for many years, the general rule of thumb was that any musicians that came into the "family" would be managed by DPO. The fact that Dio was managed by Payne, meant that the more Dio earned, the more his manager earned (rather than the DPO management). It caused conflict as both management companies worked on different commission rates.

To further muddy the waters, DPO was due to supply Elf's Roger Glover produced, and therefore DPO Production *Trying To Burn The Sun*, to MGM Records in America. With the potential of another album featuring Elf clashing with it, it caused additional complications over publishing rights.

However, the business side of things to one side, Ritchie, Ronnie, Mickey, Gary and Craig worked on the album, along with producer and engineer Martin Birch. Ritchie's girlfriend Judith was also in the studio with them. "I was especially thrilled to be working with renowned engineer Martin Birch who engineered most of the Deep Purple LPs," she recalls.

"Working with Martin was an amazing experience. Martin was a down to earth, pleasant fellow always greeting you with a smile. I remember sitting in the control room with him while he was recording Ronnie's vocals or Richard's guitar. I watched everything that he did and Martin would often explain to me what he was doing and why. It was decided by Ronnie and Richard, that I would only sing background vocals on 'Catch The Rainbow' and 'Still I'm Sad'."

But Feinstein also recalls that when she wasn't called upon to do her background vocals, Blackmore had a piano put in a room so that she had something to do when they were working on the rest of the recording.

Aside from 'Black Sheep Of The Family' and 'Still I'm Sad' the rest of the songs were joint Blackmore and Dio compositions although the late Craig Gruber claimed in an interview in 2009 that, "'If You Don't Like Rock 'n' Roll' wasn't initially gonna be on that album because if you listen to the album, it's kind of a misfit song. It was a song that Elf had come up with the riff and partially written it. It was supposed to be at the end of the *Trying to Burn the Sun* album. The album was pretty much done, in the bag, and we had that song left over. We just came up with it too late and it ended up on the *Ritchie Blackmore's Rainbow* album."

The initial studio time was extended by five days and the recordings at Musicland were initially wrapped up on 14th March. Blackmore had the small matter of a Deep Purple European tour to then contend with, starting off behind the Iron Curtain for the first time with two gigs in Yugoslavia commencing two days later.

Purple's tour concluded in Paris on 7th April. Colin Hart who had been a Purple roadie since 1971 but at that time was given the job of working with support band Elf — snapped some photos backstage after the gig that clearly show happiness on the faces of both Ritchie and Ronnie. Hart had instantly agreed to become Rainbow's tour manager when he was asked just before the show.

Ronnie and Colin Hart – Rainbow's newly appointed tour manager backstage at Blackmore's last Purple gig in Paris

JOHN PEEL'S SINGLES EVERY WEEK

sounds

APRIL 26, 1975 12p

Harley — rebel who played the game and won

BLACKMORE TO QUIT PURPLE?

RITCHIE BLACKMORE may split from Deep Purple. Rumours concerning this have been rife for some weeks now, so much so in fact that three weeks ago EMI issued a press release denying the possibility of a break up.

But SOUNDS believes that, following the completion of his solo album 'Rainbow' in Munich, Blackmore may amicably part from Purple and form a band with the musicians who backed him on his solo effort. The remaining Purple members will stay together.

A spokesman from Purple's offices this week said: "The band is splitting, but only for three or four months to enable Ritchie to promote his solo album.

Continued Page 4

WIN 50 ERICS AND 10 GUITARS FREE

Page 31

● RITCHIE BLACMORE

Purple split

FROM PAGE 1

"Also, Jon Lord is going to Germany to record his own classical album and there's a possibility that Glenn Hughes may make an album with David Bowie.

"At the moment they're having a break for a while — you'll hear about the band, obviously, though not necessarily as a unit.

"But if one of the sole ventures really took off—especially by one of the older members of the band who have been with them for five or six years — then it could be that someone could well leave for good."

A-Z OF HEAVY METAL

From Aerosmith to Zeppelin via 100 plus bands: a 4 page special

THIRTEEN VIEWS OF STATUS QUO

sounds

ELTON JOHN AT WEMBLEY

JUNE 21, 1975 12p Australia 40c South A

NEW PURPLE MAN

Blackmore out— Tommy Bolin in

RITCHIE BLACKMORE has left Deep Purple to form a new group called Ritchie Blackmore's Rainbow. Simultaneously Purple have announced that Tommy Bolin, former guitarist with the James Gang, has joined them on lead guitar to replace Blackmore.

Bolin will appear on all Deep Purple albums whilst continuing to record as a solo artist for Nemperor Records. Bolin recently appeared on the Billy Cobham 'Spectrum' album.

● CONTINUED PAGE 2

INSIDE

Tamm

ach Boys Prizes

Ea Pr

PURPLE SPLIT

● FROM PAGE 1

Deep Purple, one of the handful of top world recording acts, will record a new album with Bolin in Munich in August and release the LP around October.

Ritchie Blackmore's Rainbow will release their first album in July and a US tour is set for late Summer or early Autumn. There is a possibility of European gigs before the American dates.

The band consists of the four members of ELF, with whom Blackmore had already been closely associated, as previously reported in SOUNDS. The line-up is: Ronnie Dio vocals, Craig Gruber bass, Gary Driscoll drums, and Mickey Lee Soule keyboards.

● OWING TO an industrial dispute beyond ou control, SOUNDS is la being published t week. We apologise any inconvenience to readers and hop return to normal si publication dat week.

Blackmore: Why I quit Purple

RITCHIE BLACKMORE quit Deep Purple because, he claims, of his laziness. The split between Purple and Blackmore, reported in last week's Melody Maker, ended one of the most productive partnerships in rock. Blackmore was one of the founder members of the band which today ranks as one of the giants.

But, Blackmore tells the MM this week, he was getting lazy in the band. And there were personality clashes which, inevitably, led to the split.

His replacement in Purple, ex-James Gang guitarist Tommy Bolin, will be following two careers. "I will be touring the States with my own band for a while, but there will be no problems," he says. "What's good for Purple is good for me, and we get along very well. Purple are all amazing players, and it's a step forward for me."

● Ritchie Blackmore and Tommy Bolin interivews, see pages 8 and 9.

Ronnie and Gary Driscoll at Ritchie's apartment in Oxnard County, California.

Above right and below: Relaxing in Jamaica where a few overdubs were done for the album.

88Due to the fact that recording needed to be wound up for the tour, the album hadn't been entirely completed. The additional work that was done on it a month later has something of a Spinal Tap touch to it. Blackmore claims they needed to do some vocal overdubs for 'Catch The Rainbow'. Having returned to America, where he now resided, the option to record there was closed off for tax reasons. Blackmore, Dio, Birch and Hart headed off to Jamaica. Hart confirms his passport was stamped on arrival on April 27th 1975: "I believe the studio was Dynamic Sound in Kingston, where The Stones recorded Goats Head Soup. It was quite a shabby place and I remember that Martin Birch had a few problems with the equipment in the studio and we didn't get a whole lot done there."

The minor work done in Jamaica was followed by a brief return to Munich where Birch did the final mix and Blackmore provided a few final overdubs before the tapes were shipped over to Kendun Recorders in California for mastering.

The album was released in August, the first on the new Oyster label (in Europe) and on Polydor in North America and Japan. The cover had a Disney feel to it, not surprising when you realise that the artist David Willardson had already done paintings for Disney and specialised in cartoon imagery. He had also done a Loony Tunes cover for a Warners' album of the cartoon show! But the cover seemed more suitable for children than it did for rock fans. The overall layout of the gatefold sleeve followed the same pattern as all of Purple's gatefold releases from In Rock onwards; a monochrome inside spread, in this instance, adorned with photos by Fin Costello, mainly taken on stage from 1974 shows.

Rainbow gets Cozy

COZY POWELL has definitely joined the new-look Ritchie Blackmore's Rainbow, but it seems doubtful whether the band will make their British debut this year.

Powell was in London last week for a few days, having left rehearsals in California to attend to business matters in Britain. He was due to fly back to Los Angeles on Monday to continue rehearsals with the band, who are still looking for a keyboard player to complete the line-up. As exclusively reported in last week's MM, the singer in Blackmore's new band will be ex-Elf vocalist Ronnie Dio, who sang on the album, which is currently number 16 in the MM charts, and the bassist will be ex-Harlots player Jimmy Bain.

American dates are being set for November, but the change in line-up has caused a postponement of previously planned British gigs that were to take place before the end of the year.

Powell told the MM this week that Strange Brew, the band he has formed with ex-Humble Pie members Greg Ridley and Clem Clempson, was now defunct. He also said that Blackmore's invitation came at a time when he had seriously considered leaving the music business to become a racing driver.

Blackmore's Rainbow are expected to record a second album in the States before going on the road.

■ Last week's MM report about the changing line-up of Ritchie Blackmore's new Rainbow Band may have been a little premature, but the gist of the story was certainly correct as Cozy Powell confirmed in London last week on a lightning visit between bouts of rehearsal in Los Angeles.

■ It was only two weeks ago that Cozy received a call from Blackmore in LA asking him to come over and have a blow. A week earlier Cozy had decided to pack in the music business in favour of a motor racing career and was putting his energies into finding a sponsor for next year's racing season.

■ "Quite literally, I was going to pack it in and try my luck at racing cars," said Cozy in the Purple offices on London's Newman Street. "But I got over there and after three numbers it was all happening. Ritchie liked it. I liked it and so I got the gig."

■ Cozy was flying back to LA on Monday of this week to spend October rehearsing prior to a US tour in November. But a keyboard player has still to be found, according to Cozy, who also confirmed that the vocals will be handled by ex-Elf singer Ronnie James Dio (who sang on Ritchie's album) and that the bassist will be Jimmy Bain.

■ "It'll take us about four weeks to rehearse because there's going to be all sorts of things going on on stage . . . guitars blowing up, drum-kits disintegrating. Ritchie's always been that way inclined and he wants to put a good show on and so do I."

■ New material is being written so the music will comprise both the recently released album and a soon to be recorded album, but Ritchie, apparently, is determined not to play anything from his Deep Purple days. "I know he wants to get right away from all that," said Cozy. "He said that he'd been playing 'Rough And Ready', the Jeff Beck album, and that was the kind of drumming he wanted."

■ Blackmore's admiration for Jeff Beck is widely known, so the future looks bright for both Cozy and his new-found friend.

The music, whilst rockier than *Stormbringer,* and similar to Deep Purple's sound, didn't display the same bite or aggression that albums such as *In Rock*, or even Burn had. But it did show that working within a band structure was still very much Blackmore's chosen aim, albeit with different styles and ideas thrown in. No attempts at doing a Jeff Beck were evident, except arguably on the instrumental 'Still I'm Sad' that closed the album.

Blackmore was keen to explain his rationale shortly after the album was released; "When we formed Rainbow, Ronnie and I had the same interest in music which were basically medieval classical roots such as Bach, actually the whole LP was inspired by Johann, who was there some of the time. And a lot of the progressions we used were classical progressions. That's not as drastic as it sounds, they're still rock progressions because I believe that Bach even in the sixteenth century (sic) was still playing in a way that was very relative to the way that people are playing today. Which is very rhythmical and we both had the same interest so we tried to incorporate these medieval parts... We used a lot of modes instead of scales. And modes meant we used weird chords. But we found out it worked with a rock backing. We achieved this on about four tracks. And I'm very excited about it because I've never done this before and it's turned out very well."

EXKLUSIV

Blackmore holt sich Super-Drummer

Sensationell! Cozy Powell steigt bei Blackmore ein

Dieser Ritchie Blackmore! Da glaubt man nun, dass der exzentrische Junge mit der scharfen Gitarre bei seiner neuen Gruppe Rainbow endlich das Glück seines Musikerlebens gefunden hat. Man freut sich sogar darüber, denn Blackmore ist, wenn auch oft ein bisschen schwierig, trotz allem ein wahnsinnig netter Kerl. Und kaum hat man sich an den Gedanken gewöhnt, wird man pereits mit neuen Hiobsbotschaften überschwemmt.
Zuerst erreichte uns aus Los Angeles die Nachricht, dass sich Blackmore mit seinen neuen Mitmusikern total überworfen habe und bei Rainbow ausgestiegen sei. Eine Meldung, die sich dann bei näherem Hinsehen als nicht ganz wahrheitsgetreu erwies. Tatsache war, dass es bei der Rainbow-Truppe heftige musikalische Meinungsverschiedenheiten gegeben hatte, die zur Folge hatten, dass Drummer Gary Driscoll fristlos gefeuert wurde.
Und jetzt kommt die Sensation: Der neue Schlagzeuger, den sich Blackmore holte, ist kein geringerer als sein Landsmann Cozy «Hammer» Powell (durch seine Hits «Dance With The Devil» und «The Man In Black» auch bei uns bestens bekannt). Powell hatte im Sommer dieses Jahres zusammen mit den beiden Ex-Humble-Pies Greg Ridley und Clem Clempson das Rock-Trio Strange Brew gegründet, ein Projekt, das sich alsbald wieder zerschlug, weil Ridley zu seinem Ex-Boss Steve Marriott zurückkehrte. Powell und Clempson bemühten sich in der Folge vergeblich, die Gruppe wieder komplett zu machen. Als dann Blackmores Offerte reinkam, überlegte Cozy nicht lange und setzte sich in den nächsten Jet Richtung Los Angeles.

:s ist kaum zu glauben – Ex-Purple-Gitarrist Ritchie Blackmore hat seine neue Rainbow-Truppe schon wieder umformiert. Nachdem vor einigen Wochen Drummer Gary Driscoll an die Luft gesetzt und durch den englischen Stardrummer Cozy Powell ersetzt wurde, hat jetzt der ewig ruhelose und nie zufriedene Ritchie auch noch den Bass- und den Tastenmann gefeuert.
Ritchie und Sänger Ronnie Dio sind somit als einzige von der Rainbow-Urformation übriggeblieben. Neu hinzugekommen sind Jimmy Bain (Bass) und der Indianer Toney Caley (Tasteninstrumente). Seit dem 5. November befinden sich die neuformierten Rainbow auf Konzertreise durch Amerika. Für Februar 1976 ist eine ausgedehnte Europa-Tournee angesagt. Immer vorausgesetzt natürlich, dass Blackmore nicht vorher wieder den grossen Umbesetzungskoller kriegt.

Neuer Star in der Blackmore-Gruppe: Cozy Powell

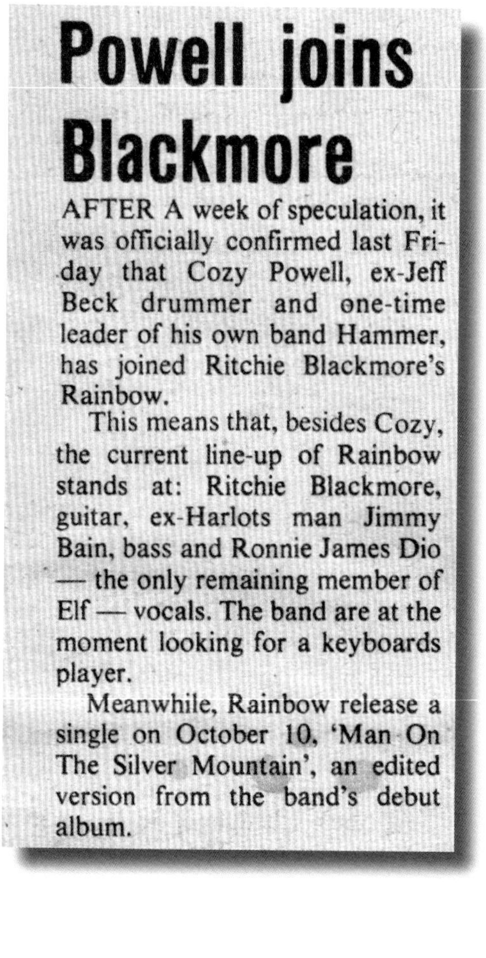

Powell joins Blackmore

AFTER A week of speculation, it was officially confirmed last Friday that Cozy Powell, ex-Jeff Beck drummer and one-time leader of his own band Hammer, has joined Ritchie Blackmore's Rainbow.

This means that, besides Cozy, the current line-up of Rainbow stands at: Ritchie Blackmore, guitar, ex-Harlots man Jimmy Bain, bass and Ronnie James Dio — the only remaining member of Elf — vocals. The band are at the moment looking for a keyboards player.

Meanwhile, Rainbow release a single on October 10, 'Man On The Silver Mountain', an edited version from the band's debut album.

If You Don't Like Rock 'n' Roll

Amongst the sleeve credits was one for the German baroque composer Johann Sebastian Bach who is credited with inspiration. Born in 1685 and passing in 1750, Bach is widely regarded as one of the greatest composers of all time. Blackmore had become enamoured with Bach's work by the time he started to put together the *Ritchie Blackmore's Rainbow* album.

Several tracks on the album use modes that were used in Bach's time. Throughout the album Aeolian and Ionian modes can be heard and 'Self Portrait' is a good example of such modes being incorporated into rock music. The Phrygian mode was also used to great effect on 'Catch The Rainbow'. Blackmore's grasp and understanding of modes also sees him working around the Phrygian mode in 'Snake Charmer'. A fine example of how highly developed Blackmore's compositions were compared to most others within the rock world. English composers in the early part of the century such as Gustav Holst and more notably Ralph Vaughan Williams used modes from hundreds of years earlier, in their cases, from old English folk tunes and adapted them for their own compositions. Whether or not Blackmore was the first rock musician to embrace Bach inspired modes, he was clearly seen as a major influence on many guitarists who emerged in the eighties, dubbed as "neo-classical".

Aside from Bach, Blackmore embraced much of the baroque style. In an interview at the time he said, "all the music I play at home is either German baroque music; people like Buxtehude, Telemann, or medieval music, English medieval music. I prefer things like the harpsichord, the recorder and the tambourine. They used very weird instruments in those days."

In his book *A Hart Life*, Rainbow's tour manager Colin Hart recalled fondly, shortly after the album's release, of a party Ritchie held at his home in California, which was gatecrashed by Rainbow fan John Bonham: "The party was in full swing, the heavily candle scented air accented by the lilting music of Bach. I dispensed cocktails and wine, the ever-dutiful barman. The doorbell rang and I glided to the door. There stood Bonham and his ever-present shadow Richard Cole. 'Good evening' says he in his heavily accented Birmingham brogue. 'I hear there's a bit of a piss up going on here'. 'Do come in,' I said, not wanting to piss him off or indeed be the one to shut the door on one of my all-time heroes. It was also the slightly lesser of two evils — pissing off Ritchie came ever so slightly second. Ritchie spied him from across the room. 'What's he doing here? Can't you get rid of him?' (like that was an option now he was in). Poor Ritchie! He had tried so hard to make this a tasteful affair and he could see his plans going down the gurgler. I served Bonzo large neat vodka as he enquired, 'What's with the morbid music? Isn't this supposed to be a party?' he said exhaling heavily. It was evident that this was not the first watering hole our drummer boy had visited this fine evening. He wandered over to the stereo system and, with that wonderfully, destructive scratching noise that can only be made with a stylus dragged over vinyl, yelled, 'What the fuck is this shit? I want to hear that 'Silver Mountain Man',' referring of course to 'Man On The Silver Mountain' the current Rainbow single. Well it was close. He rummaged through RB's record collection until he found the album and put on the track after a few more stylus scrapes. He then cranked it up to eleven and started to enjoy himself, a broad smile across his face, as did most of the other guests. Ritchie, visibly infuriated, went to his stereo and replaced his own album with Bach once more. Bonham, stopped short in mid boogie, stormed back to the stereo with a very irritated look on his face, frisbeed Bach across the room and returned the sounds of Rainbow to the assembled and bemused guests. You'd have thought Ritchie would see the compliment that this icon of rock was paying him, that a man such as Bonham would demand that he hear the latest work by Ritchie and of course Ronnie James. Well, alas no. Ritchie returned once more to regain his control of the music."

Ritchie also recalled this story, some twenty years later in an interview with Neil Jeffries: "Bonzo really liked Gary Driscoll as a drummer; it's a compliment that one of John Bonham's favourite songs was what he used to call 'Love On The Silver Mountain'. He used to come to the house and say: 'Play 'Love On The Silver Mountain'. 'John, it's called 'Man On The Silver Mountain'.' 'Fucking play 'Love On The Silver Mountain'!' 'But I'd like to play some classical stuff, because there are a lot of people here, I don't want to just play that.' 'I want fucking 'Love On The Silver Mountain'.' 'Okay, I'll put it on.' We nearly had a fight over that. We had a standoff in the house. He'd already been beaten up and had a big patch on the top of his head where he'd got stitches, and he's looking at me, going: 'I'm the fucking guest' I think he was in love with one of the fills, but it was done purely by mistake."

***

Author of *Dance With The Devil -The Cozy Powell Story*, Laura Shenton, wrote a thesis on Blackmore's career for a diploma from the London College of Music. It looked at the influences that Bach and other classical music had on Ritchie. She is happy for the relevant bits referring to the first Rainbow album to be used here:-

'Man On The Silver Mountain', has hard rock music features. As much as the medieval influence is present throughout *Ritchie Blackmore's Rainbow*, the riff in the opening track is very characteristic of hard rock music whereby perfect fourths are present.

Purple people

by Chris Charlesworth in New York

RITCHIE BLACKMORE: self-confessed loner

Blackmore—I was getting lazy

RITCHIE BLACKMORE'S departure from Deep Purple comes as no surprise to followers of Deep Purple who have watched their activities closely over the years. For almost three years now, Ritchie has been quoted publicly about his apparent disinterest in the group, and he has regularly made outspoken critical remarks about their records and stage shows.

Grimly he has carried his Stratocaster through three changes in line-up, each one involving the vocalist and bass player of the band. Equally grimly, he has read not only his own critical, outspoken comments but also harsh reviews on the band as a whole.

Finally he decided to call it a day in a search for a musical direction more suited to his taste. Recent Purple albums have not been to his taste, and he's always been big enough to admit that "Purple In Rock" and "Machine Head" were the only two Purple albums he really enjoyed making — and re-playing out on stage.

Behind the angry young man persona that Ritchie exudes with black clothes and witch's hat is a guitarist of rare talent, not only in fields of rock riff invention and motivation but also in fields of medieval music and classical or jazz chord structure.

The few who have watched Ritchie idly playing a Spanish guitar will realise that power chords and smashed Fenders are just one side of his musical character.

Like any other showman, Blackmore realises the shock value of such tactics. Unfortunately he has been misread by many who consider him a paid-up member of the crash-bang school, not an unreasonable assumption after witnessing him on stage with Purple. But a wrong one nevertheless.

Personally he has always been at loggerheads with various members of the group, keeping himself to himself apart from during an actual concert. He is a self-confessed loner, and, I think, a man very much misunderstood as a result.

"I was considering leaving about six months ago and I finally decided to go ahead four months back," Ritchie told me from his new home in California.

"I had just made my own album in Germany and I just decided after that to end it all. Seven years is a long time with any band and I realised that it couldn't go on forever.

"Everything was getting pretty heavy within Purple and the guys that are in this new band of mine are more on my own wavelength than with the old group. They all like the same kind of music as myself, while in Purple it seemed that there was always someone who didn't like what was being put down.

"Most bands seem to break after three years but Purple just carried on, and I was getting lazy and so was everybody else.

"Actually I have been thinking about making the move for the last two years, and it was the last tour that brought it to a head. It was the different musical policy that was involved."

Ritchie's new LP will be called "Rainbow," and his new group will tour initially as Ritchie Blackmore's Rainbow. He hopes to be able to drop his name from the title once they become established. He has written all the material.

The group are the remnants of a New York based band called Elf, who toured with Purple at one time or another on their numerous US outings.

Initially Ritchie used the lead singer on his own sessions, but that inevitably brought the whole band into the picture. Now they are Ritchie's band, although Ritchie himself is at pains to point out that they are a band and not just a vehicle for Ritchie's solo work.

Rainbow comprises Ronnie James Dio (vocals), Gary Driscoll (drums), Micky Lee Soule (keyboards) and Craig Gruber (bass) — the same complement, in fact, as Deep Purple. Ritchie raves unashamedly about the singer.

For his new venture Blackmore has signed with a new label, Polydor, in the US, leaving Warner Brothers, the label Purple have recorded for since breaking through in 1971. The album will be released in July.

"We've started rehearsing and we're going out live in about three months," Ritchie continued. "We'll be playing much smaller places that I did with Purple. In the past it has always been silly with Purple, playing those big arenas. The only places that were good were the small halls in England.

"The stuff I am writing now is not all that different from what Purple did. There aren't so many riffs because the singer is a more melodic vocalist than with Purple.

"It's more like medieval rock and roll, with 16th century fills and I am using modes instead of scales. That's not as drastic as it may sound but it is a change from before. It's still very hard music, harder than "Stormbringer" in fact.

"It's not the Ritchie Blackmore band, as people will think, and we'll only use my name until Rainbow sinks in. I don't want to hold the attention by guitar soloing all night long. I'm also very pleased that it's the same line-up as Purple."

Ritchie has no plans to return to England and California will remain his permanent base for the future. Like the rest of Purple, taxes have driven him out of Britain. He does have vague plans to bring his new group over for an English tour in November and December this year.

"Some of Purple were surprised when I announced I was quitting," Ritchie admitted. "And that surprised me because I thought they could all tell how I was thinking.

"Our last gigs in Europe were strange because we never hardly talked to each other. In fact, in seven years I never really mixed with them.

"At first they were going to break up but then the management persuaded them to stay together.

"The new guitarist is more of a jazz player and good luck to them. I don't mean that sarcastically because I've been with them a long time.

"There were certain things that I wanted to do myself that I could never do with Purple because everyone, including myself, was egotistical.

"Everything seemed to have to include a guitar solo or a drum solo, or an organ solo so that everyone had their share.

"When five musicians feel that way it can sometimes be an advantage but also a disadvantage.

"Everyone in Purple seemed to be doing their own thing and we never met to write together and not even to rehearse very often.

"We just met occasionally at gigs and I think the audiences were beginning to suss what was happening.

"I'm the kind of person who likes to keep proving himself, and I want to do that again as I guess I've already done it with Purple.

"I really want to prove myself once more and I'm looking forward to it."

by Chris Welch

A CURIOUS marriage of convenience. That is how the link between American lead guitarist Tommy Bolin and British speed rock band Deep Purple might appear to the casual observer.

For Tommy has never seen Deep Purple perform nor has he heard their records. Furthermore, he won't be playing any gigs with them this side of Christmas.

He'll also spend much of the year packing his pick around America, touring with his own band. This would never have done in the early days of rock, when a musician virtually had to sign in blood and give over his goods, chattels and wife to join a group.

But Tommy, with the light laughter of a musician waking up at 9 am in Los Angeles, explained all this week. The man who sparked the James Gang and went on to surprise jazz-rock aficionados with his remarkable playing on Billy Cobham's "Spectrum" album, on cuts like the hair-raising "Quadrant 4" will be recording with Purple while getting into their music.

And the freedom of the arrangement means that Tommy will be able to go off and do his own things, while Purple get the services of one of the best young guitarists to emerge in a long time.

Despite his reputation and the amount of work he's put in, Tommy is only 23. And asked about such subjects as study and lessons, he gives an amused drawl: "I don't know what I'm doing — I don't know one scale from another!"

How did Mr Bolin meet up with Jon Lord and his particular gang? "I met Ritchie Blackmore about two weeks ago and he recommended me to the band.

"The thing is I've never really listened to a lot of Deep Purple records, but when I joined the James Gang it was a step forward, and Deep Purple are all amazing players, and its another step for me.

"Ian Paice is an amazing drummer, and I have all the respect in the world for Jon Lord. I think I will be bringing out my own individuality with the band, and bring some things out in them. The LP we're making will surprise a lot of people. We start recording on August 3 in Munich.

IS THIS LUCY BROWN?

'Self Portrait', strongly demonstrates the use of classical musical influence in rock music. It is described by Blackmore in an interview as being a cross between the song, 'Manic Depression' (1967) by Jimi Hendrix and Bach's 'Jesu Joy of Man's Desiring' (1723). Also, Blackmore says of the song, 'Temple Of The King', "There are two classical guitars on that and one electric, but the electric guitar on that isn't really audible. It's got a medieval progression and a string ensemble in the middle."

There are different editions of sheet music available for 'Sixteenth Century Greensleeves'. Some are written in common time but others are written using the 6/4 time signature. Both are valid transcriptions of the song. The fact is that it can be counted in (some) bars of 6/4. Even in classical music, it is not particularly common for the 6/4 time signature to be used that is present in 'Sixteenth Century Greensleeves'. This unusual use of time signature is exemplified by the fact that the song is also interspersed with bars of common time when counted in 6/4. It gives the music a feel that is bouncy but still within the character of a hard rock piece whereby the emphasis of chords is played on the beat. A classical piece of music that makes similar use of the 6/4 time signature is *Pictures At An Exhibition* (1874) by Mussorgsky. It is considered by some that the Promenade theme in the piece was originally written by Mussorgsky in 11/4 time. Thereafter though, the piece is most commonly notated as being in bars of 5/4 and 6/4. It is argued that Mussorgsky embraced such irregular use of time signatures in order to replicate the rhythm of his own gait as he imagined himself walking around the art gallery that was the source of his inspiration for the piece. Promenade is characteristic of Russian classical music whereby the soloist leads and the chorus follows, repeating and harmonising the theme.

This characteristic is also present in 'Sixteenth Century Greensleeves'. Whilst there is no definitive quote from Blackmore stating his rhythmic intent for 'Sixteenth Century Greensleeves', it certainly has a number of features present that have less in common with popular music and more in common with the diversities apparent in a classical piece such as *Pictures At An Exhibition*.

Ritchie Blackmore:
"My favourite all-time song is the old tune 'Greensleeves', and in England I used to live just a little way from Windsor Castle, I was always up there just looking at the place. We wanted to record a song about castles and crossbows, and I was pleased that we were able to keep that hard rock thing within a classical mode."

"I really like medieval modes, I listen to more classical music than rock and roll and I think this influences my music a lot although I try to keep rock and roll as a dominant factor."
(*Sounds*, 1976).

Dio was also switched on to what Blackmore was trying to achieve: "He wants music that's really a little different than the rock and roll everyone else is doing... Therefore the medieval concept... Being able to take that classical influence and put it to raw rock and roll, I think, is a real challenge, and that's what we're trying to do."

Lyrically, Dio asserts that the songs on the first Rainbow album are consistent with the medieval theme of the music. He considers that the song 'Catch The Rainbow' is about a relationship between an upper class lady of the courts who has a romance with a stable worker. The class divide of the two protagonists makes their romance unsustainable and the overall message of the song explores what Dio refers to as "the futility of man versus women." He considers that the overall imagery of the song's lyrics is "a representative track" (Polydor Rainbow Radio Special, 1975) of the album in terms of the medieval theme.

In the same interview, Blackmore and Dio discuss the way in which the medieval theme of *Ritchie Blackmore's Rainbow* is very apparent in 'Sixteenth Century Greensleeves'. Lyrically, it is about a knight who captures a young peasant maiden from a village. He locks her in a tower and one day the peasants revolt. The song lyrics contain imagery such as "The fighting must begin before another someone dies, crossbows in the firelight. Greensleeves waving, mad men raving." Dio considers that 'Sixteenth Century Greensleeves' conveys their intent to embrace a medieval theme and concept.

As a result, Rainbow's first album is abundant in classical music influences and in particular, medieval modes blended with features typical of rock music.

SOUNDS Page 25

albums

EXCLUSIVE PREVIEW

VOLCANIC BLACKMORE

• RITCHIE BLACKMORE

'RITCHIE BLACKMORE's RAINBOW': (OYSTER OYA2001)

INITIAL REACTION from people who have heard this album has been 'yeh nice stuff, but what's the difference between this and things he was doing with Purple?'. Answer? a helluva a lot more than one might think. This album unveils many new facets that were previously unknown in Blackmore's guitar playing. It's also the debut of a tough outfit capable of kickin' enough shit to cause an earth-quake in a compost heap (e.g. mighty tough stuff). In the last three years Purple's music has gone through many a deviation, basically due to friction between musicians and tight schedules, permitting a minimal amount of time for writing. The result has been, the good, the bad and the mediocre. While 'Machine Head' was probably the definitive album for Purple Mk II, 'Who Do You Think We Are?' was an abysmal effort to hold the crumbling structures of a band together. While 'Burn' was an exciting declaration of new strength from what promised to be (and most certainly was, while it lasted) a hot new band, 'Stormbringer' indicated that Blackmore's talents were receding into the background and opposition of musical ideas was inevitable — a change was a-coming. Rainbow has a band feel that has been lacking, more spiritually than musically, in Purple for a long time. The Rainbow album has released something that has been building up inside of Blackmore, like an awakening volcano, ready to explode. Vocalist Ronnie Dio is undoubtedly the catalyst, the man who lit the fuse. His vocals and lyrics capture the mood and atmosphere of Blackmore's music with perceptive accuracy. The moody, Germanic qualities appear in 'The Temple And The King' which features a haunting acoustic melody line, and '16th Century Greensleeves', powered by a hypnotic riff battling against Dio's abrasive vocals which cut through with searing intensity. Then there's the out and out sheer energy-laden rock and roll like 'Snake Charmer' and 'Man Of The Silver Mountain' which both vaguely sound Purplesque but still carry the solid identity of the Rainbow band. Gary Driscoll's explosive percussion combined with Craig Gruber's vibrant, belching bass lines create a thunderous cacophony of rhythm allowing keyboardman Mickey Lee Soule to embellish or attack with some hypnotic clavinet work. Blackmore is his ever excellent self, playing some unusually calm leslified guitar on 'Self Portrait' which is very reminiscent of early Cream. He only steals all the limelight on one track, an instrumental version of The Yardbirds 'Still I'm Sad', which has his Fender and fingers working at full pace. The man even hides himself on 'Black Sheep Of The Family'" and 'If You Don't Like Rock And Roll', although his presence is always felt when that strident chordwork shatters your tweeters to smithereens. 'Catch The Rainbow' captures the dramatic, lyrical qualities of the band. OK, so this is a snivelling, syncophantic review from a self-confessed Deep Purple fanatic but just listen to this album (even if you're not a DP fan) it almost captures the live excitement of Blackmore's playing ... and that's saying something! — **Pete Makowski.**

SOUNDS Page 31

THE DEVIL MOVES ON

'I Get Around' should be Cozy Powell's signature tune. He's just joined Ritchie Blackmore's Rainbow. Kid Barton reports

• *COZY POWELL: "It's nice to do something positive for a change"*

THE SOAP-OPERA so far: Moody guitar hero Ritchie Blackmore leaves the top rock band Deep Purple. Flabbergasted, Purple begin a desperate search for a replacement. They try out Clem Clempson, a one-time Humble Pie, but it's no good, he just doesn't fit in. Not dispirited, Clempson rallies to the rock and roll cause and forms a band called Strange Brew with bassist Greg Ridley and ex-Jeff Beck, Hammer drummer Cozy Powell.

Meanwhile, Blackmore's own band Rainbow record an album which, on release, shoots up the charts, and Purple find a new axe man in Tommy Bolin. Then, suddenly, Strange Brew split: Ridley joins Steve Marriott's Allstars and Powell joins Rainbow. Now read on.

Permanent

Episode 23: 'Why Did Cozy Do It?'

"You mean it's permanent?" asked the young journalist in a disbelieving tone. His mind flashed back to his very first rock interview: it had been with Cozy Powell, while he was with his band called Hammer. It seemed quite a turn-around.

"That's right, yeah," replied Powell, his gruff voice reminding the kid that he should do his best not to offend.

"It's quite a surprise."

"Yeah, a surprise to me as well." Powell took a noisy swig from a can of light ale. You could see it begin to buckle under the pressure of his twitching right hand. Obviously, he was anxious to get hold of a motorcycle throttle once again. "I got a phone call from Ritchie in the States last week. He was on the look-out for a ... ballsy drummer, if you like, so I decided to go over and have a play with him.

"It was nice. Things went well. I decided to join. So I'm going back to America shortly, to start rehearsing. The band'll probably be on the road over there in mid-October, we'll be coming over to Britain at the end of the year or in early '76."

"But haven't you got various contractual and managerial commitments that could prevent you joining Rainbow?" asked the journalist, gingerly.

Powell brought the beer can crashing down on the varnished dark wooden table top. He chipped it. "No — none at all." Composing himself, he continued, "The Mickie Most situation resolved itself in March and I haven't done anything since then, except a spot of motor racing.

"It's nice to do something positive for a change. For a while I was going to pack in the music business and take up racing as a career—I still will, eventually, it's just a matter of *when* — but Ritchie's tempted me to get back into it once again."

"What happened to your teen idol image?"

"Teen idol? Me?"

"Uh-huh."

"I dunno ... " For the first time, Powell hesitates. Unaccustomed to moments of indecision, he grips the arms of his chair, tightly. "It was nice to have hit records and it was nice to be able to play to kids who possibly hadn't heard of me before. But I could only take all that for so long — and it wasn't doing my mental state any good, either.

"My band, Hammer, was very good musically, but it was wasted just playing to kids of 14 or 15 who just wanted to hear 'Dance With The Devil' and a drum solo. I was just knocking my head against a brick wall."

"And what about Strange Brew?"

"It fizzled out, it was doomed from the start." Powell picks up the wood chip and begins playing with it, carelessly, between a calloused thumb and forefinger. "The basic problem was lack of incentive from myself, Clem and Greg. There was also a lot of contractual difficulties. It would have taken a long time to get the band together. It sounded nice at the time, but in practice it would never have worked out."

"How," the journalist wondered, "do you find you get on with Blackmore?"

"I get on great with him." Powell squeezes the chip strongly. The tips of his thumb and forefinger begin to redden. "I've been through the same scene as he has, you know, I've done numerous German tours, I've been up and down the States and everywhere else, we get on OK.

"If it'll last — who knows? We may have a punch-up on our first gig, but it's looking good at the moment. I mean, Jeff Beck has to be the most difficult musician to get on with and I stood him for two years — so I think that after Jeff, anybody's easy. And anyway, I'm not the easiest of guys to get on with either am I?"

"Now that you've joined, Ronnie Dio, the vocalist, is the only remaining member of Elf in Rainbow, isn't he? Which sort of scotches the initial rumours that Blackmore had left Deep Purple to *join* Elf ..."

"I think Ritchie used Elf as a means to get his career off the ground, to get some of his own music on record." Powell increases the pressure on the small piece of wood. "Now he wants to put a band together that's equal to him — rather than have just a few backing musicians, Ritchie wants to be part of a band."

Splinters

"But isn't that rather callous, using Elf as a vehicle like that?" A searching question. The kid smiles secretly.

"I dunno if it was a vehicle, I just think that after a while Ritchie realised that one or two of the members weren't quite up to scratch. From talking to him, I don't think he realised this until after he'd done the album and rehearsed a bit. I don't think he had the intention of slinging them out from the start, it just happened that way. Only Ritchie can answer that question though, I don't know what's going on inside his head. All I do know is that I'm playing with him now, so ...". The wood chip splinters in Powell's hand. He begins to smile, but he ends up smirking." ... you'll have to work it out for yourself."

Watch out for episode 24 — coming soon!

Track By Track

1. Man On The Silver Mountain (Blackmore / Dio)

The opening cut from the album has gone on to become one of Rainbow's most popular songs. The fact that the riff isn't actually that dissimilar to 'Smoke On The Water' might have something to do with that. Lyrically, Ronnie Dio explained at the time; "It's a semi-religious song. The man on the silver mountain is the kind of God figure that everyone is crying out to come down and save them, and give them money and chicks! Cures from diseases and all that! They basically cry out for him to come down and make them holy and full and rewarded."

In his typical dry humoured way, Blackmore told one journalist the song was inspired by Edmund Hillary and Sherpa Tensing! Blackmore throws in some fancy runs over the top of the riff and the power in Dio's voice clearly shows that Blackmore had secured the services of a highly talented singer.

2. Self Portrait (Blackmore / Dio)

Compared to the opening track and indeed the rest of the album, 'Self Portrait' is a more laid back offering. Full of interesting textures and a memorable melody, it is indicative of the variety and abundance of ideas on Rainbow's debut.

3. Black Sheep Of The Family (Steve Hammond)

In retrospect the song that kicked-started the whole Rainbow thing is arguably one of the weakest tracks on the album and one has to question what appeal Blackmore saw in it in the first place. Principally, the best thing about it is that it gave Blackmore the impetus to create his own band and all the great stuff that followed thereafter. Lyrically the song was quite fascinating and again Dio puts in a good performance, though strangely Blackmore's own work on the song gives a very "poppy" sound to the finished track that is rather at odds with the rest of the album.

4. Catch The Rainbow (Blackmore / Dio)

With Blackmore having total control, Rainbow gave him the scope to branch off into different directions and bring in new dimensions without having to be overtly concerned about whether or not it fitted into the pigeonhole of "heavy rock." Whilst some critics saw 'Catch The Rainbow' as Blackmore's attempt at replicating the ballad 'Soldier Of Fortune' from *Stormbringer*, others said it owed more to Hendrix's 'Little Wing'. Fundamentally it is a beautifully crafted song that once again sees Blackmore using modes. In this case, a form of the Phrygian mode, but the song also has a basic structure that was the perfect platform for extending it in the live arena. It was also highly indicative of the future direction Blackmore was to take Rainbow in, with a greater emphasis on melody and subtlety than had sometimes been the case with Deep Purple. Judith Feinstein under the stage name Shoshana makes her professional recorded debut on backing vocals.

5. Snake Charmer (Blackmore / Dio)

Although some fans were expecting something akin to a "solo guitar" album, Blackmore has always preferred to work within the framework of a band. Though at least with a track such as 'Snake Charmer', there are numerous overdubbed guitar parts for the fans to enjoy, plus the use of wah-wah — something Blackmore frequently used in the first couple of years of Purple and another example of the Hendrix influence at play.

6. Temple Of The King (Blackmore / Dio)

As Blackmore explained in interviews at the time, J.S. Bach was hugely influential throughout the album. 'Temple Of The King' is a fine example of this and once again stood out as a track where Blackmore was happy to do something different. Both he and Dio combine wonderfully to produce a piece of music with an historical feel to it.

7. If You Don't Like Rock 'n' Roll (Blackmore / Dio)

A little bit of light relief amidst the modes and medieval flavours that pervade throughout the album, this track is more suitable for Chuck Berry fans than Bach. Baroque 'n' roll anyone? Mickey Lee Soule's piano solo was in typical rock 'n' roll style and the track is the only one on the album that allows the keyboard player the chance of a cameo role.

8. Sixteenth Century Greensleeves (Blackmore / Dio)

Another highlight of the album, and another track that combines rock tradition with a medieval ambience. Blackmore was also keen to have lyrics that added to the overall effect. Very few lyricists in rock were writing such things at the time, but Dio was equally enamoured with kings, castles and all things from the age of chivalry.

9. Still I'm Sad (Paul Samwell-Smith / James McCarty)

The album concludes with this instrumental version of The Yardbirds' song. The fact that The Yardbirds had originally been inspired to write it after hearing a Gregorian chant suggests that Blackmore's interpretation isn't as wide of the mark as some have suggested. It also appeased those who wanted a record with lots of guitar solos. Blackmore delighted those who clamoured for such, as the track is ultimately one long solo. Although buried in the mix, Shoshana's voice is an added instrument.

A billboard announcing the debut album right in front of the Chateau Marmont Hotel on Sunset Boulevard.

2.
Paint Me A Picture: The First Tour

"I'm the kind of person who likes to keep proving himself, and I want to do that again as I guess I've already done it with Purple. I really want to prove myself once more and I'm looking forward to it."

Having returned from Jamaica and with a final mix back at Munich in May, Ritchie, Ronnie and Colin Hart returned to their new Los Angeles base, where the rest of the band were as well. Meanwhile, in the same month, Purple began the arduous task of finding Blackmore's replacement. They first tried out Dave "Clem" Clempson following the disbandment of Clempson's group Humble Pie, but something didn't click for them. Clempson and his fellow Humble Pie bandmate, bassist Greg Ridley then wasted no time in putting a new band together and the same month announced the formation of a power trio called Strange Brew along with former Jeff Beck drummer Cozy Powell.

With Purple having recently announced their replacement for Blackmore in the shape of former James Gang guitarist Tommy Bolin, an element of potential competition was at play as well. Indeed Blackmore had a high opinion of Bolin: "I originally heard him on Billy Cobham's *Spectrum* album, and thought, 'Who is this guy?' Then I saw him on television and he looked incredible. Like Elvis Presley. I knew he was gonna be big. When I heard that Purple hired him I thought it was great."

By June, Rainbow rehearsals started at the former Columbia sound stage. Robert Simon, formerly of the sound company Tychobrae, had taken over the unit and created his own company Pirate Sound. From their homes in Oxnard County, just over an hour away, it was a convenient place to start rehearsing.

Pirate Sound was large enough that it could be divided and two bands could work there simultaneously. Colin Hart recalled, "One day, noticing that a large amount of equipment was being shipped to the stage next to ours, I, inquisitively as ever, asked who it was. 'Deep Purple for four to five days' came the amused reply. 'They start rehearsals next week.' I told Ritchie who also saw the irony and ordered a week off to avoid any embarrassment to anybody, despite him still having to pay a daily rental to the studios. Nevertheless, Ritchie asked me to 'drop in' to spy on their rehearsals and report back, which I dutifully did. Bolin was good, very good and fitted into the jazz funk direction that Glenn and David were determined to follow. Ritchie's curiosity could not be contained and I drove him down to the studios one afternoon. We quietly entered our sound stage and like two sneak thieves stealthily cracked open the double doors leading to Purple's stage. They were in full flow. Ritchie's face showed no emotion and he listened there for nearly half an hour. He finally looked at me, just shrugged as if to say, 'No competition there' and said, 'Okay, let's go'."

Robert Simon recalled this situation as well, albeit slightly differently: "That was a total nightmare for me. I was caught up in the middle. Ritchie was right in my face. More demands, more demands. I could divide the studios in half they were so big and one band could have the day session and one could have the night session. Whoever paid the most money got the choice of the session, which was normally the night's session. And we had them like that but he didn't even want them in the same building, so I moved

Purple to stage three and I had Ritchie in stage four. I had my own sound system and I was splitting it half with Ritchie and half with Purple. I'd work with Purple in the day mixing them and Rainbow at night. Then it just got to the stage when he came up to me and said, 'you know what, you're not mixing for them anymore. You're mixing for me and they're not using any of your PA we are using the whole PA.' I said, 'shit I don't care as long as someone is paying for it. Whoever pays the most can have the most.' But it got really political. The next thing I knew I had everything set up for Ritchie and Coverdale and the rest of the band are all standing behind me 'Si, what are you doing this to us for?' 'I didn't want you to take it personal I thought it had all gone through Cooksey and Colin and everyone else' but they took it personally. They thought I'd fucked them over for Ritchie and I found out later that was kind of what it was. He wanted to snuff them."

Robert Simon might well have seen this act as one of sheer bloody-mindedness, but there was certainly no bad blood between Blackmore and Bolin. Upon joining Purple, Bolin leased a house close to where Ritchie was then living. In 1991 when speaking to *Guitar World* about their relationship Ritchie said, "he was always so humble. I remember he would always invite me out to his house in Hollywood to see his guitar. One day I went to his place. I walked in and tried to find him, but no one was around. There were no furnishings — nothing. I stayed there for ten minutes before he finally appeared. He showed me his guitar, and the strings must have had a quarter inch of grime on them, as though he hadn't changed them in four years. I asked him when was the last time he'd changed strings, and he said very seriously, 'Gee, I don't know. Do you think I should change them?'"

With the Rainbow album complete but still to be released, Blackmore did a round of interviews in early summer. Not a man keen on such, he was clearly aware that he was now the spokesman for his new venture and everything was on his shoulders.

In an interview with Chris Charlesworth for *Melody Maker*, published on 26th June, Blackmore said, "Everything was getting pretty heavy within Purple and the guys that are in this new band of mine are more on my own wavelength than with the old group. They all like the same kind of music as myself while in Purple it seemed that there was always someone who didn't like what was being put down."

"Actually I have been thinking about making the move for the last two years, and it was the last tour that brought it to a head. It was the different musical policy that was involved. We've started rehearsing and we're going out live in about three months. We'll be playing much smaller places than I did with Purple. In the past it has always been silly with Purple."

Elsewhere, Ritchie was also high in praise for his new writing partner and singer, whilst at the same time cryptically condescending of some of the other singers he had worked with, "Ronnie is very versatile. He sings on the single 'Love Is All', he used to play the trumpet in an orchestra, that's why he knows so much about scales. I like working with Ronnie, he is never out of tune, he never makes mistakes: Most vocalists I have worked with don't know what they are doing, they just hope it fits. With Ronnie you know it fits. He might be small but his voice isn't!"

But despite speaking highly of Dio, when rehearsals began, as Colin Hart observed, Blackmore wasn't so happy with some of the other band members. "Even at rehearsals before we had done one show, I knew the signs of discontent in Ritchie were surfacing. He has this thing he does which, although he says nothing, his actions shout, reverberating around the room. He simply stops playing, slowly turns round, slips his guitar over his head and lays it on top of the stack, switches off and walks slowly and silently away. He did quite a bit of that at rehearsals. He admired Ronnie, of that there was no doubt as a singer and a lyricist, but he was used to virtuosos in Purple and I think he missed that, more than he would ever admit. He was funding Rainbow personally, so I guess he took the view that he had made his bed and he would have to lie on it for the time being."

Craig Gruber endorsed Hart's recollections: "We had bought houses out on the Coast. The band was a viable band, and then we got into actual rehearsals to go out on tour. The rehearsals just weren't going good. I mean Ritchie kept putting the guitar down and walking away and it was like Deep Purple all over again."

Unfortunately for Gruber, it was he who was Blackmore's initial reason for dissatisfaction and by July he was out of the equation. "Ritchie just could not suffer him any longer," recalls Hart. "This was made worse by Craig's obvious belief that the guitarist had hijacked Elf and his antipathy showed. Ronnie seemed unfazed on the surface that his band was being ripped apart; no doubt the obvious financial implications had a bearing."

On a trip back to the UK, Blackmore soon found Gruber's replacement when he checked out Scottish bassist Jimmy Bain at London's Marquee club. Bain was playing with a band called Harlot and during the summer of '75 they had secured a regular spot at the legendary venue. Playing predominantly on Sundays they performed there six times: 22nd May, 22nd June, and in July on 6th, 20th, 22nd (Tuesday) and 27th.

It's unclear exactly which show Blackmore was at but Harlot's drummer Ricky Munro had been in the short-lived Mandrake Root with Blackmore back in 1967 and recalled, "we had a residency at the Marquee and Jimmy Bain had a message, 'could you go and meet somebody in the pub down the road who wants to speak to you.' I went along with him because he didn't know who it was and there sitting at a table in the corner is old Blackmore and that was the end of Harlot. I was just thinking the bastard's coming back to haunt me again. He had exactly the same personality before he became a success. He always had a high opinion of himself but unfortunately it didn't extend to him being civil. He was very difficult to get on with because you never knew when he would turn around and say you're sacked. I couldn't believe it when he came and took Jimmy Bain. He bought me a pint. I rather we'd kept our bass player because we were going to be the first band on The Rolling Stones' label so all that fell through because one main songwriter had been poached. He'd been well and truly poached and promised the earth. Blackmore was so single-minded and he got there by his own means."

In an interview with David Lee Wilson in 2002, Mickey Lee Soule relayed his own recollections of how the situation unfolded: "What happened was we all moved to Malibu because that is where Ritchie was living and we started rehearsals and we didn't get very far at all and Ritchie wanted to replace the bass player. That was more of... it wasn't a musical choice really it was just a whim of Ritchie's or a personal thing. So, the bass player was replaced with Jimmy Bain and we rehearsed a little longer and then Ritchie wanted to replace the drummer and I was very disappointed in that. He was my best friend and we had gone through a lot together and he was a great drummer. It was just that it was his style, his style was more like the American R&B style of drumming and Ritchie had been used to a different style, you know, Ian Paice, so I was very disappointed in that decision and that is kind of one of the things that led me to leave. It is very hard to talk about really because I don't want to sound like I am bitter about anything. You know, Ronnie and I are still very good friends to this day although we have kind of gone our separate ways and I don't run into him that often anymore but back in those days we were all much younger I guess."

Seven years later in an interview with Jeff Cramer, Craig Gruber recalled things slightly differently with his memory certainly playing tricks on him: "So there was a band meeting and they wanted to make some changes. They wanted to bring in Cozy Powell. Cozy Powell was and still is in my mind, first of all, a great person. One of the sweetest guys and one of the funniest guys you'd ever meet in your life. He's an amazing guy and a machine on drums. Gary, our drummer from Elf, was amazing in his own way too. Gary had an R&B kind of a groove, funk feel where Cozy had like a metal feel. Gary kind of dabbled around in between the beats and played a little bit too many little fill kind of things, if you will, for that type of music. Cozy just laid it down, played across the beat and just like laid down this monster thing."

"So they brought Cozy in to rehearse for a week and didn't tell Gary. Here's Gary, living right down the beach from me, not even a hundred yards from my house, and we're going in to Hollywood every day to SIR Studios and we're fucking rehearsing to go out on tour. Oh my God, how fucking horrible."

Gruber's comments that Powell was tried out before his departure should be taken with a pinch of salt but well over thirty years after the event, it's understandable if the time elapsed plays havoc with the memory. It's quite possible that someone relayed the story of Driscoll's departure to Gruber at a later date, who went on to say, "that caused a huge upheaval in the band. Mickey Lee and Gary were in the band for so many years before I joined. Mickey Lee had a fit. He didn't show up one day. Mickey Lee got so smashed. I mean he just drank an incredible amount of scotch and he just got fucking trashed. We couldn't find him for a couple of days, and then finally, Colin came in and said, 'I found him. He's at the beach now.' Mickey Lee said, 'If you're getting rid of Chops that was Gary's nickname then I'm leaving too. This is not the band I want. This is not what we did. This is not what we worked our lives, heart, lungs and liver out for, to be sliced and fucking diced.' So Mickey Lee quit."

But Mickey Lee was still there for a short while after Driscoll had been given his marching orders. It's been well documented that a huge number of drummers were auditioned. Perhaps less well documented is that amongst them was Bobby Berge, who had previously been in Zephyr and Energy with Blackmore's Deep Purple replacement Tommy Bolin. "They had a small kit set up and Ritchie said I could use it if I wanted. But no! I had to take up a bunch of time and set up my whole damn kit. Then, sad to say, as Tommy used to say, 'I blew my cookies in the first bar!' I overdid it and tried too hard and played way too much. Ronnie Dio's comment to me, when I asked what he thought, was, 'Man, it looked like you were dying!' Probably so as I was out of shape and just tried too hard. Now, if I would have just used their small kit and laid it down simple and solid! I had been listening to 'Man On The Silver Mountain' and really dug it and also knew what kind of drumming was called for. Anyway, it was great meeting the guys and getting a crack at it!"

Step forward one Cozy Powell who blew them all away with his ability to play a fast shuffle with no let up or speed fluctuations. Blackmore was already familiar with Powell from his time with the Jeff Beck Group but his ability to play consistently and nail rhythms quickly had also resulted in him becoming a much in demand session drummer, from which producer Mickie Most went on to cut three chart successful singles with Powell over the previous two years — a phenomenal feat for a drummer to have such commercial success under his own name. And to think that after the short-lived Strange Brew with Clem Clempson had gone nowhere, Powell was so disillusioned that he had initially decided to give up music to focus on his other passion of motor racing before the call to try out for Rainbow came in. It couldn't have come at a better time.

If Powell was a more familiar face to add to the ranks, the same couldn't be said for Mickey Lee Soule's replacement Tony Carey, a twenty-two-year-old American who was in place by October. Also, if

Blackmore had to fly back over the Atlantic to check out a new bass player, the complete opposite applied with Carey, as the man himself told the author, some years back, "I was never really a hard rock player and Rainbow was the only hard rock, progressive band I was ever involved with. The band I had before (Blessings). I was nineteen, twenty, and we got signed in Connecticut with ABC Dunhill and they sent us up to Hollywood to get high and fuck girls and maybe make a record! It was crazy times in Hollywood in the seventies. I'd heard 'Man On The Silver Mountain' on the radio and I liked Deep Purple but Ritchie was actually looking for drummers and keyboard players — Cozy and me. We were both rehearsing. My band was rehearsing in SIR studios in Hollywood, and Ritchie was holding his auditions I guess across the hall or something. I always played loud and somebody heard the loud Hammond and said to Ritchie 'check this guy out maybe you can steal him from his band.' Which was perfect timing because we would sit there in Hollywood for a couple of years and not be able to get a record finished because of various outside influences! I was fed up with the thing anyway. We were like a country band and I was classically trained, can play anything. So Jimmy Bain came over and introduced himself and said, 'Do you want to come over to Pirate Sound', which is the old CBS movie lot in Hollywood: Big sound stage, 'and try out for the band?' I said 'yeah I'd love to', so I went down with a buddy of mine and I was early, and I was like playing this little mini concert... about six keyboards — loud! I thought I was actually alone but Ritchie, Cozy, Ronnie and Jimmy were all in the back, seated against the back wall about fifty yards from me in the dark, so I got the job before I played with the band just by warming up."

With the new line-up completed by late October, Rainbow could set about final rehearsals for its first North American tour that was creeping up on them and was due to start on 5th November. But before the band had been finalised, Ritchie already had a vision of wanting to present Rainbow in a more visual way, more so than had been done with Deep Purple. The wooden Rainbow that adorned the stage at the California Jam the previous year had given him an idea for the stage show. "I remember when he was just forming Rainbow and he walked into my studio Pirate Sound and said, 'okay I want you to make a big arcing rainbow from one side of the PA to the other and all these flashing colours,' recalled Simon. The lighting company See Factor in New York was commissioned to build the huge electronic rainbow to span the stage. The first of its kind in the world, containing 3,000 light bulbs and operated by a portable computer. Though the technology was advanced for its time, it was highly primitive compared to today's computer sophistication and caused more than a few problems.

The large backdrop of the album cover that would hang at the back of the stage was far less technical but was another major visual attraction.

In addition to the visual situation, Ritchie also commissioned Robert Simon to build a sound system. Concerned by the mounting cost, as Ritchie hadn't specified anything exact, when Simon mentioned that the price had escalated to about $75,000 Ritchie just replied, "I don't care how much it is. I know you will do it the best so just do it and whatever it is I'll pay for it. I trust you and I don't want to know about it at all."

"When I was done with the equipment I got this phone call from Fergie (Ian Ferguson, Ritchie's guitar technician). 'Ritchie wants you to have all the gear set up because Ritchie is going to have someone come and play on it tonight and test it out.' I had the stack of equipment set up and a brown Rolls Royce turns up and out of it pops Felix Pappalardi. I said 'hey Felix what's happening man?' He said, 'I'm here to test out Ritchie's gear. He wants me to play though it and give him my opinion.' So Felix just started jamming by himself. He just played for about an hour. We all just stood around and went 'whoa!'"

With only one album's worth of material to rehearse from, fans who had bought tickets for the shows might have expected to hear some old Purple tunes as well. However, during rehearsals Ritchie and Ronnie wrote three new pieces to compliment some of the songs from the album released in August. Therefore a good proportion of the show consisted of songs no one had heard. In fact, one of the new songs opened the show. Whatever the strengths of the album that had just been released, Blackmore clearly felt that there wasn't anything on it that was rousing enough to be an opening song of a live show and of the new songs, 'Do You Close Your Eyes' became the set opener. Amongst the tracks from the album, some of them were stretched out live, to give a ninety-minute set.

The disruption caused by line-up changes with Carey only joining in October — as well as technical issues with the electronic rainbow — meant that some of the shows had to be re-scheduled. With the tour originally planned to start on the 5th November it commenced five days later. According to Carey, not a great deal of rehearsing was called for before the first show, but obviously the other four would have rehearsed before he joined them. When I interviewed him though, he recalled that they did, "astoundingly little. We liked... play a song, learn the chords a few times. I don't remember exactly, but we didn't work anything out except the structure, like you solo here, Cozy solos here. Everything was very free-form, really progressive rock. We weren't The Sweet, learning all these harmonies and hooks and hit singles. We played very long songs sometimes because everybody was having fun. And that was an ass-kicking jamming band. One of the unsung heroes of that band was Jimmy Bain, a fantastic bass player who kept it going and never let up a second, and Cozy too. He was so consequent in his playing. Ritchie's idea of a drum audition was to start a fast shuffle and play of for half an hour until the drummer collapsed. Not pull a grimace, not look at him just keep playing at this thunderous volume until he had enough and the drummer went home."

The standard set list was:-

Do You Close Your Eyes
Self Portrait
Catch The Rainbow
Sixteenth Century Greensleeves
Man On The Silver Mountain
Stargazer
A Light In The Black
Still I'm Sad

Of the shows where audience recordings exist, only one appears to capture an encore number of 'If You Don't Like Rock 'n' Roll'. It's my gut feeling that it was the standard encore but because the rainbow caused so many interference issues, it would appear that several shows didn't include encores.

Original US promo poster.

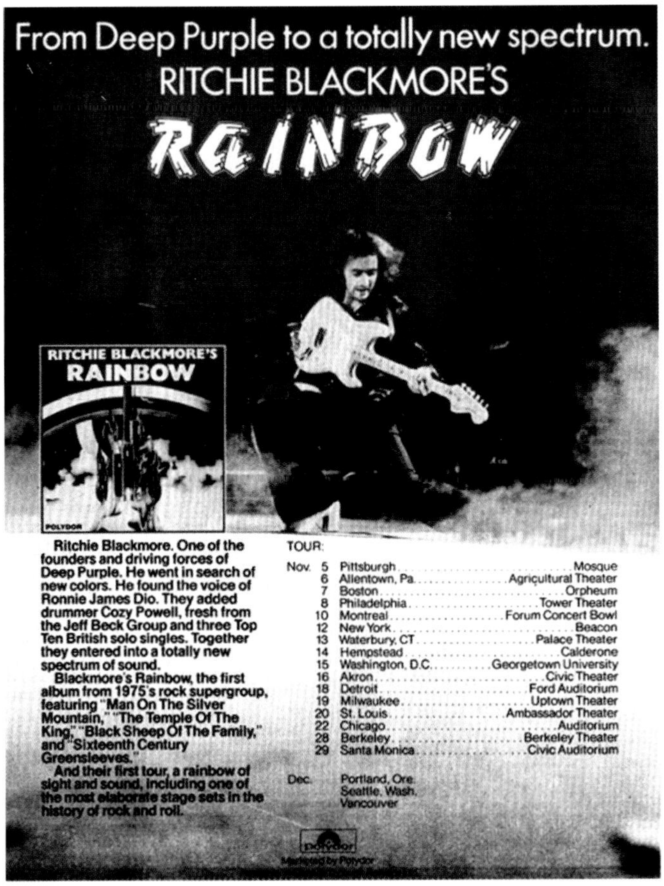

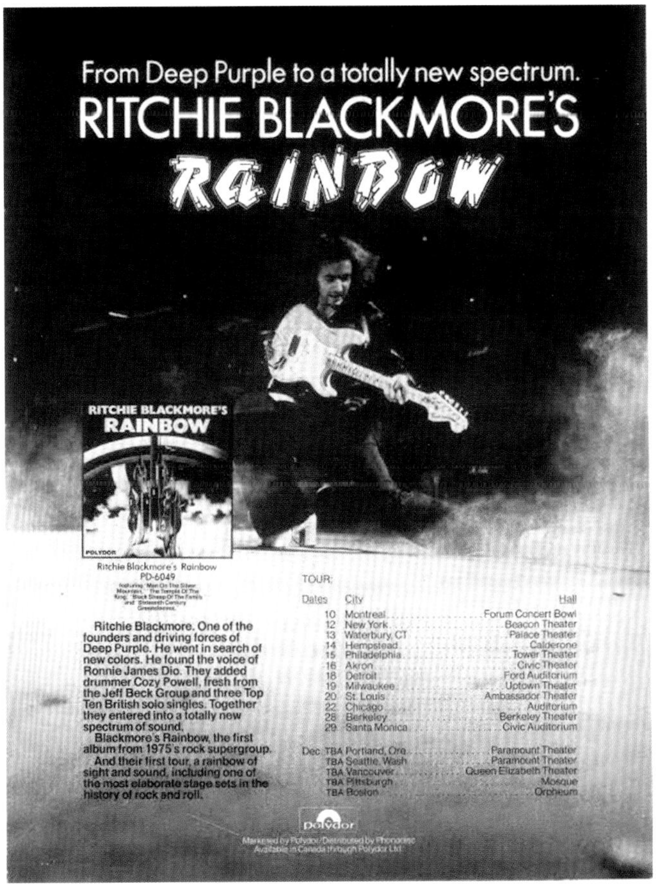

An original tour advert and a later one with a partially rearranged schedule. Some of the shows ended up never taking place.

Wednesday 12th November
Beacon Theatre, New York City, USA

The first batch of colour photos in this section are by Frank White and all come from the second ever show at the Beacon Theatre in New York. All of the black and white photos were taken by John Oster at the penultimate show of the tour at the Community Theatre, Berkeley.

Ludwig
Cozy

Marshall
Ludwig
Powell
Marshall

Powell
Marshall
Marshall

Wednesday 5th November
Syria Mosque, Pittsburgh, USA
This would have originally been the first gig but was rescheduled for the 17th November.

Thursday 6th November
Fairgrounds Agricultural Hall, Allentown, USA
Rescheduled for December.

Friday 7th November
Orpheum Theatre, Boston, USA
Rescheduled for December but probably never happened.

Saturday 8th November
Tower Theatre, Philadelphia, USA
Rescheduled for the 15th November.

Monday 10th November
Forum Concert Bowl, Montreal, Canada
Support act: Argent
The first show eventually took place at the Montreal Forum, a venue capable of holding approximately 17,000 people but Rainbow only drew about 1,500 as Dio recalled some years later. It was suggested that this bruised Blackmore's ego, but if it did, he didn't let it show. When people have something to prove, it invariably brings out the best in them. In the case of Blackmore, Rainbow may have started off on a sticky wicket but such was Blackmore's passion and belief in what he was doing that it just gave him additional impetus.

I put the question to Tony Carey who said, "I never saw Ritchie throw any ego tantrums, that wasn't his style. His style was, he'd disappear into the dressing room with a bottle of Scotch and keep it to himself, then show up on stage. He never played like a drunk but he played like Paganini a little bit, like he'd sold his soul to the devil... or to Johnnie Walker! I don't have much sympathy when I hear a story like that, that it didn't sell out in Montreal, the very first Rainbow gig. We were delighted and excited to play."

Raymond D'addario explains why such a large venue was used. "It was a big ice arena in Montreal and we played to half the arena. They put the stage in the middle but they couldn't have played in a smaller place because we were trying to drag that big rainbow around."

The show started later than planned as technical problems caused delays. This was a regular problem during the early shows as the electronic rainbow caused interference with the equipment, particularly Blackmore's guitar and amplification. At this opening show, the band supposedly played 'If You Don't Like Rock 'n' Roll' which was rarely performed, although it is sometimes claimed the recording comes from the show in Hempstead four days later. But the performance is high energy and played at a faster pace than on the album. It also includes a vocal guitar interplay that Blackmore had originally done to great effect with Ian Gillan. This is followed by a Dio and audience interplay, that was later done with 'Long Live Rock 'n' Roll'. But strip those aspects out and the song could have worked well as a set opener and it's a shame that it was played so infrequently.

Wednesday 12th November
Beacon Theatre, New York City, USA
Support act: Argent

For the second show, this much smaller New York theatre had a capacity of just under 3,000. At these early shows, Dio seemed very fired up and appeared to be agitated sometimes as the audience responses were often quite reserved. As an example, after 'Sixteenth Century Greensleeves' Dio twice asks the audience if they feel alright before shouting back at them "well do you fucking really feel alright? Well then, shout it. This is the first time we have played in the United States for anyone, the first time... and New York is the place we wanted to play first. Make us feel this like we want to play every other place and come back to you again."

This show was reviewed by Dan Nooger for the *Village Voice*:

The Rainbow that came to New York was in a very real sense a brand new band. Ritchie Blackmore, who walked away from Deep Purple and the security that comes with selling untold millions of records, had assembled a completely new group around himself and singer lyricist Ronnie Dio since recording their successful debut album. When the new Rainbow stepped on stage at the Beacon Wednesday night it was their first-ever gig and the atmosphere was electric with tension and anticipation.

Ronnie Dio fits perfectly into his roll of foil to Blackmore's serious demeanour. Strutting across the stage shaking his mane, pulling those old Stewarty microphone moves, flipping like a flag on a pole, Ronnie rocked the house down while Blackmore stood stage left whipping up storms of electric frenzy. Tony Carey's lush keyboards came to the forefront on the balladic 'Catch The Rainbow', the lyrics almost lost in deep echo as streams of colour poured through the huge Tony Mazzucchi-designed rainbow overlooking the stage. Black-

more's brief solo was his best of the evening.

'Man On The Silver Mountain' was stretched to nearly double its recorded length. Dio's voice recalled Robert Plant in full cry as Cozy Powell's perfectly timed drum smashes pushed him on. Blackmore has always been a staunch admirer of Jeff Beck and Rainbow's show-stopping rock out of The Yardbirds' 'Still I'm Sad' made the instrumental album version sound like a warm up for the real thing; Dio making up lyrics on the spot, Blackmore soaring, Powell, climaxing in an orchestrated explosion. As bits of the '1812 Overture' roared through the PA, the former Jeff Beck drummer let loose with cannon shots and explosions.

Any litany of the great vocalist/guitarist combinations of the rock age includes Jagger and Richards, Stewart and Beck, Plant and Page, Daltrey and Townshend. Add to that list the two newest stars in that exalted heaven — Dio and Blackmore.

The show was also reviewed for *Billboard* magazine by Joe Bivona, but he was far less impressed. "*All the stage gimmicks in the world could not disguise the fact that its music was mostly tedious heavy metal that failed to sustain interest.*"

Bivona also went on to say, "*like Purple, excessive volume was used to drive this band's high points home. The only exception, curiously enough, was Blackmore himself, who brought the only touch of variety and humour to the music. His emotive blues intro at the start and his precisely picked intro into 'Greensleeves' were the most musical moments of the evening. The sludge created by the rest of Rainbow effectively blurred many of Blackmore's other exceptional moments.*"

For the young Frank White — whose colour photos adorn this section of the book — it was his first year of photographing bands, with the aid of his mum's camera. It was also the first time he had not only seen Blackmore, but also Dio, who left a lasting impression. As Frank forged a career in photography he would go on to take numerous photos of Dio as he followed the singer's career. A Dio book of Frank's photos was published in 2018.

Frank's recollections of Rainbow's first ever show in America also adds context regarding why some of them were poorly attended, or in the case of others, why they were cancelled due to a lack of advance ticket sales: "I just happened to see an ad for Ritchie Blackmore's Rainbow. I heard Deep Purple broke up but didn't know what happened to the band members. Back then, it was harder to know where band members ended up after they left the band you knew of for years and then I found out about Ritchie. Rainbow was playing with Argent at the Beacon Theatre in NYC but I had never been there before. So again, I left my parent's house with one of my mum's cameras, telling them I would be at a friend's house, got some film before I left and headed to NYC.

"This time I took a bus to the George Washington Bridge bus station in the Washington Heights section of NYC and took the subway downtown and walked a few blocks to the theatre. I bought a ticket at the box office and the seat was towards the back of the theatre and again as soon as the lights went out I ran to the front of the stage. When the stage lights came on a rainbow appeared over the stage.

"The singer who I didn't know wore an all-white outfit with snakeskin boots. His voice sounded amazing and the band had the crowd on their feet. I blended into the crowd and started taking photos. I was right on the isle in front of Ritchie Blackmore, who was doing all kinds of moves with his guitar playing. Some of the songs I remembered they played that night were 'Man On The Silver Mountain', 'Catch The Rainbow' and 'Stargazer'. Even though I was only thirteen at the time, I thought Ronnie was a special singer and became a fan of Rainbow and him that night. Over the next several years I would listen to his amazing voice on the albums that Rainbow produced."

Rainbow biographer Roy Davies says, "The gig was again delayed due to problems with the rainbow electrics interfering with the PA, producing a hum/feedback. If the various bootlegs of the earliest live set known to exist are anything to go by, the Judy Garland 'Over the Rainbow/Wizard of Oz' tape intro was not used yet, the band simply tuning up on stage and launching into the opening number.

"'Catch the Rainbow' had not yet matured into the fully extended epic seen in 1976. Ronnie improvised different lyrics from the recorded versions in slower tempo takes of 'Stargazer' and 'A Light in the Black'. 'Man On The Silver Mountain' featured a mid-song guitar blitz into a slow 'blues' which was originally a part of the live 'You Fool No One' back in Deep Purple days. The French press mentioned an encore of 'If You Don't Like Rock 'n' Roll', which was for decades thought to be an error, but is now confirmed by attendees. A bootleg version of the track has circulated, possibly from this night or from Calderone Hall, as the New York gigs remain the most widely recorded. However, press references to a live 'Temple of the King' was indeed a mistake!"

Thursday 13th November
Palace Theatre, Waterbury, USA
Support act: unknown

Friday 14th November
Calderone Concert Hall, Hempstead, Long Island, USA
Support act: UFO
Originally advertised for the 8th November, the opening salvo to this show is quite similar to that of

'Burn' from *Made In Europe*. Sound problems yet again caused by the electronic rainbow meant both a late start and a forty-minute break in the show after 'Sixteenth Century Greensleeves'.

Overall a fine performance with Dio making some particularly witty comments throughout the gig with the English style of humour that he had been surrounded by over the past three years in the company of Deep Purple, but once again making comments about the crowd's attitude: "Are you preparing to enjoy yourselves tonight then? It doesn't seem like it. Get into something, anything. Here's a song inspired by Robin Hood. One of our main people who made Marian so to speak. This one, 'Sixteenth Century Greensleeves'. This takes some special preparation this one does, you have to get into the mood of Henry the eighth, the ninth, the tenth, the eleventh, all the way to sixteen — Sixteenth Century Greensleeves..."

'Man On The Silver Mountain' is particularly impressive with a bluesy intro — Ronnie sings unaccompanied before Ritchie starts playing blues over the top and takes over with some lengthy doodling for nearly three minutes before kicking into the more familiar song structure.

A hesitant embryonic version of 'Stargazer' featured, though the longer extended format of 'Still I'm Sad' (with keys and drum solos) was already established. Cozy had by now fully developed his drum solo from one he had first performed with Hammer, utilising a reel-to-reel backing tape of Tchaikovsky's '1812 Overture' as played by the Minneapolis Symphony Orchestra.

After 'A Light In The Black' Dio says, "Let me give you just one little bit of history about this song. One reason being that if we don't, our drummer will collapse. Secondly if we don't, our bass player will die. This is a new band right? Let me introduce you to a couple of people in this band. Bass player Jimmy Bain. Tony Carey on the keyboards. I've forgot who plays guitar. I think it's Les Perrin... Les Perrin on the guitar, maybe somebody else. If in this song you hear thunder or cannons going off, well that's the way it goes. We cried all the way through this song when we recorded it. I hope you don't cry when you hear it. This is a Gregorian chant and it makes us so sad; I hope it doesn't make you sad. It's a song called Still, and Still, and Still, and Still ... Still I'm Sad. I'm sad, I'm sad."

Ritchie then starts a gentle piece of playing with Ronnie singing "oh I'm sad, oh I'm sad, oh I'm not really sad, because you make me glad, you make us all glad." After Bain announces Ronnie, Ritchie then kicks in with the riff.

It is reported that 'If You Don't Like Rock 'n' Roll' was played as the encore but as mentioned for the opening show in Montreal, it is unclear if the tape circulating is from that show or this one.

For anyone wondering who the hell Les Perrin is, he was a publicist who represented many artists.

Saturday 15th November
Georgetown University, Washington DC, USA

With the original dates being rearranged, this show got cancelled and it's unlikely that it got reinstated.

Saturday 15th November
Tower Theatre, Philadelphia, USA

Support act: Argent

Another show that was considerably delayed due to problems caused by the rainbow. This was accurately detailed in a review by Jack McDaniel for *The Villanovan*:

It had the makings of a great evening. You knew when Ritchie Blackmore stepped on stage you would be besieged by smoke, fire, bombs and volume. When the show was moved back a week to permit proper stage preparations, you figured dark glasses might be in order. When the show was moved back an additional hour though, you feared there may be trouble. There was.

Settled down in your seat, feeling just great, the lights went out and the electricity began. A loud drone accompanied by the toll of a bell introduced the opener, Argent. You hadn't heard many of the songs, but were entertained by a classy blend of funk plus rock 'n' roll. Rod Argent played a steady keyboard which, accompanied by impressive guitar work, comprised a genuinely satisfying opening set.

Now Blackmore was coming up. It had to be tremendous. There was a huge rainbow arched triumphantly over the stage and four Marshall amps over where Blackmore usually stands. A fight breaks out behind you and as you turn to see the action you're greeted by hosts of neo eyes. Yes, everything was perfect for the occasion. Finally, after a very long wait, the show begins.

The curtain ascends and the crowd gasps at a backdrop of castles under stars and a quarter moon, colours flashed magnificently across the rainbow and amidst streams yellow light, Ritchie Blackmore achieves the stage. Leering at the crowd, he turns up that Stratocaster but something is wrong. Above the ordinarily clear, crisp Blackmore sound is a mysterious cosmos pervading buzz. It seems to be coming from one of the Marshalls and is bothering the hell out of Blackmore. After two songs he leaves the stage for repairs. An agonising hour passes before the crowd is told the lights interfered with the speakers. Thus the elaborate light show, that demanded weeks of preparation was now just ordinary.

The Rainbow played pretty well though. Despite all else, Blackmore did a good job. He's one of those guys who just seems to look good with a guitar. He got down hard, but it was useless. No one could salvage the evening at this point. The crowd was disenchanted and the band felt it, resulting in a very short set and no encore. Too bad. It really could have been a great show but turned out to be a disaster. You can't blame Blackmore though. The crowd was simply beyond responsiveness. So we can only sit back and await a hopefully triumphant return of the Rainbow. As it was though, they were the first band to be outplayed by a buzzing amplifier.

Sunday 16th November
Civic Theatre, Akron, USA
Support act: unknown

Monday 17th November
Syria Mosque, Pittsburgh, USA
Support act: UFO
This show was rescheduled and would originally have been the first gig. Some claim that it took place on the 18th.

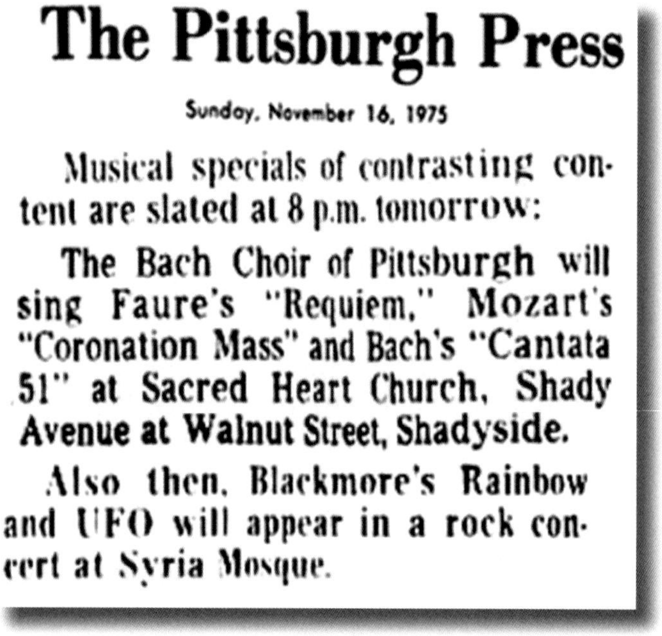
The Pittsburgh Press

Sunday, November 16, 1975

Musical specials of contrasting content are slated at 8 p.m. tomorrow:

The Bach Choir of Pittsburgh will sing Faure's "Requiem," Mozart's "Coronation Mass" and Bach's "Cantata 51" at Sacred Heart Church, Shady Avenue at Walnut Street, Shadyside.

Also then, Blackmore's Rainbow and UFO will appear in a rock concert at Syria Mosque.

Was Ritchie tempted to cancel the show so he could catch the Bach Choir in action?

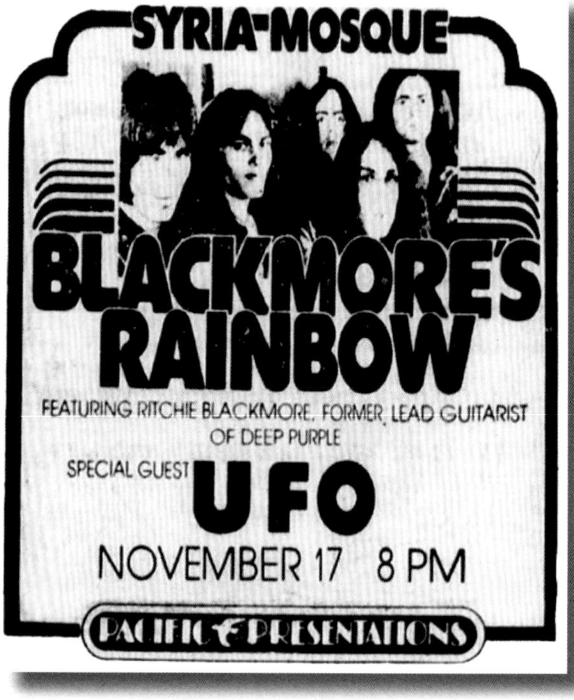

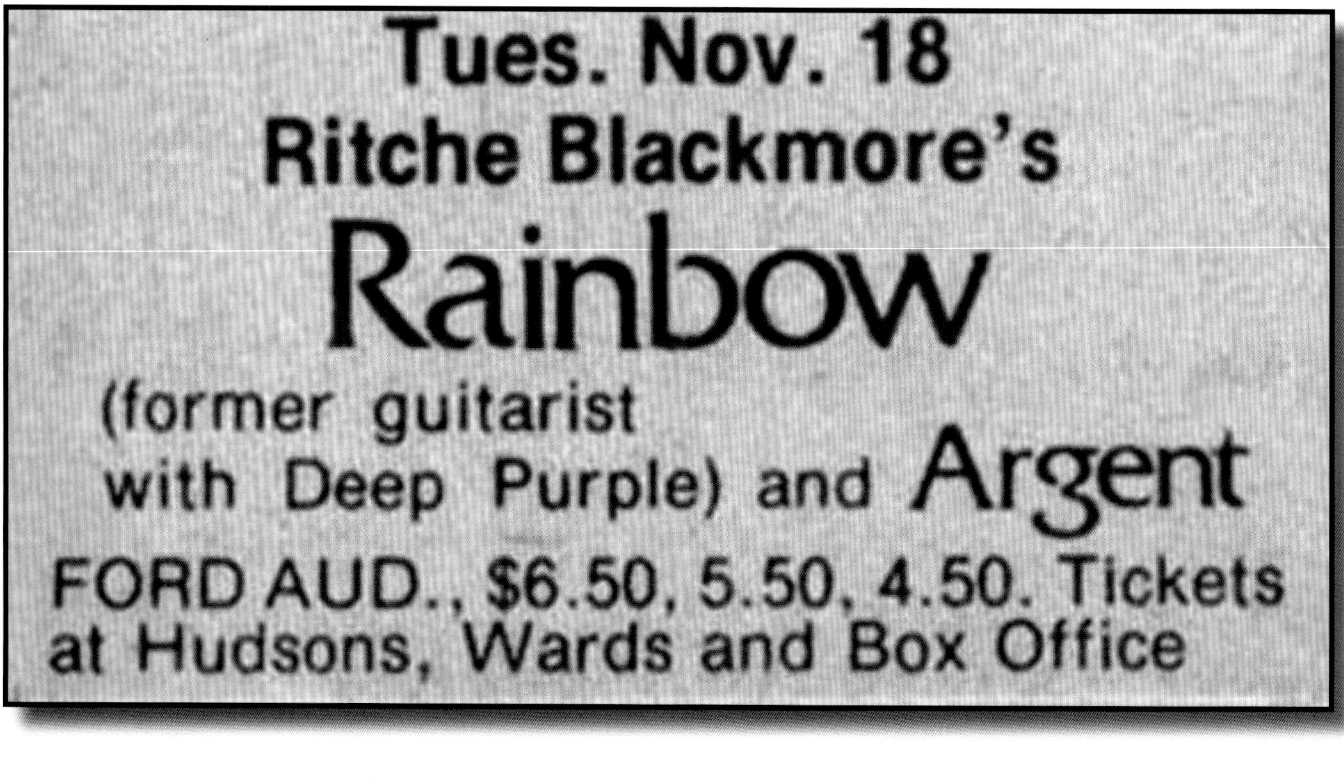
Tues. Nov. 18
Ritche Blackmore's
Rainbow
(former guitarist
with Deep Purple) and Argent
FORD AUD., $6.50, 5.50, 4.50. Tickets
at Hudsons, Wards and Box Office

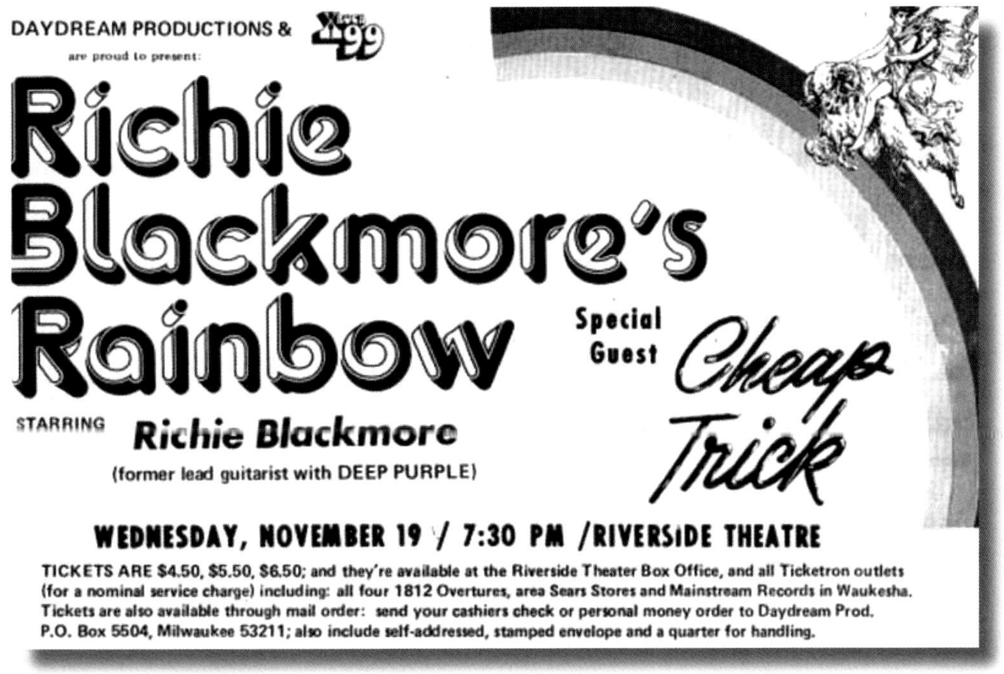

]Wednesday 19th November
Riverside Theatre, Milwaukee, USA
Cancelled. The support act was planned to be Cheap Trick.

Thursday 20th November
Ambassador Theatre, St. Louis, USA
Support act: unknown

Friday 21st November
Ford Auditorium, Detroit, USA
Support act: The Mutants (Argent was advertised as support)

This show was originally scheduled for the 18th as the original adverts testify. Part of the rainbow fell down during preparations for the soundcheck but luckily no one was hurt. Argent were advertised as the support but it was The Mutants, a local Detroit band (not the cult Californian punk band of the same name) and the first of some hastily arranged supports for Rainbow.

Seen listed variously as taking place on the 18th, 20th or 21st. Newspaper adverts (and various bootlegs) all state the 18th, however various promotional posters and photos filed in photographer Fin Costello's archive date the Detroit concert as the 21st. Arguably the best of the 1975 shows, the opener was preceded by a Blackmore opening guitar blitz. 'Self Portrait' remained a five minute punchy version with extra guitar, while the nine minute 'Man On The Silver Mountain' at this stage started with a nice understated blues intro and had a short solo guitar/vocal interplay rather than what would become the more familiar 'Blues' section.

A lovely lyrical guitar intro led to 'Sixteenth Century Greensleeves'. An excellent 'Still I'm Sad' and a frantic 'A Light in the Black' following on directly after a ten minute 'Stargazer'. Again, both latter tracks were still work-in-progress with alternate lyrical takes.

Saturday 22nd November
Auditorium Theatre, Chicago, USA
Support act: Rush
Although the Canadian power trio was billed as the support act, they cancelled. Rush had a show the day before in Terre Haute, Indiana and although it was only a three hour drive due north to Chicago, the following night they had another show in Indiana, two hours south of Terre Haute, and probably made the judgement that additional travelling, just to play a forty minute or so support slot couldn't be justified. It's unclear if another band was brought in or whether the show went ahead with no support.

Wednesday 26th November
Selland Arena, Fresno, USA
Support acts: Steppenwolf
This show was billed as the Winter Festival of Rock. The band did a round of press interviews at the Fresno Hilton hotel. The then-current version of John Kay's Steppenwolf stepped in to support at very short notice when it seems that Argent pulled out.

Friday 28th November
Community Theatre, Berkeley, USA
Support act: Sammy Hagar
Blackmore was in one of his more playful moods with lots of improvisations, the set extended to nearly two hours long.

Saturday 29th November
Civic Auditorium, Santa Monica, USA
Support act: Argent

Earlier in the day, the English Formula One racing driver Graham Hill died at the controls of his Piper PA-23 Aztec twin-engine light aircraft when it crashed near Arkley, Hertfordshire, while on a night approach to Elstree Airfield in thick fog.

Undoubtedly instigated by Cozy Powell, 'Still I'm Sad' was dedicated to the two-times former world champion at this show.

Perhaps it fired Cozy up more than normal, if the review by Todd Everett in the *New Musical Express* was anything to go by:

New drummer Cozy Powell was monstrous as he wielded drumsticks resembling baseball bats and laid down a solid locomotive beat. His interplay with Blackmore after just eleven shows was remarkable. A drum solo near the end of the show came complete with dry ice smoke, flash bombs, and strobe lights.

Material consisted mainly of the "Rainbow" album, and included 'Man On The Silver Mountain', 'Catch The Rainbow', and 'Still I'm Sad' (which was dedicated to racing driver Graham Hill). A new piece titled 'Stargazer' showed Ritchie branching out into lengthier and more complex music and managed to whip up some interesting (if not too emotional) guitar.

Ritchie Blackmore is a master, a shadowy figure on stage whose fingers have coughed up some remarkable guitar. As a musician his career is really just beginning and one can be sure that on his next trip around, the show will be every bit as powerful as he is.

Sunday 30th November
Swing Auditorium, San Bernardino, USA
Press adverts for this gig claimed "by popular demand" but the show was cancelled just four days before it was due to go ahead because of low ticket sales. According to a report in the *San Bernardino County Sun*, Orange Show ticket manager Bob Lewis claimed that only 342 tickets had been sold. The venue had a capacity of around 10,000. Given that the previous year Blackmore had been playing huge venues with Purple, this must have been a harsh reminder that brand names are vital. Despite being regarded at the time as one of the top guitarists in the world, it's easy to overlook that quite often individual band member names don't register with large swathes of the audiences.

As a combination of cancelling at such short notice and largely relying on word of mouth, it was reported that between fifty to a hundred people, largely from the Los Angeles area, turned up for the show clutching their tickets. Just three months later, Deep Purple went on to play to the same venue, and whilst it might not have been sold out, a substantial audience witnessed the band with Tommy Bolin.

The following shows are thought not to have taken place:

Paramount Theatre, Portland, USA

Paramount Theatre, Seattle, USA

Queen Elizabeth Theatre, Vancouver, Canada

Orpheum Theatre, Boston, USA

Fairgrounds Agricultural Hall, Allentown, USA

Curtis Hixon Hall, Tampa, USA
An article in *Beat Instrumental* mentioned the tour ended in Tampa but it's unconfirmed.

1976.

Rainbow
Rising
RITCHIE BLACKMORE
A RAINBOW RISING...
polydor
Oyster

3.
I See A Rainbow Rising

"All the songs on the first album were written at my own house, then I put them down on tape and said to the band, 'play this'. But now, with the new line-up, it's every man for himself. We're writing, funnily enough, in the same way that Purple used to write — if they used to write at all — during rehearsals and in the studio. It's very hard, very much like early Purple in 'In Rock' days. There are some involved tracks, but I don't think we ever lose sight of our original objectives."

Despite upheavals with the tour schedule and endless problems with the electronic rainbow, the '75 dates quickly forged a band chemistry. The addition of three new songs played on the tour also meant that there was already half an album's worth of material for the follow up album. And what an album it would turn out to be!

To all intent and purposes, with the first Rainbow album having been recorded with the members of Dio's band Elf, Blackmore had used musicians who were convenient for the job in hand. By the time Rainbow went back to Munich to record the second album, an established group line-up was in place. Within the short space of time together, they had developed into a formidably powerful and tight outfit. Furthermore, a more democratic approach was brought in for the recording and performances. It was decided that the share of mechanical royalties for the album would be split 56% to Blackmore, 24% to Dio, 15% to Powell and 5% to Bain. Whereas the youngest member of the band Tony Carey received no royalties and was merely considered a session player.

From a musical standpoint, Blackmore and Dio's writing partnership was flourishing. Between them, they wrote six songs, which for most Rainbow fans still hold together today as the group's finest album.

Returning to Germany to start working on the album was a breeze, as Tony Carey relayed to me back in 2005: "Well we went to Munich, and I'd never been to Germany, and I got my new passport. Jimmy and me we were kind of a team, we roomed in the seventeenth floor of the Arabellahaus Hotel. I've since lived in the Munich area for twenty-five years so I know the hotel, in fact the same guy's on the door by the way as it was in 1976. It's amazing and he still remembers me! 'Hello Mr Carey'. We rehearsed in an old farmhouse and if you told me where it was today I'd know. I would say somewhere like Fürstenfeldbruck around Munich. We drove out and rehearsed with really tiny, minimal equipment.

It was in December, [*late January or early February. Ed.*] it was freezing cold and we rehearsed the same way we always rehearsed, which was basically 'here's some riffs.' Ronnie would have his pad and paper and be writing lyrics and mostly we played without Ronnie singing because he would be brainstorming his demons and wizards thing."

When I interviewed Cozy Powell in 1997, he recalled, "from what I can remember we ran through the stuff in a disused club outside Munich just to run through the ideas for the songs. Ritchie kind of let me get on with it as far as the drum tracks were concerned. Once I knew the format, we'd worked out 'A Light In The Black' which was sort of fifteen minutes of mayhem or however long it was. 'Stargazer' was kind of worked out. We got the basic track worked out but we hadn't got the beginning so I kind of just worked out a drum fill for the beginning of that."

Indeed, during the performances of 'Stargazer' in '75, the drum intro was somewhat perfunctory compared to Cozy's bombastic statement that ended up on the record. In fact at some shows, it almost sounded like they were still discovering the song. During the fourth show at the Calderone Concert Hall, the whole song almost falls apart at one point, before Cozy picks it back up and the rest join in, but before long it comes to a rather anti-climactic end and sounds more like a rehearsal outtake than a live performance. "The other tracks were pretty straightforward," concluded Cozy.

Tony Carey: "Then we went into Musicland, which at that time was a state of the art studio in the basement of the Arabellahaus Hotel. I remember they carved a drum room. This was kind of revolutionary at the time, now everybody does it. Everybody sets drum kits up in bathrooms and tiled rooms to get this crashy, banging sound. But in those days studios had rugs on the walls. This dead sound from Abba to The Beatles. Everything was this dead studio seventies sound and we wanted to definitely make a little more damage, a little more noise. I don't know if they did construction or not, I think they did. They somehow hollowed Cozy out a concrete room to put the drums in. Everybody does it these days but it was revolutionary then. Martin Birch produced and engineered... I don't know if he produced, actually I'd say Ritchie produced, he knew what he wanted but Martin engineered and was the liaison with everybody's egos, a lovely guy. Great guy. I really loved working with Martin."

Cozy Powell concurred with Tony about the drum set up: "To get the drum sound we actually went into the corridor and built a kind of shed if you like, for me to play in. It was the corridor that goes down to the cellars, and a concrete staircase, and concrete is always very good for drum sound. It's very ambient. So instead of using the actual studio which I thought was a good studio, but it didn't have a very good room for drums, we actually built this kind of alcove I could actually play in inside the corridor."

For Tony Carey it was his first time making a professional recording and despite it being over before you could blink an eye, he has one underlying memory of the whole recording process: "I don't remember his name [*Reinhold Mack, Ed*], the guy from Musicland, the Tonnmesiter came in, in an SS uniform one day! It was fantastic. Not the black, but the brown shirt uniform with a red and black swastika, complete Nazi uniform. Now I just thought it was funny, but being American I can just wear anything I want all the time. But being German in 1976 that's a serious crime, but he came in and the whole day his demeanour was 'sieg heil' but perfectly done, really funny guy. He never cracked a smile. He would say 've vill do it zis vay'. Real German in his Nazi uniform. That stuck out from the recording."

"I did that only once," recalled Mack in 2014. "Ritchie always asked me about WWII stuff — as if I would know. So me and my assistant rented the gear and stormed into the control room cussing and shouting, almost scaring Ritchie to death. Fairly good acting on my part."

"I remember it was done very quickly. It was done in the winter of '76" recalled Cozy. "I think the actual recordings were done in a week. Backing tracks. Very, very quickly. I think the idea was to try and capture it as quickly as we could. I think I was there for a week, ten days and then once all the drum tracks were done then Ronnie did the vocals which took forever and a day. Ritchie and Ronnie used to go through quite a lot of grief trying to get that sorted out and Wendy was of course on tour with him as well, so as soon as I'd finished my stuff I got out of there and let them get on with it. I remember it was done very quickly. It wasn't a sort of manufactured record. It was done spontaneously and the musicians input is the way you hear it. Which is possibly why it's one of the better albums that we did. I think it's generally regarded by the fans as the classic."

Once again Tony Carey echoes those thoughts, "we zipped through the record. 'A Light In The Black' — basically the band cut the track without me, 'Stargazer' too and I overdubbed the keyboards. And they wanted an introduction for 'Tarot Woman' so everybody left and I sat with Martin for about an hour and a half and we did 'Tarot Woman', and on the same day we did the solos for 'A Light In The Black', the fast synthesiser solo, some stuff on 'Stargazer', the orchestra things, which I simulated and were later done with a small orchestra. Once again I'm looking back through thirty years of whatever but compared to making records today it was effortless. It was a breeze, a piece of cake because basically what we did was what you are supposed to do when you make a record, and nobody ever does because everybody's too neurotic, is go in and play the fucking thing! Then Ronnie came down with his notebook and sang 'my eyes are bleeding' and all that shit! And it was done."

Tony Carey had been brought into the band for a specific reason as he explained in a more recent interview; "My part of Ritchie's band was to support his guitar parts, and give him support while he soloed. He played a lot of open fifths on the guitar and I basically doubled his parts, on organ and clavinet — loudly — and once in a while got to show off with a solo. I used all the synths popular at the time, but the real deal was the Hammond organ. I don't think I played a major chord in all the time I was with the band, as major chords never sound in tune between a keyboard and a loud guitar, and open fifths sound, uh, heavy."

In a contemporary article in *Circus* magazine by Jon Tiven, published just after the album was released, Tiven reported that during some free time in the recording schedule, Rainbow enjoyed a night at the local ice-skating rink. There was also a band playing there and as the Rainbow chaps were skating one of them suggested they gatecrashed as they rounded the bandstand. On Ritchie's cue they all jumped into the band pit, grabbed the instruments away from the musicians, and proceeded to run through a few numbers. "Everyone was shocked at first," Ritchie commented, "but most of them knew who we were — we're quite well-known in Germany — and they sat down and watched us play the 'Ice-Skating Blues.' We stayed up there for an hour, and then just handed the guitars back to the band, jumped into the rink and resumed skating. It's the first time I've played on ice skates, and I must say it was enjoyable. Good fun."

Back to the recording and it was soon completed. Tony Carey summed up his feelings about it: "I just know that the record was real, made for the right reasons, and got something down on tape that was unique to that band at that time in that place. Cozy played like a madman, Ronnie knew what he wanted to sing about and how he wanted to sing it, Ritchie seemed sure of what he was doing... Bullseye."

Carey has nothing but praise for Blackmore and his vision for what he wanted: "When I did all of my solos, every time, he said to Martin 'I'll come back...' I did two different solos to 'A Light In The Black' and one of them was a low one that made the record and before that I did a high one, more your standard keyboard solo about two octaves higher. He came back and said, 'boy that's fast that's good, don't like it, do another one' and he left again. I said 'okay' and Martin suggested I do something completely different. We did this low one and he came back and said, 'That's the mark of a good musician when you do something different'. He was only a control freak in the sense that had he not liked that solo I would have played a third one and if he hadn't liked that he would have got another guy to play it. But as far as letting people do their jobs he was great. He hired me because he thought I was the best he could find at the moment and he didn't need to sit there and tell me how to do my job. If anybody would be the one to do that it would be Martin who was ostensibly producing."

Whilst the album was indeed recorded very quickly and with a simplistic production, 'Stargazer' was the exception to that rule, being the big production number on the album with the Munich Philharmonic Orchestra being brought in to add to its grandeur. It made perfect sense. Blackmore had originally come up with the riff whilst playing his cello in a melancholy way. In May '75 his girlfriend Judith had recently broken off their relationship, something that devastated Blackmore and took him a long time to get over. In fact he continued to make contact off and on up until 1990.

Rainer Pietsch was brought in to score the piece. Pietsch was used to working with rock musicians and in the sixties had toured with the likes of The Who and Herman's Hermits. In 1969 he had begun working as a producer. By the time he had moved to Munich he soon became one of West Germany's most sought-after studio arrangers. He was also a prolific songwriter and the previous year his song 'Ein Lied kann eine Brücke sein' was Germany's Eurovision Song Contest entry. Even though performer Joy Fleming only managed to score a meagre seventeenth place in the international final in Stockholm, the song became an evergreen in Germany and beyond.

Arranging the music for the orchestra to compliment Rainbow gave Pietsch a much wider palette to work from. But typical of Blackmore, his seeming inability to ever achieve satisfaction even applies to this piece and to Pietsch's contribution. In Pete Makowski's Rainbow article in *Classic Rock* in 2014, he quoted Blackmore as saying, "the orchestra was too flowery, and there was too much detracting from the simple melody. We kept taking out parts, and I felt sorry for Rainer because he was so proud of this grandiose piece he had written. We got down to the bare bones and mixed in some Mellotron to even out the orchestra not sounding cohesive or in tune."

Recording the album so quickly ensured they were back in California to escape the German winter before the end of February. Soon after their return the band found themselves at the Long Beach Arena on the 27th. Carey recalled, "We went to see Deep Purple in Los Angeles with Ritchie and we sat in the tenth row. There was no problem that way. I didn't think there was a problem. I wasn't in direct competition with anybody and I worshiped Jon Lord. So he said 'do you want to go and see Purple tonight?' so we said 'okay we'll go', and we sat there in a row like school kids and everybody was polite, there was no kind of vibe. I loved the band. That was the first time I saw Coverdale and Glenn Hughes together and it was unbelievable, I thought they were great." With that particular show being recorded for a radio broadcast and subsequently officially released, there are probably still many Rainbow fans unaware that Rainbow was amongst the audience that night.

Blackmore and the rest of the band were of course strictly there in an observational capacity — no Blackmore getting up to join his old band for the encore of 'Highway Star' (interpolating 'Not Fade Away'). But the following month on the 24th at the Civic Auditorium in Santa Monica Ritchie guested with The Sweet.

On the 19th, Free guitarist Paul Kossoff died on a flight from Los Angeles to New York. That evening as a tribute, The Sweet encored with 'All Right Now' with Free fan Blackmore joining in, such was his admiration.

Back in 1996, Mark Welch interviewed Andy Scott about this event in our then publication *More Black Than Purple*. Scott started by explaining how it came about: "It was completely spontaneous. We had met him the night before or a couple of nights earlier, and the one thing that he'd said to our tour manager, who used to work for Deep Purple — a guy called Mick Angus — was 'You'd better let me get into the gig tonight'. Because the last time we'd played Los Angeles he hadn't been able to get into the show, because our management at that time, and record company, had virtually sold out the gig before tickets even went on sale. There were only a certain amount of tickets down in the auditorium that were available, because the record company had basically bought all the tickets. That's how 'in demand' that concert was; we should have done more nights there at the Santa Monica Civic that first time, but that's the way they wanted to play it. So the second time we did it, the tickets were sold out — not so much record company stuff — by the end of the day. And one thing that Ritchie said to him (Mick Angus) was: 'I'm gonna come, and I'm gonna get in this time'. And we said: 'Of course you are!' And somebody made the joke: 'If you want to get up, put your guitar in the boot...' You can definitely tell which is Ritchie's sound because he is the cleaner guitar sound, and I am the more driven Marshall sound — because there was an offer to set up another stack , but I think Ritchie just said: 'Plug me into anything, I'll be alright'. And I think the only amps on my side of the stage that were available for him to plug into were the amps that I think were monitoring the synthesisers, which had a couple of horns in them, which left him with a rather loud and clear sound."

It was a memorable night for Scott, as he had always admired Blackmore and was heavily influenced by him. "In the really early days when I first joined the band we used to do 'Hush' and 'Kentucky Woman', and we also did a version of 'Black Night' — but these were because we were playing 'popular' dance halls that wanted to hear not only our music but also some other music of the era. It was a generally accepted thing in less heavy bands, more commercial bands. We all wanted to play numbers like 'Speed King' and 'Flight Of The Rat', but we had to keep it down to the more commercial things."

"I could probably still play the 'Black Night' guitar solo exactly the same as it was on the record. I actually had — this shows how much of an influence Ritchie was — I used to play a Stratocaster , but I also had a (Gibson) 335 which I used all the way through the early Sweet era with a certain type of solid body Bigsby, because the 335 had a solid centre to a semi-acoustic guitar. I could put this solid body Bigsby arm on there which gave you a much greater height of tremolo arm, and I also used to use a Hornby-Skews treble booster, which I found out that Ritchie used to use. So the reason I probably sounded quite like him was that I was using a very similar set-up."

During the recording of Rising at Musicland.

Ritchie playing with Sweet 24th March, 1976

© Colin Hart

Rainbow Rising was released in May '76. As far as Blackmore's homeland was concerned, putting everything into context, Deep Purple's album *Come Taste The Band* was released late in '75. It received mixed reviews and only two months before the release of *Rising*, his former band had received terrible reviews for their British tour. For many, Blackmore's absence from Deep Purple was the key factor.

With that in mind, all Blackmore had to do was come up with a half decent album and he was onto a sure-fire winner. The debut album had been a good start but for some it was a little too constrained. *Rising* on the other hand was a full-on assault. No 'Catch The Rainbow' or 'Temple Of The King' style songs were evident. The mellower Blackmore of the first album was replaced with a far more aggressive one for *Rising*, no doubt the breakdown of his relationship with Judith was a contributory factor.

If chart positions were anything to go by (see the full details of chart places at the end of the recording guide section), *Rising* didn't set the world alight. But reviews were positive and it was generally considered a stronger album than the first.

Even the cover was far more striking than its predecessor. Cover artist Ken Kelly specialised in fantasy art but was only just starting out in album artwork. In fact, he had just done his first album cover a few months previously with *Destroyer* by Kiss, which was in more of a comic book style.

Forty years after the album's release, Kelly recalled his memories: "I have to preface it with what happened before I came to Rainbow. Rainbow itself was a very simple cover to do but I don't want to misrepresent that. It was a difficult cover, it was a unique cover, but I have to give Ritchie Blackmore the credit for it. He knew exactly what he wanted. So, when I came into his office and after we greeted each other and sat down and started talking about the cover, I believe it comes from one of the songs — the actual reaching of the hand out to the rainbow. I had just been completely overwhelmed with Kiss and what I did for them, so I was very prepared when Rainbow called and then I went into their office and they dictated the cover."

"So I left the office with a complete painting in my head, I simply had to go home and use the disciplines that we're taught as artists and do what Ritchie said and that's what I did. I didn't think about it much at the time, but it's stayed alive for forty years, it's amazing, it's incredible and it was a masterpiece because that's what Ritchie asked for. He still knows what he's doing to this day and he did back then. I would love to say I created everything and it's all mine, but that's simply not true."

A great cover and a dynamic six songs — with reports in the press that Deep Purple was about to call it a day, forgive me the obvious pun, but the world was indeed Blackmore's oyster.

Rainbow on the rise

RAINBOW have completed recording their new album which has been tentatively set for release at the end of April — but they won't be seen in Britain before August when they plan to do a tour.

Titled 'RAINBOW Rising', the album was recorded in 10 days at Munich's Musicland Studio but the tapes are being taken to America for mixing. All compositions are from within the group — Ritchie Blackmore, Ronnie James Duo, Tony Carey, Jimmy Bain and Cozy Powell.

Blackmore told SOUNDS: "I can't take the music to pieces but if I'm forced into a description I'd say it's a kind of long, heavy rock with a lot of melodic content that seems to be missing from a lot of today's rock and roll groups."

A single from the band, likely to be 'Tarot Woman', will be issued in mid-April shortly before the album and before the band start their American tour.

BLACKMORE

Excessive costs of RAINBOW personnel

E. H Reid CHARTERED ACCOUNTANT

7 11 WOODCOTE ROAD, WALLINGTON, SURREY SM6 OLH

Telephone: 01-647 0831/2/3/4

PN

18th March 1976

R.H. Blackmore Esq.

Dear Ritchie,

re Recording in Munich

Enclosed is a photocopy of the bill received through Acton Travel for damages done at the Arabella Hotel in Munich. This converts to £609.40.

You must appreciate that, because you are the only member of the group who is presently in credit, the effect is that you personally are paying this bill.

May I suggest that, until people have enough money to be able to afford to cause damage and pay for it out of their own money, you might feel inclined in your own special way to indicate that you do not altogether approve of being asked to pay for their hi-jinks.

I think you should also know that exactly the same applies to the extras incurred during the same period while you were recording in Munich. In particular, the extras incurred were as follows:

Jimmy Bain	£103.69
Cozy Powell	365.78
Martin Birch	184.12
Yourself	346.83
Ronnie Dio	1,156.26
Colin Hart	249.76
Ian Ferguson	182.28
Bob Adcock	211.69 + 127.27
David Needle	45.73
Ray D'Dario	102.38
Colin Oxford	8.74

All this adds up to the not insubstantial sum of £3,084.53 + 609.40
As your own particular expenses would appear to be only

cont....

-2-

£346.83 (which you can afford) I fail to see why you shouldbe called upon to foot the bill for an additional £3,347.10. Do you? I certainly don't and I know you would not accept it if I advised you that it was.

You might let me know what you decide to do about it please. What I would like to do is to deduct the cost of the extras from their salaries week by week until they have paid them off. But that is a matter for you to discuss with Bruce, I think.

There are also extras entered against your name in addition to all the above for £1,894.94 some of which have been approved by Colin Hart. I have sent Bruce an analysis of these charges so that he would be in a position to explain to you what they were.

When I told you that the money we have so far received from Polydor is even insufficient to pay for the cost of the first album and to remind you that the first tour did not (as we expected) make a profit, I think the time has come to take a sharp pull on the reins.

Yours sincerely,

c.c. R.S.Bagehot Esq.
J.L. Coletta Esq.
R.J. Cooksey Esq.
M.A. Edwards Esq.
B.A. Payne Esq.

The band might have been happily ensconced back in sunny California but during their time in Munich, large bills had been racked up for damages caused to the hotel.

RAINBOW: 'Rainbow Rising' (Oyster 2490 137) ****

"WITH RAINBOW'S music I intend to carry on and expand upon the essence of Deep Purple — aggressiveness — and at the same time add a kind of medieval feel to it all,'

Thus spake Ritchie Blackmore in a SOUNDS interview dated August 2, 1975 — the last time, to my knowledge, the one-time Deep Purple guitarist visited Britain. Of course, it's been even longer since he actually played here and while this is disappointing I can't help but feel, in a twisted, abstract sort of way, that this lengthy absence from his home country hasn't altogether worked to his favour.

Bearing in mind the recent, much-discussed poor British displays of the Tommy Bolin incarnation of Deep Purple, Ritchie Blackmore is now, to most people, a hazy, indistinct, albeit fond, memory. A good deal of mystique surrounds not only the man but his band as well.

For, at the moment, Rainbow is an uncertain, undiscovered property, not being the band that appeared on last year's amorphous debut album. Gary Driscoll, Mickey Lee Soule and Craig Gruber have long since left the fold, only Blackmore and vocalist, lyricist Ronnie James Dio now remain. The rest of the group is, to British audiences at least, new and untried.

The Rainbow has, however, been carefully crafted, put together with no small amount of precision by Blackmore and Dio. The outfit now comprises, besides the aforementioned duo, Scottish bass player Jimmy Bain, late of Harlot; Tony Carey, Keyboard player, California-born, ex- of a band called Blessings; and old-timer Cozy Powell on drums, whose past credentials vary from the 'Ruff And Ready' Jeff Beck Group to a teenscream 'Dance With The Devil' solo career.

What can I say? This new line-up fits together as neatly as the guitar lead into the socket of Blackmore's well-worn Fender. It works.

'Rainbow Rising' is right, it achieves Blackmore's prime objective, as described in this review's opening quote, on the button — hard rocking, exciting music with an underlying medieval influence.

The album's accompanying biography lays great emphasis on Blackmore's admiration for German Baroque music and this comes through strongly — especially on the LP's standout track 'Stargazer' which has a deep-throated, brooding background (which Itake to be Tony Carey's mellotron work) coupled with some sweeping violins, all of which boosts an already potent, awesome rock sound. If court minstrels of yesteryear had had electric guitars instead of lutes, their odes could well have sounded like this.

But, first and foremost, 'Rainbow Rising' is thermo-nuclear rock 'n' roll, Blackmore's boundless enthusiam for his band shining through like the stark oil-painted rainbow on the album's cover (stylishly conceived by Ken Kelly, the man behind Kiss' 'Destroyer' sleeve). His riffs are fluid, freely-flowing, far removed from the tedious churning exercises that penetrated so many of the songs on his post-'Machine Head' Purple albums; his breaks — notably a soaring, searing solo on 'A Light In The Black' — are dextrous, never derivative.

Of the rest of the band, Dio and Powell shine above the others. Through his work with Elf, Dio has always been recognised as a talented vocalist. Yet with this album, lyrically, he comes into his own. His words lean towards fantastical, sword and sorcery subjects, the epic tale; his book lines (i.e.: 'Lady Starstruck, she's nothing but bad luck/Lady Starstruck, running after me') make an instant impression. Powell, meanwhile, bruises through the album like Bonzo Bonham, his drum work possessing the finesse of a punch-happy boxer whose fists have been hardened by years in the ring.

RITCHIE BLACKMORE: thermo-nuclear rock 'n' roll

Rainbow's high-flying sorcery

This is not to slight either Bain or Carey, both of whom pull their weight and make their respective presences felt throughout.

There are a mere six tracks, four to the first side, two to the second. Unlike the first album, which had the slow, somewhat reflective 'Catch The Rainbow', all are unflagging, powerful numbers — 'Tarot Woman' (refined, many faceted), 'Run With The Wolf' (solid and more simplistic), 'A Light In The Black', 'Starstruck', 'Do You Close Your Eyes' and the already-cited highlight, Rainbow's devil-may-care 'Stairway To Heaven', 'Stargazer'.

Playing the album at home, the remark being bandied about the most of all was, "With a few exceptions, this is better than anything Blackmore ever did with Deep Purple".

I tend to agree, and it's odds-on that you will, too —**Geoff Barton.**

Ritchie Blackmore: "I'm suspicious by nature."

Ronnie Dio: "I'd rather go out and play than go out and find chicks."

Rainbow: "Dio was one of the guys who fell to Earth and I found him in a ditch."

Nearer My Dio To Thee

The Blackmore & Dio Interviews

by Scott Cohen

Rainbow
Rising
RITCHIE BLACKMORE
A RAINBOW RISING...
polydor
Oyster
WORLDWIDE ON POLYDOR RECORDS AND TAPES

Track By Track

1. Tarot Woman (Blackmore / Dio)

In a very unconventional way for a Blackmore album, *Rainbow Rising* starts with the lengthy Minimoog intro of this track. With the album being recorded so quickly, Tony Carey commented; "The only time I ever played 'Tarot Woman' was the day I recorded it."

"I especially like the Minimoog solo Tony does," said Blackmore in recent years. "It was the first solo he did for the song. He said he could do much better, and went back and played for about an hour, but it never compared to the first solo."

Blackmore's guitar comes soaring through the mix and the introduction of Cozy Powell to the band clearly shows what a bonus he was to the line-up as he relentlessly drives the track on. Dio continued with the mystical lyrics that featured so prominently on the first album. It was a superb opening track and seemed the logical choice to open the live set as well. Blackmore reckons they tried it out in rehearsals but weren't happy with the outcome. Hence he wrote 'Kill The King' to be the stage opener and 'Tarot Woman' was sadly laid to waste!

2. Run With The Wolf (Blackmore / Dio)

A short punchy number, and once again Dio is singing about things that aren't entirely tangible to the average listener but are nevertheless fascinating. Blackmore's middle eight solo is quite subdued but he more than makes up for it with the second solo during the closing section of the song with some fluent and intricate runs on his trusty Stratocaster.

3. Starstruck (Blackmore / Dio)

If the lyrics to 'Run With The Wolf' are somewhat puzzling, 'Starstruck' is much more discernible. In Purple, Ian Gillan had sang about "a strange kind of woman" but none could be as strange as the woman who was the inspiration, if one can call it that, for this song: A female fan called Muriel who stalked Blackmore for many years! He claimed he even spotted her once in the bushes of his garden and in order to get rid of the crazy fan he set the dogs on her! Musically the intro is quite offbeat before settling into a very straightforward 4/4 riff. Blackmore makes good use of his slide technique during the solo. Unlike so many other players who use a conventional slide, what Blackmore produces isn't the typical "steel" sound but a more blended, smooth and rounded sound. Something he used extensively on the following album.

4. Do You Close Your Eyes (Blackmore / Dio)

The first of the three tracks — written prior to going into the studio — that had been performed on the '75 dates. Another straight ahead no-nonsense rocker, it had opened the shows in '75 but was used as the encore number for the *Rising* tour, and when the mood took him, Blackmore would do one of his famous guitar demolitions whilst Powell and Bain kept the rhythm driving along.

5. Stargazer (Blackmore / Dio)

It's hard to eulogise about this track without going overboard. Quite simply the best thing that Rainbow ever recorded bar none: Indeed one of the greatest rock songs recorded by anyone! 'Stargazer' clearly shows Blackmore's depth and breadth of musical vision to the full, with the Munich Philharmonic Orchestra giving the composition a grandness of epic proportions that it so richly deserves. "It's amazing how many guitarists use the same old lines," said Blackmore. "They never dare touch Arabic or Turkish scales."

Dio spoke about the song before the album was released to Don Snowden of the *L.A. Vanguard* in March 1976: "I always wanted to write a song about a very oppressed person. To me the most oppressed person I could think of was a slave, more or less in Egyptian times, who was always led around by chains, whipped, and never had an identity. I wanted to write it from the standpoint of the slave, through his eyes, give you his impression of The Wizard, who doesn't seem to have feet, who has a big long flowing robe. I picture The Wizard's eyes being totally turned back so he has no pupils.

"So here's this totally oppressed individual, who's speaking not only for himself, but for all the other slaves around him, and he still believes that The Wizard will take them all out of this oppression and lead them to his star. At the end of it, he climbs up to the top of the pyramid, this tower of stone that took them nine years to build. He launches himself off the top of the tower and there's total silence as he falls instead of rises, and they still believe until they see splat! and he's just a little lump of blood on the sand.

"It correlates itself with the way almost all of the people in this country believed in Richard Nixon up until the time he decided he was going to take a leap off the tower and fell flat on his ass and became just a little lump of blood and putty. That was my way of saying that the common man will always rise above the leader who oppresses them. I don't feel that you can ever give social comment without making it a fable in some way, of having a little story that keeps the interest."

6. A Light In The Black (Blackmore / Dio)

With 'Stargazer' and 'Do You Close Your Eyes' already firm staples of the live show, 'A Light In The Black' just required some honing in the studio. As previously mentioned, Carey reckons he did two try outs of his solo section, but yet another song recorded very quickly. The instrumental section is the highlight with Blackmore and Carey combining superbly with solos of astonishing speed. The riff appears to have also inspired songs from both 10CC ('Good Morning Judge') and Whitesnake ('Don't Mess With Me') that appeared within two years of its release. Dio said that lyrically it was a continuation of the 'Stargazer' story.

***

As time passed, the band itself expressed mixed views on the album. For Carey, as it was the only studio album his finished work ended up on, he was rightly proud of it. Dio and Blackmore both tended to blow hot and cold. Whilst both liking it and accepting that is was a fan favourite, Dio always favoured the first album, believing the songs were better. Blackmore, in his usual downbeat way often cites 'Stargazer' as good but generally gives little credence to the rest of the album.

Jimmy Bain, like Carey, only got one chance to be immortalised on a Rainbow studio album and said, "you could tell how much fun we were having. It's got that attitude."

Cozy Powell was also upbeat about it when I spoke with him in 1997: "I'm certainly very proud of it. I think it was a real milestone at that time. I mean we were competing with the likes of Zeppelin and obviously the Purple sort of thing. We had to come out with something that was seriously contender stuff. Ronnie was singing really well, the band was gelling pretty well."

RITCHIE BLACKMORE
Marshall
Marshall

The Japanese typically went one better than anyone else. As well as including a four-page lyric insert, the first 50,000 included a Ritchie Blackmore poster (opposite). Second press versions can be distinguished as the obi strip wasn't as wide as the one displayed here. The rare promotional version (page 67), distinguished by the white label with blue text, also included a red flexi disc of 'Tarot Woman'. These are often seen for sale separately and it is reported that they were also issued with a magazine.

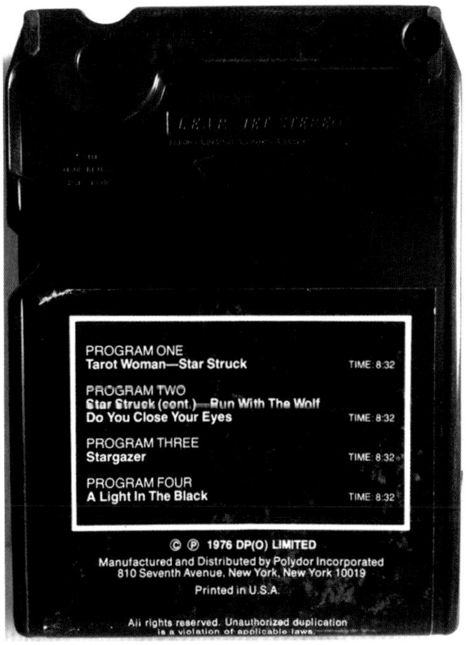

8 track cartridge releases were popular in the States largely thanks to players being installed into cars. Because they played on a tape loop that made each side equal in length, it necessitated splitting 'Starstruck' in half.

Different pressing plants in the States did things differently. Although the album was released on Oyster as the Terre Haute pressing showed, the Hauppauge pressing plant simply used Polydor labels. Naughty Hauppauge!

Label variations from around the world.

Germany

Greece

Mexico

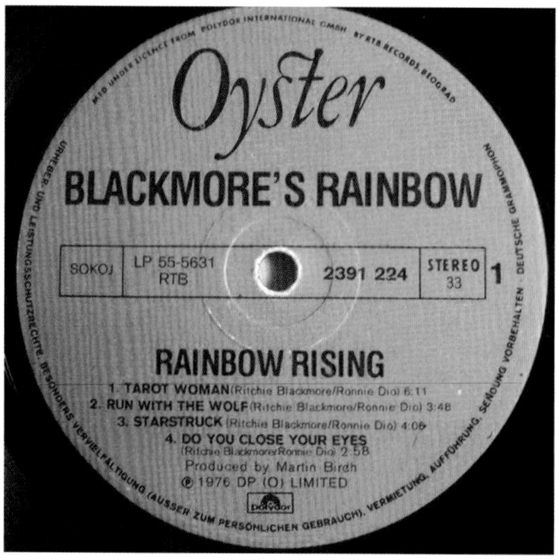

Yugoslavia

Austria

Singapore

Netherlands

Mexico

Rare German test pressing, date stamped 6th May 1976.

Most countries issued it as a gatefold, but the back of this example from India shows that it was released there in a single sleeve.

The 1983 UK re-issue like the Indian release, stripped it down to a single sleeve albeit with a different back design.

.

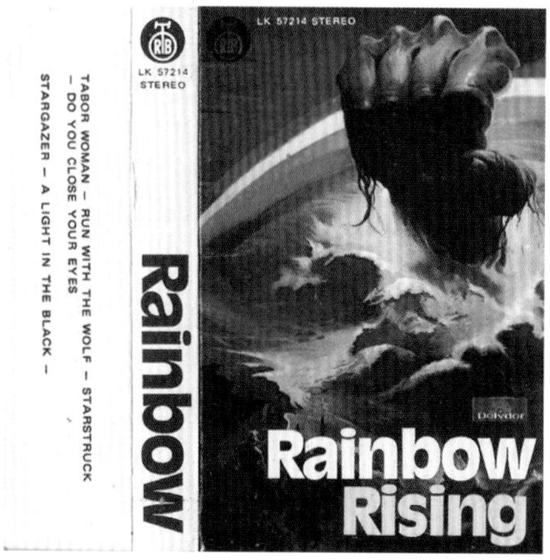

And finally a few cassette versions. Top left: Italy, top right: USA & below: Yugoslavia.

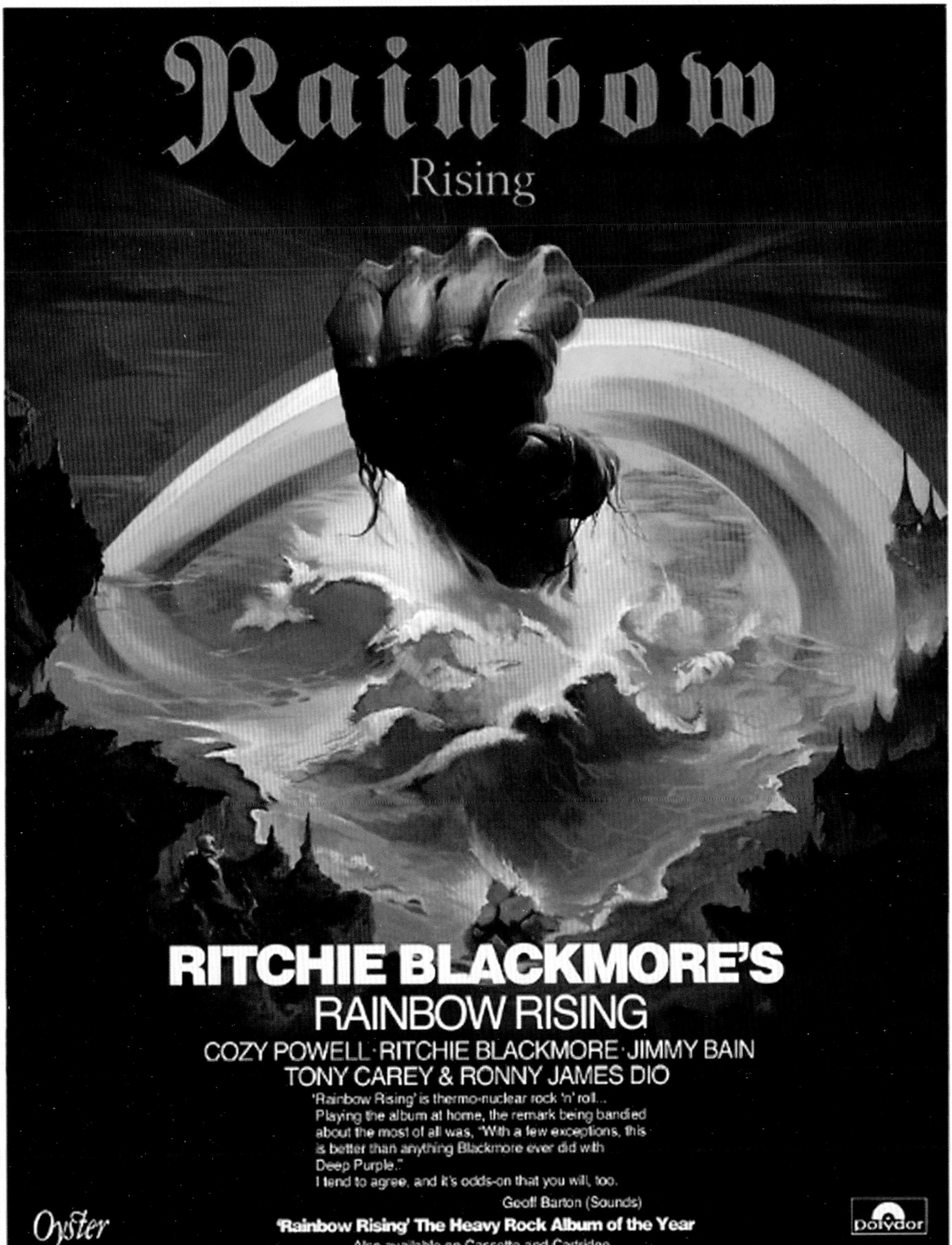

Rainbow
Rising
RITCHIE BLACKMORE'S
RAINBOW RISING
COZY POWELL · RITCHIE BLACKMORE · JIMMY BAIN
TONY CAREY & RONNY JAMES DIO
'Rainbow Rising' is thermo-nuclear rock 'n' roll... Playing the album at home, the remark being bandied about the most of all was, "With a few exceptions, this is better than anything Blackmore ever did with Deep Purple."
I tend to agree, and it's odds-on that you will, too.
Geoff Barton (Sounds)
Oyster
'Rainbow Rising' The Heavy Rock Album of the Year
Also available on Cassette and Cartridge
polydor

A SOARING SEQUEL FROM BLACKMORE'S RAINBOW: "RISING"

When guitarist Ritchie Blackmore left Deep Purple, he found his musical future in Rainbow, with Jimmy Bain on bass, Tony Carey on keyboard, vocals by Ronnie James Dio, and drummer, Cozy Powell. It was easy to expect more virtuoso axmanship, but no one thought Blackmore would gain access to new, undiscovered rainbow hues.

Now, on "Rising," Rainbow's second powerhouse album, Blackmore and company have consolidated their newly-colored energy to create more and better rainbows, the likes of which have never been heard before.

"Rising," a soaring sequel from Blackmore's Rainbow.

WATCH FOR BLACKMORE'S RAINBOW:

6/6	Stateline, Idaho	6/17	New York City, NY	6/25	Chicago, Ill.
6/11	Columbus, Ohio	6/22	Dayton, Ohio	6/26	Indianapolis, Ind.
6/13	Allentown, Pa.	6/24	Milwaukee, Wisc.	6/27	Davenport, Iowa

4.
We Feel That Our Time Has Arrived:
North America, 6th June - 3rd August

"It was an exciting time, yeah. It was one of those kind of line-ups that just worked. At the time it was really good. It was only sort of after the first tour that the various problems with individual members started coming to the surface. First person to suffer I think was Tony Carey."

Cozy Powell

Rising was recorded quickly in February and released in mid-May. According to press reports in various European publications, the first dates for Europe were scheduled for March. Whether or not this was down to a promoter getting ahead of himself, or whether it was decided to cancel the dates because the album wasn't ready for release is unclear. For the record, dates that were listed are as follows:

Wednesday 3rd March 1976
Palasport, Torino, Italy

Sunday 7th March 1976
Stadthalle, Erlangen, Germany

Monday 8th March 1976
Eberthalle, Ludwigshafen, Germany
Tuesday 9th March 1976
Stadthalle, Offenbach, Germany

Thursday 11th March 1976
Philipshalle, Dusseldorf, Germany

Friday 12th March 1976
Westfalenhalle, Dortmund, Germany

Sunday 14th March 1976
Stadthalle, Wolfsburg, Germany

Tuesday 16th March 1976
Musikhalle, Hamburg, Germany

For the '75 shows, tour income had been split 40% each to Blackmore and Dio with 15% to Powell and 5% to Bain. For the *Rising* tour, a greater share was given to Powell and Bain and the split became 36¼% each for Blackmore and Dio, 20% for Powell and 7½% for Bain. For both tours, Carey was simply paid a wage with no potential share of tour profits.

Tour rehearsals were once again held at Pirate Sound. Bizarrely, given that the band now had two albums of material, Blackmore was still not happy with a potential set opener. 'Tarot Woman' had apparently been tried out according to Blackmore although Carey claims he only played it the once in the studio. In exactly the same way that had happened the previous year, a new song developed during rehearsals — 'Kill The King'. When it materialised on record the following year, Cozy Powell was also credited as a composer in a three-way split with Blackmore and Dio.

Equally as baffling, with more than enough material for a ninety-minute show, Blackmore also decided to fall back on a Purple tune, namely 'Mistreated'. As much as Rainbow's own songs shone at the gigs, 'Mistreated' was just as much a highlight. The set list that developed at rehearsals would remain constant throughout North America as follows:

Kill The King
Mistreated
Sixteenth Century Greensleeves
Catch The Rainbow
Man On The Silver Mountain
Stargazer
A Light In The Black
Still I'm Sad

Having opened the shows in '75, 'Do You Close Your Eyes' was now switched to the encore, which invariably saw Blackmore do his guitar demolition in the process.

Although the '75 dates had suffered with numerous problems with the rainbow, they were generally ironed out by the time that the *Rising* tour began. But there were still other issues to contend with. For the first leg of the tour across America, despite Blackmore's past, Rainbow still hadn't captured the imagination of the American public to anywhere near the degree that Purple had.

Even though it was a much lengthier tour than in '75, starting in June and going through until early August, some of the dates saw quite small attendances and some shows were cancelled due to poor ticket sales. It would appear that some shows were arranged at relatively short notice and poorly promoted. An advert placed in the bi-weekly magazine *Rolling Stone* on 17th June, the day of the fourth show, only listed nine gigs in total!

Rainbow even did a few shows as the support act as they simply weren't big enough to play the big arenas as a headlining act. There are also some sizable gaps between gigs. Either other shows were pulled or there are still a few more that have not been documented. Given the rather low-key coverage, either suggestion is possible.

In addition to this, the original plan was to have Thin Lizzy as Rainbow's support but Lizzy was forced to withdraw just before the tour started.

Thin Lizzy had been touring the States since April. Buoyed by being signed to Thames Talent, they had supported several acts in support of their *Jailbreak* album including Rush, Be Bop Deluxe, Aerosmith, Blue Öyster Cult and Nazareth and were just beginning to break through. Unfortunately though, by the time they got to Ohio to begin the campaign with Rainbow, Phil Lynott collapsed in Columbus. Lizzy guitarist Scott Gorham said, "The day we got to Ohio, Phil more or less nearly collapsed with exhaustion and was taken to the hospital where he was told that he had contracted hepatitis and was to immediately fly back to London. Back in London he was put in the intensive care unit for a couple of weeks. It´s a shame, because it would have been a great tour for Lizzy."

Musically, few fans are in doubt that the '76 tour was a pinnacle in Rainbow's career. However, reading some of the press interviews that follow, you would certainly question that. It shouldn't be forgotten that for reasons I simply cannot fathom, Rainbow struggled to get the attention of the American public at this time. Ultimately, it played a big part in Blackmore's decision to change style, which followed in late '78 with the departure of Ronnie Dio.

But for the meantime Blackmore's improvisational skills that had been a big part of Deep Purple's shows carried over and were certainly a highlight of the *Rising* tour, particularly as far as one American was concerned, namely Tony Carey: "'You improvise until I do this and hold my hand up in the air.' That's the thing, when I say progressive rock, with this band it was never 'I solo for sixteen bars then we go somewhere else.' It was like 'I'll play until I don't feel like playing anymore.' It's trial and error — you find out what works and when a solo peaks and when you tend to leave it and repeat it the next time. But you put any four or five good musicians together and tell them to jam it's going to work and the solos are going to fit and it sounds like they've been playing together all their lives. It was a very democratic band. The interplay developed from the first gig and it wasn't the sound of seventies metal. It had more in common with Weather Report than Black Sabbath."

Sunday 6th June
Nor' Wester Rock Festival, Stateline Speedway, Idaho, USA
Rainbow's first date of the *Rising* tour was supposed to be as the headlining act on the final day of this three-day festival. Unfortunately it never got that far. The show was beset with financial problems and the first night — with headliners Blue Öyster Cult — started five hours late. Bachman Turner Overdrive were due to headline on night two but by mid-afternoon the show ended abruptly when the sound company, realising that they were not going to get paid, basically packed up their equipment. This sparked a riot amongst the 5,000 or so present and a hasty end to the festival.

Friday 11th June
Veterans Memorial Auditorium, Columbus, Ohio, USA
So the *Rising* tour eventually got underway in Ohio, but as previously mentioned, without support act Thin Lizzy. It's thought that no support act was put in their place.

Sunday 13th June
Allentown, USA
The *Rolling Stone* tour advert listed this. Either in error, or it was cancelled and replaced with the Albany show. Possibly this was the festival at the Fairgrounds that went ahead on 1st July, or it was at a different venue and cancelled and replaced with that gig.

Sunday 13th June
Palace Theatre, Albany, USA
As with the first gig, it's thought that there was no support act to replace Thin Lizzy.

Monday 14th June
St. Denis Theatre, Montreal, Qeubec, Canada
This show was rescheduled for 20th July.

Tuesday 15th June
Allen Theatre, Cleveland Ohio, USA
This show went ahead with no support act.

Wednesday 16th June
Broome County Veterans Memorial Arena, Binghamton New York, USA
Just two days before the show was due to go ahead, the local paper reported that Thin Lizzy would be performing with Rainbow. The announcement of the show's cancellation appeared in the press on the day of the concert.

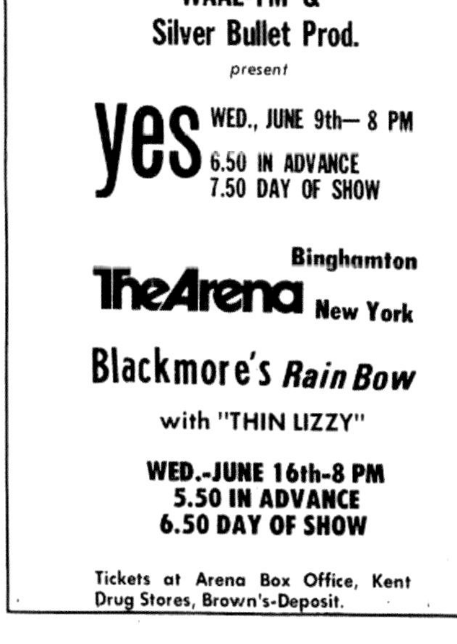

At Arena Wednesday

Blackmore's Rainbow, from left, Jimmy Bain, Cozy Powell, Ronnie Dio, Ritchie Blackmore and Tony Carey, will appear in concert Wednesday. On the same bill will be Thin Lizzy. Tickets are available for the 8 p.m. concert at the Arena box office.

Thin Lizzy will appear on the same bill with Blackmore's Rainbow Wednesday at the Broome County Veterans Memorial Arena at 8 p.m.

"Blackmore's Rainbow" and "Thin Lizzy" have canceled tonight's scheduled performance at the Broome County Veterans Memorial Arena.

June 16, 1976 PRESS, Binghamton, N.Y.

Arena Concert Canceled

"Blackmore's Rainbow" and "Thin Lizzy" have canceled tonight's scheduled performance at the Broome County Veterans Memorial Arena.

Bud Becker, of Silver Bullet Productions, promoter of the concert said it was his decision to cancel when illness forced "Thin Lizzy" to stop all of their shows for an unspecified time.

Becker said the concert would be re-scheduled later this summer with "Blackmore's Rainbow" and another group. If possible, "Thin Lizzy" would also be re-scheduled, he said.

"We didn't feel it was right to bring in just one band after the kids paid $5.50 to see two," Becker said.

"Since 'Thin Lizzy' canceled, 'Blackmore's Rainbow' has been playing a single, but longer, set. We tried to get another act comparable to 'Thin Lizzy' but we couldn't in the time we had.

"We've been trying since January to deliver what we promised for the kids in Binghamton and if we can't deliver, we don't want to substitute something less," Becker said.

About 1,000 advance tickets have been sold, he said, and the money would be refunded. "We didn't expect that this was going to be a concert that would attract 6,000 anyhow. But it is unfortunate because 'Thin Lizzy' is getting really popular, their last album is taking off. And Ronnie Dio, the lead singer of 'Blackmore's Rainbow,' is from Cortland and has a strong following in the Binghamton area."

Doug Thaler, concert manager for Thames Talent,Inc. in New York City, said "Thin Lizzy" had to cancel because of the illness of lead singer and founder of the group, Phil Lynott.

He said Lynott came down with infectious hepatitis about a week ago and spent two days in the Ohio State University hospital before returning to London Saturday.

The rest of the group returned to London yesterday, where they will main until Lynott recovers before continuing their tour.

"I hate to see stories about hepatitis because the first thing people think, because they're rock stars, is that its because of drugs. That is absolutely not the case. Phil and the other guys are good kids.

One of the major causes of hepatitis is from using dirty hypodermic needles while taking intravenous drugs like heroin.

"We think they may have caught it on the West Coast where they met a lot of different people. There were groupies all over the place."

Thaler said "Blackmore's Rainbow" would continue to do concert performances in smaller auditoriums until they can be joined by another rock group to work in the larger arenas.

Thursday 17th June
Beacon Theatre, New York, USA
Support: Southside Johnny And The Asbury Dukes

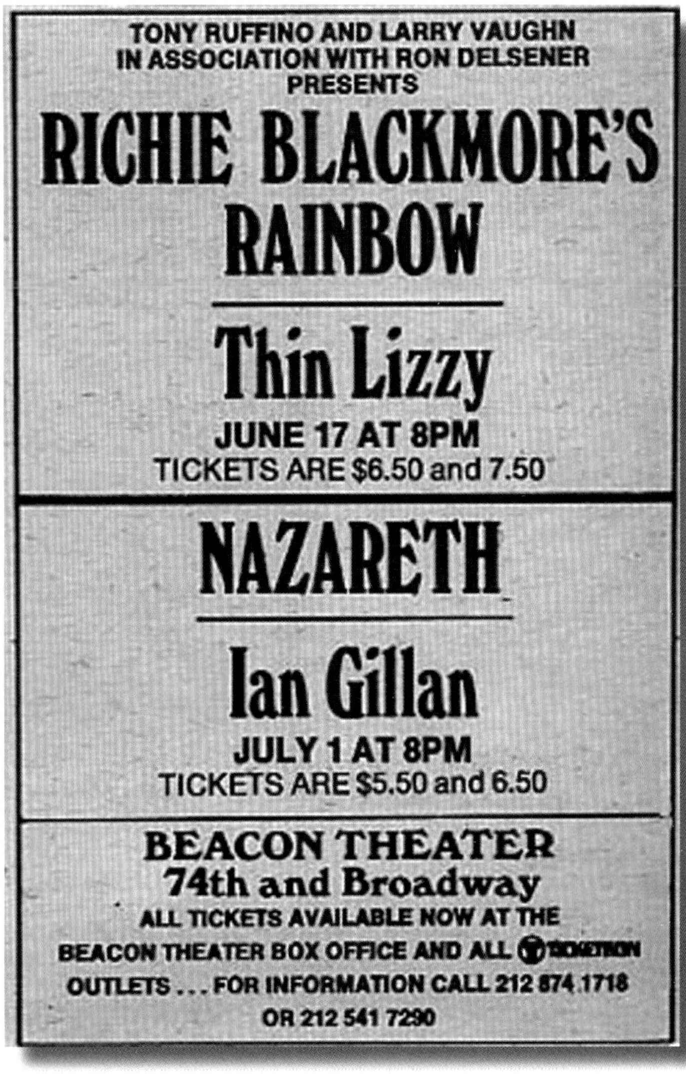

Peter Crescenti reviewed the show for *Circus* magazine, albeit getting a couple of song titles incorrect:

It may be a few months before Blackmore's Rainbow appears in Britain for the first time, but even if they have to wait until distant '77, Blackmore freaks, when they finally do see the band live, will no doubt decide that the wait, no matter how long, was damned well worth it. Rainbow, now in its second version, is simply one of the most dynamic and energetic heavy rock outfits in the free world.

Ritchie Blackmore is a happy man again, happy because now that he's left Deep Purple, he's once again free to make the kind of rock 'n' roll he loves best — visceral and explosive, an atomic dose of chordal calamity — and by no coincidence, it's the same sweaty brand of rock thousands of rockers have become addicted to over the last ten years, hooked, mainly, by fixes served up by the Main Man of heavy metal, Ritchie Blackmore.

The rowdy mob at Rainbow's Beacon Theatre gig were Blackmore Junkies alright. Not one wouldn't have sawed off a hand for a piece of the Stratocaster Ritchie smashed during the encore of 'Do You Close Your Eyes', and the lucky boys in the front rows who shook the Man's hand as he leaned out into the audience a few times probably still haven't washed their hands. And their throats are probably still raw from all their ecstatic wailing... and smoking. Blackmore's, ironically, is one of the dopiest crowds going.

Opening with 'Temple Of The King', a blues, and then 'Sixteenth Century Greensleeves', Rainbow simply knocked the crowd on their collective tails. People were running around the hall in delirious glee, but before the audience could slip from Rainbow's grasp, they cleverly eased into the moody 'Catch The Rainbow', which featured some soulful, sensitive singing by Ronnie Dio and some of Ritchie Blackmore's tastiest playing ever.

When the guitarist walked to centre stage for his solo, the rest of Rainbow could have been transformed into porcupines, and no one would have noticed, that's how transfixed everyone was, not only by Blackmore's playing but by his overwhelming stage presence. All the same, I kept my eyes on Cozy Powell a lot too. What a dynamite addition Cozy is to Rainbow, providing that ass-kicking back beat Blackmore's high energy music so desperately requires. On his kit, Cozy's easily Blackmore's match, but they compliment rather than battle each other. Cozy pummelled hell out his drums all night, especially giving 'Man On A Silver Mountain' a drive it sorely lacked on the first Rainbow album. Blackmore himself was amazing during 'Mountain', shaking hands with his right hand while continuing to play with his left.

'I have done a little show, at certain gigs,' says Ritchie, 'like breaking my guitar up. I felt the audience needed that. I haven't done it for a year, but I felt that it was necessary because the audience weren't that musical.' 'They wanted to see some violence, actually,' Cozy agrees.

Rainbow's show is visually powerful as well. At the front of the stage, arching from stage left to stage right, is a mammoth rainbow, operated by a digital computer that sends waves of colours and shapes through the construct. Backdrops, huge blow-ups of rainbow's two album covers, are also used, the first during the first half of the set, and the 'Rainbow Rising' fist during 'Stargazer' and 'A Light In The Dark'.

Add it all up, and it's nirvana for Blackmore's Rainbow fans. Just watch out for Stratocaster fragments when they come to your town.

For fan Frank Aziza, it was his first time seeing Blackmore and Rainbow and it clearly made an impression: "It was a very memorable night, so memorable that I still talk about it frequently. The setting was beautiful, a two balcony theatre in New York City. With a huge statue on each side of the stage. A guy decided to climb one statue, as the crowd cheered him on. Then after about twenty minutes there came the announcement, 'The show will not start until the man climbs down' and the crowd turned against this young man.

"I was nearly twelve years old. My older brother took me to the show. I will always thank my brother, if it were not for him I would have missed all this great music. This was my second concert, earlier that year I had witnessed Deep Purple with Tommy Bolin, another memorable night.

"Standing there in the pitch-black theatre, except for the little red lights on Blackmore's Marshall heads, I was shaking. Then I heard Judy Garland tell us 'we're not in Kansas anymore, we must be over the rainbow...' then it happened, the chilling power chords then he broke into the fast paced 'Kill The King'. Just as the tears stopped, I saw a little man come walking out from the side of the stage. Dressed in purplish top and velvet pants with his hands up in the air. I always remembered 'Danger, danger' and some magical melody that I would later find to be 'fly like the wind'.

"Ritchie's lead in that song on that night was the most amazing thing you could witness. His fingers looked as if they weren't touching the neck on the guitar. They sort of glided like he was playing air guitar. It was without a doubt the heaviest thing I have ever seen, yet crystal clear sound, and loud as hell. Then Ronnie announced the second song, the Deep Purple song, 'Mistreated' which shocked me. I didn't expect any Deep Purple that night. Ritchie's guitar intro blaring through the theatre still makes me numb just thinking about it and Ronnie's version of this song was stunning. He sang it so powerfully.

"The rest of the night was so good, it changed my life forever. There were moments during the night, when the band got so low that you could hear a pin drop. While Ritchie would play some beautiful leads and put his

index finger over his lips to shush anyone that would scream his name. What made this group so special was their ability to take things down to a whisper and then at the drop of a hat, be the loudest (yet melodic) band you could ever see.

"'Man On The Silver Mountain' was a gem. Ronnie's singing was beautiful. 'Do You Close Your Eyes' was the encore and it would be the first ever smashing of the guitar in Rainbow. I'll never forget the way I felt when 'Somewhere Over The Rainbow' was playing over the PA after the show. I was emotionally drained from the show, and so pumped up... Judy Garland's classic was music that tamed the savage beast."

Friday 18th June
Calderone Concert Hall, Hempstead, Long Island, USA

Saturday 19th June
The Century Theatre, Buffalo, USA

Sunday 20th June
Erie County Field House, Erie, USA

Tuesday 22nd June,
Hara Arena, Dayton, Ohio, USA
Support act: Ted Nugent
Thin Lizzy should have been part of a three-band bill.

T-105 and Windy City Present
BLACKMORE'S RAINBOW
Super Special Guests
TED NUGENT
THIN LIZZY
Tuesday, June 22—7:30 PM
Dayton Hara Arena
Tickets: $5.50 Advance—$6.50 Day Of Show Tickets Available ALL TICKETRON outlets—Cincinnati, Hamilton, Middletown
Phone: 278-4776

Thursday 24th June
International Amphitheatre, Milwaukee, USA

Friday 25th June
Aragon Ballroom, Chicago, USA
Support acts: Heart, Frank Marino & Mahogany Rush, The L.A. Jets

Saturday 26th June
Expo Centre, Indianapolis, USA
This show was cancelled at short notice. Probably due to poor ticket sales.

Sunday 27th June
Orpheum Theatre, Davenport, USA
It's unclear if there was a support act at this show.

Monday 28th June
Sports Arena, Toledo, USA

Orpheum Theatre, Boston, USA
It's claimed by some that there was a show in Boston in June but given that the venue is the same name as the Davenport show, it's possible that some confusion arose over the two venues.

Saturday 1st July
Summer Rock Celebration Festival, Fairgrounds, Allentown, USA
An open-air festival starting at 6pm, featuring Chumbi, Moxy, Angel, Leslie West with Rainbow headlining to an audience of around 4,000.

THE MORNING CALL, Allentown, Pa., Friday, July 2, 1976

Hard rock pleases 4,000 as summer series opens

By JONNA BARTGES
Of The Morning Call

Hard rock was the menu last night at the Allentown Fairgrounds grandstand, and nearly 4,000 fans sampled the smorgasbord.

From Angel's white satin to Richie Blackmore's Rainbow 30-foot neon arch, five bands catered to every rock taste.

The six-hour marathon was the first outdoor grandstand concert sponsored by the Council of Youth for the 1976 summer season.

Judging from enthusiastic crowd reaction, Angel was the band many came to see. The five-man band from Washington was discovered by Kiss, another top group which has played the Lehigh Valley.

Garbed in flowing and feathered white costumes, Angel members immediately took command of their audience with their classic rock sound and their stage theatrics.

Greg Giffria was outstanding on the keyboard, and Frank Dimino was a powerful lead vocalist. When Angel lit into hard rock and roll, dozens of fans danced on the track in front of the grandstand stage. Guitarist Punky Meadows was spotlighted during a jam.

At the close of the hourlong performance, the crowd applauded Angel back for a lively rock and roll encore climaxed by a wild percussion solo featuring Barry Brandt. Mickey Jones was on electric bass.

Richie Blackmore's Rainbow was the second favorite band. Blackmore split the heavy metal Deep Purple and formed Rainbow with the members of the Southern group Elf.

Rainbow is into heavy metal and performs inside the arc of a huge neon rainbow, which colorfully pulsates to their music.

The arc took six months to design and build, and crews spent the entire day erecting it at the front of the stage.

"Mistreated," a powerful driving rock number, was well-received by the enthusiastic crowd.

Chumbi, a local group, opened the concert.

Friday 2nd July
Auditorium Theatre, Rochester, USA
Support acts: Gentle Giant, Angel
An audience of around 1,500 saw Giant Giant — replacing Thin Lizzy — play in the middle of a triple bill. They were also well enough received to return to the stage for an encore or two. Their audience ovation continued even after the house lights finally went up. In a published interview in 1980, Gentle Giant's bassist Ray Shulman recalled this concert fondly, claiming that his band upstaged Rainbow.

Saturday 3rd July
Boardwalk Casino Arena, Asbury Park, USA
Support act: Henry Gross
Blackmore finished this show by using the stage monitors as the target for his guitar smash-up.

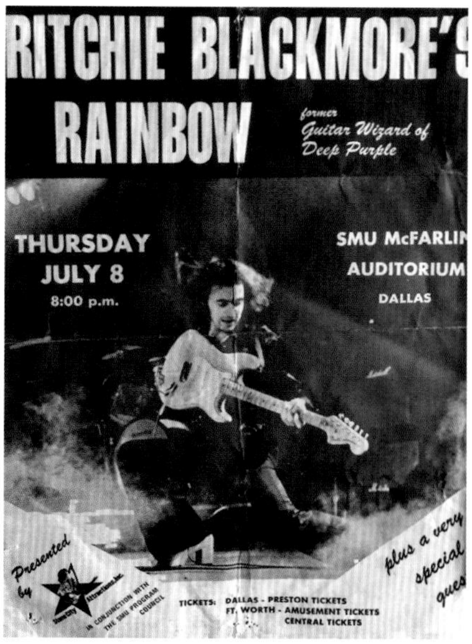

Thursday 8th July
SMU McFarlin Memorial Auditorium, Dallas, USA

Friday 9th July
Municipal Auditorium, San Antonio, USA
Support acts: Mott, Starz, Rainbow
Headlining act: Blue Öyster Cult
Rainbow had to be content with playing second fiddle as the main support to Blue Öyster Cult. As a consequence, it's almost certain that the electronic rainbow would not have been used at this show. It's also unlikely that Rainbow would have performed their full set. Also, even though listed, it is thought that Mott did not perform and the show was opened by Starz.

Saturday 10th July
Music Hall, Texas, USA
Support act: Don Harrison Band
At least parts of this show were filmed, although it is unclear as to the reasons why. In the days before video machines were household items, there was no commercial outlet for a concert film. A ten-minute film was put together. It showed the crew erecting the electronic rainbow, plus brief clips of 'Man On The Silver Mountain', 'Stargazer', 'A Light In The Black', Powell's drum solo and 'Do You Close Your Eyes'. It's often referred to as a promo film and was broadcast on Australian TV in November. It might well have been done for the purpose of promoting the Australian tour.

Wednesday 14th July
Curtis Hixon Hall, Tampa, USA
Support act: unknown.

Thursday 15th July
Jai Alai Fronton, Miami, USA
Support acts: Savoy Brown, Roy Buchanan
Rainbow played to a relatively small audience as Dio was quick to point out after 'Kill The King'. It was the same venue that would go on to witness the last performance of Tommy Bolin six months later.

This was one of the best performances from the whole tour and typical of Rainbow and Blackmore's improvisational skills. 'Mistreated' is given a completely different feel to it; what would initially be the start of the guitar solo sees Ronnie ad-lib for a couple of minutes. Even when Ritchie then takes over, his laidback solo is utterly unique.

His intro to 'Man On The Silver Mountain' briefly flirts with 'White Christmas' and 'Lazy', but the latter is stopped before the rest of the band can break into it. 'A Light In The Black' at this show is quite phenomenal — Carey's solo is as good as can be. He initially plays it on the synth before switching to the Hammond and then back to the synth for the last part.

Blackmore's playing is like a demon, stopping the band midway through his solo for some blistering unaccompanied runs up and down the fretboard before kicking the band back into action. Definitely a tour highlight. He continues at such a high level during 'Still I'm Sad'. Following a quiet introduction, his solo is extensively lengthened before he takes it down for the lead into Carey's solo, but Blackmore continues to solo for an age more, playing very jazzy stuff, eventually leading into some interplay with

Carey before the latter gets to finally have his say. Cozy, in typical rumbustious fashion, brings down the final curtain on the song.

Of the support acts for this and the following show, Savoy Brown had supported Purple on their first 1974 American tour. At that point, Blackmore's friend, guitarist Stan Webb — formerly of Chicken Shack — was a member of the band and it's clear that the tour had created some rapport.

Roy Buchanan is cited by some as having a style not dissimilar to Blackmore's. He was also greatly admired by Blackmore. In an interview with Cameron Crowe for *Creem* magazine, published in June '75, Blackmore said: "Roy Buchanan is brilliant. He goes way above people's heads, and that's what worries me. I think, what's the point of being up there, if it's going to go over everyone's heads? You're not going to get anywhere. Pete Townshend once said that it's great to progress, but unless you take your audience with you, it's pointless. I think sometimes Buchanan is too far up front. People don't know what he's doing." Buchanan's '76 album, *A Street Called Straight*, also appeared on Oyster Records, albeit only in Germany.

Friday 16th July
Bay Front Centre, St Petersburg, USA
Support acts: Savoy Brown, Roy Buchanan
This gig was reviewed in both the*Tampa Bay Times* and *St Petersburg Times* by Bob Ross:
'I'd say 1,462.'
'Looks like 1,342 to me.'
'I'd just put down an even 1,500.'

Midway through Friday night's heavy-metal rock concert at the Bayfront Centre Arena, three Bayfront staffers were trying to outguess each other as to the exact attendance. The Bayfront Arena holds 8,400 spectators.

The Rainbow/Savoy Brown/Roy Buchanan show was a box office bomb. The music — with the exception of show-opener Buchanan — was loud and coarse. Relatively few fans were on hand — the average age seemed to be in the late teens. Scarcely a wince was visible when Savoy Brown inflicted a decibel count that challenged the pain threshold of a twelve-year hard-core rock-concert veteran. The mood backstage in promoter territory was dark and ugly.

Within a five-minute span, Gulf Artists chief Marjorie Sexton shrieked full volume at two unauthorised visitors, one hapless security guard and a reporter who had written something that displeased Mrs. Sexton three weeks ago.

Happily Fox the $6-a-toss ticket-buyers, the atmosphere on the fun side of the stage was diametrically opposite the backstage unpleasantness. The youthful audience was bewildered temporarily by Roy Buchanan. 'Look at that old dude,' said one observer. 'That shirt even has a penguin on it.'

Indeed, Buchanan's blue knit shirt did have the squaresville signal penguin. His strew hat covered thinning hair. The full-bearded cat with the incredibly beat-up old guitar looked his thirty-six years. But he made that shoddy-looking axe sing, shout, cry and croon. Roy Buchanan long has been hailed as one of the world's finest electric lead players, and his first major Bay area appearance showed why. One is entitled to wonder why such wizards as Eric Clapton, Jimmy Page and Keith Richards (all white British guitar superstars) would express intense public admiration for a shy, serene American picker who spent most of his career playing small bars near Washington, D.C.

Buchanan was simply amazing. He smiled a bit when the appreciative guitar-lovers cheered his superb catalogue of sounds. Flamenco, blues, country, old-style acid-rock and unclassifiable original noises came in six mangy-looking strings.

Whoop, beg and holler as they might, the few connoisseurs in the crowd could not get an encore from Buchanan. He finished a knock-out set with his quasi-religious 'Messiah' composition, and then made way for Savoy Brown.

Savoy Brown, the loudest, moat tenacious second-rate band in rock history (a title they won when Brownsville Station folded) actually is the creation of one person — Kim Simmonds. Simmonds is a British long-timer who has made at least sixteen American tours with bands named Savoy Brown. The members of the band have all changed many times over, except for Simmonds. Savoy Brown never has risen higher that second-billed, and probably never will. Their forte is obnoxious volume and long, long, silky hair that they shake in unison when the beat gets heavy. That is all the time.

Show closer Ritchie Blackmore obviously is not headline draw in St. Petersburg. Being the former lead guitarist for Deep Purple does not make one a $6 attraction. His heavy-metal version was not as offensive as Savoy Brown's pulsating migraine thump, but another dose of Roy Buchanan would have been far preferable from a musical standpoint.

Saturday 17th July
Civic Auditorium, Jacksonville, USA

Support act: unknown.
This show was reviewed by Roy Simpson in *The Florida Times Union*. The review was published in the European tour programme:

Rainbow's performance was excellent. Ritchie Blackmore stunned the crowd with a multitude of brilliant lead guitar solos throughout their entire set. Through his association with Deep Purple, Blackmore long ago established himself as one of the top "heavy metal" guitarists in the world.

A monstrous electronic rainbow, arching high above the stage, had remained dark, but not unseen by the crowd. As Rainbow took to the stage it became a dazzling array of colours dancing across the sky. 'Kill The King', a yet to be released tune, presented the people with a faultless example of what to expect from the band. The sound was heavy and laden with power chords, but never once bogged down.

Loud applause came from the audience as the group broke into 'I've Been Mistreated', originally done by Blackmore's former cohorts, Deep Purple. The guitarist appeared comfortable with this one and proceeded to show the rapid spit-fire guitar work that has gained him international respect.

Introduced as a nice medieval-renaissance tune, 'Greensleeves' turned out to be a high point of Rainbow's performance. The show continued to follow the same power-packed course. Songs such as 'Catch The Rainbow' and 'Stargazer' brought the fans to their feet.

Though Blackmore continued to be in the spotlight, drummer Cozy Powell, keyboardist Tony Carey, and bassist Jimmy Bain never let the audience forget their presence. They attacked each song with unyielding determination, so necessary for a young group.

When the group got into 'Man On A Silver Mountain', off their first LP, the crowd jumped to its feet and seemed to feel this would be Rainbow at their heaviest. This was without a doubt their hottest, most rockin' number of the night. Blackmore's fingers became a blur on his guitar as the rest of the band came thundering behind.

Rainbow put on a satisfying show, both audibly and visibly. Words could not do the awesome stage rainbow justice. It has to be seen to be appreciated.

Tuesday 20th July
St. Denis Theatre, Montreal, Canada
Support act: Max Webster

Reviewed by Juan Rodriguez for *The Gazette*, who was clearly more enamoured with support artist Max Webster:

Ritchie Blackmore's Rainbow inaugurated a series of concerts at the Cinema St. Denis last night, before an audience clearly in the mood to revive the intimate Fillmore like rock hall. The promise of Blackmore, the British heavy rock guitarist formerly with Deep Purple, and his Rainbow (figuratively, as well as a stage wide fluorescent rainbow) attracted a young crowd stoked up and rarin' to get blasted.

The atmosphere was just what Max Webster, the opening act, needed and the Toronto band didn't miss a trick in winning over the ripened fans in their first local appearance. Webster, a singer and guitarist backed by three strategic sidemen, has obviously researched the rock market before designing his act. He has adopted numerous popular styles — from the jigsaw structures of Queen to the pop boogie of the Doobie Bros to the Bowie-Jagger syndrome of stage presence, and even a little Frank Zappa kitchen sink measures thrown in for effect.

Unlike many Toronto bands that play Montreal, Max Webster performed with the kind of confidence that strikes straight at the hearts of the local buzzed-out rock cognoscenti. He was careful to include several 'Merci's in his patter, and the bass player added a few bon mots himself. Lo and behold, Max Webster won over the Montreal crowd — perhaps the day is not far off when he joins Shawn Phillips and Genesis in the affections of the local audience.

Meanwhile, Blackmore took a long time getting his electronic equipment and his head together, just as he did at the Forum last year. He's a moody fellow — you can tell by the way he rolls his head limply on the axis of his neck. One gets the impression that his "wasted genius" stage looks (the stringy bedraggled hair, the black cycle jacket) are more convoluted than his guitar playing: he makes you wait for his solos, and that's how he wins over his eager audiences. It's all a big act — Blackmore rarely shows he can cut the mustard with Jeff Beck, Eric Clapton, B.B. King et al.

Monday 26th July
Civic Arena, Pittsburgh, USA
Headlining act: Jethro Tull.

After all the years with Purple, for Blackmore to find himself as a support act, as was the case with Blue Öyster Cult, couldn't have been easy for him to take. But if you have to be the support act then what better than going on before your favourite band? Jethro Tull's typically English style had really resonated with American audiences and throughout the mid-seventies they were one of the top box office draws

Monday 10th November
Forum Concert Bowl, Montreal, Canada

© Harold Kruyck

COZY
owell

St. Denis Theatre, Montreal, Canada, 20th July 1976

St. Denis Theatre, Montreal, Canada, 20th July 1976

© Harold Kruyck

St. Denis Theatre, Montreal, Canada, 20th July 1976

St. Denis Theatre, Montreal, Canada, 20th July 1976

© Harold Kruyck

St. Denis Theatre, Montreal, Canada, 20th July 1976

St. Denis Theatre, Montreal, Canada, 20th July 1976

in the States. Blackmore adores Tull's output, citing their '74 album, *War Child*, as a personal favourite. Whilst there is always a crossover with rock fans, in general Tull's audience was a different beast to Rainbow's. Tom Doyle who reviewed this show for the *Beaver County Times* is a perfect illustration of this:

Jethro Tull rolled into Pittsburgh Monday for their sixth appearance at the Civic Arena. I've seen them every time they were in town and was only disappointed once. Monday's show was definitely a crowd-pleaser. Ian Anderson and the band started the show with 'Thick As A Brick', and from then on it was a very enjoyable show.

I didn't get as excited as usual — this was my sixth time seeing them after all — but I notice the rest of the crowd was just as enthusiastic as every other Tull show I've seen.

Of course, I knew Ian would play the devil out of his flute, but I think this was the best I've ever seen him play. As for the material they played, the show included all of Tull's favourites with a few new numbers which also went over well. It was quite noticeable that the Aqualung material is still the favourite of Tull fans.

Naturally, Ian is the focal point of Tull's shows, but during times he left the stage, the band carried on very well. I could have been satisfied with an entire evening of just the band playing. As far as Ian is concerned, he is still the king of the prancers on the stage. He's just as great to watch now as he ever was. The show, for both old and new fans, was a complete success. Even though Tull's albums are going downhill, they maintain a good position on top of the hill in live shows.

Ritchie Blackmore's Rainbow opened the concert, and that was about their only accomplishment of the evening. Their show was too loud, and Ritchie's usual fine playing was just jammed into a total sound mess.

I kept waiting for this band to get cooking, but it just didn't happen. Every time they got near the point of good kicking music, they lost their shoes. The high point of their show was Cozy Powell's drum solo. It started out to be just another standard solo, but halfway through he was accompanied by taped symphonic music and he began to murder his drums. He received a rousing standing ovation for one of the best drum solos ever.

Basically though, I was bored by Ritchie and his Rainbow. The good songs from their second album didn't come across well, just as 'Mistreated', a Deep Purple number, failed to do much. With such a vast amount of good Purple music to play, he picked a real dud for the only Purple number of the evening.

Keep trying, Ritchie, because you need it. Blackmore fans, stick to the albums until the rest of Rainbow catches up to Ritchie. When that time comes, they'll put on a good show.

Around this time, Lita Ford of The Runaways was spotted hanging around with Blackmore at some of the gigs. Their relationship is touched upon in her autobiography, *Living Like A Runaway,* published in 2016. During promotion for the book, when asked by *Guitar World* magazine about her relationship with Blackmore, she was pretty evasive and merely replied, "Richie is a wonderful, incredible and intriguing man. He's a mysterious and interesting guy as well as a phenomenal musician. He was my number one hero on guitar because of his double picking — especially the solo on 'Highway Star', which was the song I auditioned for the Runaways with."

Tuesday 27th July
Market Square Arena, Indianapolis, USA
Headlining act: Jethro Tull.
The second show supporting Tull.

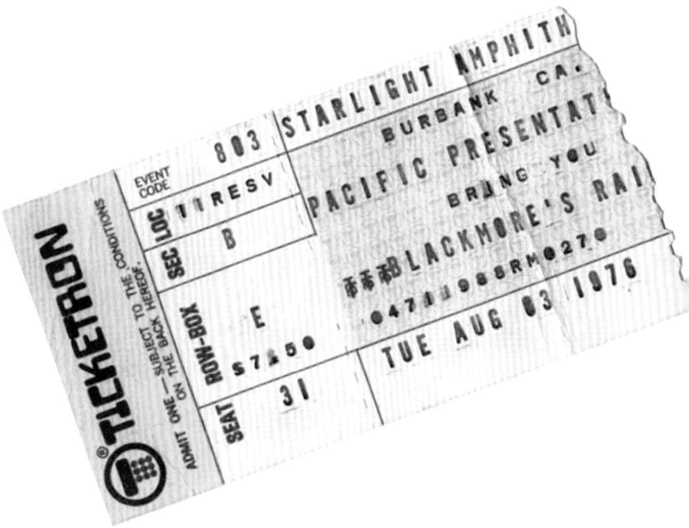

Friday 30th July
Hirsh Memorial Coliseum, Shreveport Los Angeles, USA

Monday 2nd August
Aladdin Theatre, Las Vegas, USA
Support act: unknown

Tuesday 3rd August
Starlight Amphitheatre, Burbank, USA
Support act: Man

The show was almost cancelled when the local council tackled the promoters over their reassurances that they would fulfil their commitment to supplying ballet and drama as well as music as they had only booked rock acts to date. Original support act Paris cancelled. Welsh band Man stepped in as the replacement.

Michael Hooker reviewed the show in the *Los Angeles Free Press*, published ten days after the show, and after the tour had finished:

It's virtually impossible to see Richie Blackmore without realising that he has an empathy for the guitar which might be unexcelled in rock. On a level of sheer feeling for the instrument, Blackmore lives up to much of his claim of being the world's best guitarist, but why he chooses to do so little with so much is something of a mystery.

Blackmore's Rainbow isn't even good heavy metal. At the Starlight Amphitheatre, Blackmore was boring beyond belief, seeming content to restrict his attack to a series of mindless trashings of distasteful discordances, interspersed with directionless doodlings, no doubt intended as displays of soloing expertise.

For as involved as he appeared with the proceedings, it's a wonder he bothered to show up at all. As a last-minute replacement for Paris, Man provided a solid opening performance which only underscored the deficiencies of Rainbow. In contrast to Blackmore's self-indulgent excesses, Man was the epitome of a fully integrated and powerful sound. If Man isn't ever going to shake the earth with its lyrical cleverness, or instrumental progressiveness, at least it has a firm hold on the concept of taste — something the Blackmore dinosaur seemed unable to grasp.

It was around this time in Fresno, California — although the exact date is unknown — where the well-documented prank of Blackmore setting fire to Jimmy Bain's bed happened, during time off between shows.

Friday 6th August
Civic Auditorium, San Jose, USA
Support acts: Mile Hi, Man
Another show where the 3,000 capacity venue was reportedly only half full.

Saturday 7th August
Community Theatre, Berkeley, USA
Support act: unknown
The final show of the tour. The first, lengthiest and most arduous leg of the world tour. Things could only get better. Blackmore's comments in reference to Roy Buchanan about taking the audience with you are somewhat ironic when quite a large chunk of audiences at some of these shows failed to grasp or appreciate the moments where Blackmore would play quiet interludes, often playing pieces of Bach and such like.

12 Pt IV—Thurs., Aug. 5, 1976 Los Angeles Times ★

STARLIGHT'S STAR BRIGHT—Burbank's Starlight Amphitheater is ready to take on the "big three."
Times photo by Larry Bessel

Starlight in Search of the Stars

BY LEE GRANT
Times Staff Writer

It is a majestic setting indeed, this Starlight Amphitheater carved in the mountains high above Burbank—particularly at night when the shimmering lights of the city form a spectacular backdrop and the thick brush and chaparral lend a rustic aura of camping out under the stars.

And there is another factor adding to the positive mood. The other evening, for instance, during a rock concert by a group called Richie Blackmore's Rainbow, the combination of reserved seats down front with the unreserved in the back lawn area created, somehow, a pleasant intimacy between audience and performer.

Fender STRATOCASTER

Civic Auditorium, San Jose, USA, 6th August 1976.

Civic Auditorium, San Jose, USA, 6th August 1976.

Civic Auditorium, San Jose, USA, 6th August 1976.

5.
"I'm Coming Home"
UK, 1st - 16th September

"I think one is always compromising, but I'm compromising in a nice kind of way. I'd like to be playing classical music, but I'm not capable of playing it in the way I'd like to. Rock 'n' roll still has that excitement. It's like a party. But I like the audience to think a bit, too. That's why we throw in the classical clichés.
I'm very into classical music. Bach is eighty per cent of what I listen to."

Ritchie Blackmore

Blackmore's return to his homeland was originally planned to be preceded by festival appearances in France. The first planned was the Orange Festival in Nimes on Thursday August 26th. The three-day festival with Rainbow due to headline on the opening day was cancelled following protests by local residents. The rest of the bill was scheduled to be Kevin Ayers, Rory Gallagher, Eddie And The Hot Rods, The Troggs and Curved Air. Acts for the other two days were to include Ted Nugent, Status Quo and Patti Smith.

A second festival appearance two days later on Saturday August 28th in Corbierres also got cancelled. This was to have a supporting cast of Chuck Berry, Dr. Feelgood, Ange, The Mighty Diamonds, Mallard and U-Roy. Other acts planned for different nights included Rick Wakeman, Procol Harum, The Groundhogs, Caravan, Gong and Van Der Graaf Generator.

Somewhere around this time, Blackmore also showed up at the Marquee during an AC/DC gig and so the story goes, went backstage to suggest a jam. AC/DC played the Marquee on the 16th, 23rd and 24th. Apparently the Aussie rockers were still reeling about events with Deep Purple the previous year at the Sunbury Festival when Purple's show overran and AC/DC never got to play. As a consequence they told Blackmore no, politely or otherwise.

The set list omitted 'A Light In Black'. Whilst in hindsight this was clearly disappointing to UK fans, it's unlikely that many at the time were even aware what the set list had been in America.

The support act for the UK tour was Stretch, a band who had recently seen bass player Paul Martinez depart to team up with Blackmore's old Purple chums, Ian Paice and Jon Lord in Paice Ashton Lord.

Tuesday 31st August
Hippodrome, Bristol, England

The first gig couldn't have been closer to home for Blackmore. Just a few miles from his birthplace in Weston-super-Mare and the hometown of his mother. It was more than two years since Blackmore had performed on stage in England. Prior to that it was during Deep Purple's *Burn* tour. With it being the first show, the band did a longer than normal soundcheck-cum-warm-up in the afternoon that included a full-length version of 'Lazy.'

Given Blackmore's status at the time, it's no surprise that the Bristolian crowd showed their appreciation by chanting "Blackmore is God." Well, seriously deluded people had been proclaiming the same thing about Eric Clapton for almost a decade, and he isn't even fit to be Blackmore's roadie! Not only were fans seeing Blackmore's new band for the first time but compared to Deep Purple, a far more visual act as well. Upon seeing the stage set at the Hippodrome, one reviewer said, "the stage scenery was like something from a Christmas fantasy on ice production. A painting of a castle hung at the back of the stage with a cunningly designed flashing rainbow in the foreground."

Apart from Blackmore, Cozy Powell was hugely familiar to British audiences, but the others were generally unknown. Of course Ronnie Dio has performed in the UK back in '74 when his then band Elf, supported Purple, but if many of the audiences had seen Purple, then, how many remembered the support act, or indeed bothered to watch them?

Brian Harrigan reviewed the show for *Melody Maker*:

Ritchie Blackmore is back, and nobody sleeps when he's on. There simply aren't words strong enough to describe how loud he and his band are. But in a masochistic way it was quite a gig. It was Rainbow's first concert on British soil, and they systematically blitzed the good citizens of Bristol who crammed into the Hippodrome.

Blackmore's following is quite startling, not all leftovers from the Deep Purple days, either. Fresh-faced kids not yet out of school went as barmy as their older counterparts.

Blackmore, ever-enigmatic and threatening in his all-black outfit, has surrounded himself with like-minded musicians dedicated to the proposal that "heavy makes you happy." Ronnie James Dio, who must have the most muscular tonsils in the world, sang like a giant, but commandeered the centre of the stage like some demented figment of Tolkien's imagination. Tiny, crouching and very evil, he punctuated songs like 'Sixteenth Century Greensleeves' and 'Man On The Silver Mountain' with the weirdest gestures since Dave Berry discovered itching powder. His line of between-song patter was corny to the point of parody, but it worked like a dream. Consummate performer.

Tony Carey displayed a different persona, that of a backroom wizard, but he was as hunched as Dio, with a creeping slouch and a liquid, sideways slither which moved him from one keyboard to another. It was hard to distinguish most of what he was playing, and his solos failed to flow properly, but he did winningly display an aggressive, high-speed, Wakemanesque style.

Jimmy Bain played bass like a freaked-out lumberjack toting a tree trunk; solid, strong, and dependable; it says a lot for him that he could provide such a sturdy underpinning to Blackmore's guitar. And Cozy Powell is the wickedest drummer around.

The King of the Stage, however, was (naturally) Blackmore himself and he was in spectacular form. Nimble, witty, very composed — he is probably one of the most heroic of guitar heroes.

For unrelenting pressure Rainbow are hard to beat; for professionalism they are the peak. But God knows, I could have used a little subtlety in their performance. Still, they are in business to overwhelm people. I, for one, was overwhelmed.

Harrigan's review didn't mention that the backing tape of the 1812 Overture failed to work for Cozy's drum solo (in fairness he probably wasn't even aware it was supposed to have been part of it). He also omitted the fact that Blackmore did his guitar sacrifice during the encore.

Wednesday 1st September
De Montfort Hall, Leicester, England

Not everyone was impressed with this gig. Fan Doug Parsons wrote to *Melody Maker*, explaining how his favour for Blackmore had waned after the concert. Dissatisfied with Blackmore's playing he wrote, "as an amateur guitarist myself perhaps I noticed things that everyone else around me missed, or at least, it appeared that way."

"I was appalled to see the man who is widely acclaimed to be the world's greatest rock guitarist pretending to play notes that simply weren't there and generally making a comparatively simple piece look near impossible! This I noticed on a couple of occasions. In my view this is unforgivable, but I lay most of the blame on his fans who go along expecting him to play at the speed of light.

"Ritchie Blackmore is a great guitarist but when he has to resort to this, and excessive amount of sound distortion and sustenance to the point where it doesn't matter what he does with the guitar or plays, it is pitiful and not at all clever.

However, having said all that there were moments when he showed his class and the band as a whole were very good, especially Ronnie James Dio on vocals but I couldn't make the bass out at all."

Blackmore's preoccupation with wanting the bass buried in the mix wasn't an unusual occurrence, but as for the other comments, this particular fan clearly failed to appreciate both the humour and importance of visuals that are so much a trademark of Blackmore's on stage demeanour, including the guitar demolition that he did once again.

Friday 3rd September
Empire Theatre Liverpool, England

For Liverpudlian fans, only a few months had passed since Deep Purple bowed out with their final gig at this very venue. Fans who had witnessed that show now had the opportunity of comparing Blackmore's new band to the one he had walked away from the previous year.

This show highlighted the dichotomy that faced Blackmore as he wanted to educate and entertain the crowds at the same time. During the quiet sections, many in the audience just chatted. At the other extreme, the over-enthusiastic crowd in the front stalls demolished the seating, quite a common occurrence at gigs in the mid-seventies. As another example, Eddie And The Hot Rods fans did the same at the Rainbow Theatre the following year

The Empire's management claimed that somewhere between £1-2,000 pounds worth of damage was caused and other venues were notified. Blackmore told the *NME*, "they are trying hard to get the tour stopped."

Saturday 4th September
Playhouse, Edinburgh, Scotland

Following a refurbishment, the Playhouse had only just re-opened but local residents who were annoyed by the noise emanating from the new generator sabotaged it prior to the gig and the show was in possible jeopardy. Rainbow refused to go on without power for the electronic Rainbow, and repair work started at 5pm.

Although they went on an hour late, the show at least went ahead. Like Liverpool, some damage was done to the seating. The *Edinburgh Evening News* reported on the show, some of which is quite

unintentionally comical: *Mr David Evans, general manager of John Reid Enterprises, who are promoting the Festival of Popular Music said: 'Residents had complained earlier in the week about the noise made by the generator, which boosts Queen's lightning. But we smoothed out most of the complaints. It could have been that somebody wasn't satisfied with the compensatory arrangements we made — although we've not discovered who exactly knocked out the generator.'*
Blackmore, who had to be admired on Saturday for their exhibitionism more than their music, don't go on without their gimmick — a 28ft high rainbow of over 3,000 light bulbs in red, blue and green with a 40ft span, designed and made in New York at a cost of £40,000.
It certainly caught the imagination of the fans, many of whom were on their feet for the entire concert. And there was damage. Most of the seats in the front row of the stalls were broken and, while repairs were being made in the time for this week's concerts, ticket holders for the front row at last night's performance by the New Seekers were placed elsewhere and invited backstage after the show to meet the group. Mr Evans added: 'We were apprehensive about Saturday's concert, because the previous night at Liverpool Empire, Blackmore's band was so high powered that there was over £1,000 worth of damage. The Edinburgh fans got plenty to shout about but with few exceptions, they behaved remarkably well.'
Lead singer/guitarist Blackmore capped his performance with one of his endearing little tricks — smashing his guitar, reputedly worth £350. It seemed the only way to go.

Sunday 5th September
Free Trade Hall, Manchester, England

The gig at Manchester was considered one of the best by those who witnessed it but in keeping with Blackmore's reputation he once again caused controversy in the eyes of some. As with the Leicester show, at least one fan took it upon himself to condemn Blackmore's antics, even though there is a suspicion that it might well have been part of the publicity drive. "Before he came on there was an announcement asking the crowd not to do any damage, and if there were any smashed seats it would be the last rock concert to be held at the Free Trade Hall," wrote A. Twambley of Fleetwood in a letter to one of the weekly music papers.

As Twambley observed, "all went very calmly until Blackmore started smashing his Fender against the speakers. Then after his guitar was totally ruined he swung it around his head and threw it into the crowd. Apart from half-killing the girl it hit, there then proceeded a mass riot as the audience fought to get a piece of the guitar. Fights broke out and damage was caused. Blackmore deliberately incited a riot, which could cause the end of the Free Trade Hall as a rock venue. Blackmore is bad for rock."

Since the fifties, with wild antics by the likes of Jerry Lee Lewis and Little Richard, people have made similar claims about numerous rock musicians, but to suggest that Blackmore, or indeed Townshend, Hendrix, Lewis or anyone else who has done damage to their instruments on stage are bad for rock, is like suggesting elections are bad for democracy!

Twambley would undoubtedly have been in a minority with his views but nevertheless it was left to Rainbow's manager Bruce Payne to defend Blackmore's behaviour: "Yes he did break the guitar," Payne stated candidly, "but there wasn't a riot — in fact it's about the only gig on the tour where there wasn't a riot. We purposely turned it down." Twambley's claims that a girl was half-killed (how do you half kill someone anyway?) were also dismissed by Payne. "It wasn't a girl — the guy who caught it came backstage afterwards. And there was no damage; we didn't have to pay a single pound in damages."

If Twambley's account had been a bit melodramatic, another fan also wrote a letter to the weekly music press, with his own personal account of the guitar trashing incident: "After three visits to Manchester Royal Infirmary, now I can tell you what happened," said Robert Kincaid. "The Rainbow encore was 'Do You Close Your Eyes' and halfway through it Ritchie Blackmore smashed a Fender Stratocaster and tosses part of it into the audience. The body of the Strat ended up exactly at the back of me and I grabbed it by the strings. A few minutes later I realised I was bleeding, and due to the fact that I found myself getting two stitches in my pinky right hand. I was just a rock fan who was very high. In fact I never felt any pain. What happens if a Strat comes flying straight at you? I only got two stitches but for some it could have been worse. Now I don't hold a grudge against Mr. Blackmore. In fact I can't wait until Rainbow tour again."

Bruce Payne's response to Twambley's remarks may well have played things down a bit too much, but for Steve Mills who was our resident photographer for *More Black Than Purple*, his recollection of Blackmore's Strat demolition — and the gig in general — are far more realistic: "I was fifteen at the time. I'd never been to a concert. What a concert, a tour and a band to be your first! Well, this was to be it. We rushed straight to our seats. A band called Stretch was playing. Where was everybody else? In the bar, of course. Didn't think their guitarist was bad at all. Then they left the stage. We sat in the centre balcony, with a great view of the stage, watching the roadies as they went about their business. Ritchie's amps appeared out of the clutter, the covers came off Cozy's double bass. The rainbow hugged the stage. The sense of occasion started to get to me as people filtered in from the bar. Shouts of 'Wally' abound the hall. 'Who's Wally?' Amid a crescendo of whistles, more people filtered in from the bar. The crew had done its job... the crowd grew impatient as another ten minutes passed.

"A slow but deliberate darkening of the lights announced the band's intention. This was it. One by one the band members took their positions in the gloom. The audience were whipped into a rabid frenzy when the unmistakeable figure of Blackmore lurked in the dark, last on. It was the cue for Judy Garland to set proceedings ahead.

"As the lights went on, it was the first time I'd stood in awe at finally seeing what was frankly a giant musical influence. The sight of RB in full flow for the first time. 'Kill The King' was a new number to me at the time, but the way Ritchie just stroked the guitar to start the number, I will never forget. Watching Ritchie's technique was just inspiring, especially after watching the previous outfit. I really couldn't imagine anyone else playing as well as this. To me it just wasn't possible. I probably still think that today.

"'Mistreated' was up next, Ritchie making full use of the acoustics during the intro and solo. The intro was unique, the solo similar to the studio recording at first, but with superb echo in the hall. Ronnie was brilliant, just as good as Coverdale had ever been and singing with such clarity. He introduced the next song as 'needing the instruments in perfect tune', slightly tongue in cheek, as it's 'Sixteenth Century Greensleeves'. A lovely treat from Ritchie at the beginning as he played 'Greensleeves', lulling the crowd into a false sense of security, a favourite Blackmore trick, only to unleash a crashing intro to the familiar riff. An exceptionally heavy version is delivered. What a contrast. Brilliant stuff!

"Ronnie asks John for a colour for Manchester. To the fury of some, red is the colour as the rainbow is lit. Tempers are quelled as we are treated to the majestic 'Catch The Rainbow'. To me, this is everything I imagine Ritchie could never do with Purple, and he was by now convincing me that he had done the right thing in leaving the previous year. In assembling Ronnie, Cozy, Tony and Jimmy around him, there appeared no bounds to which he could explore his freedom during this track. Again, Ronnie's voice was incredibly impressive and clear. Between songs, Ronnie has the crowd in the palms of his hands. Ritchie kicks off the next song with the deceptive 'Lazy'; the crowd go bonkers before it leads into 'Man On The Silver Mountain'. A strange intro to this one as Jimmy and Cozy get a rhythm going before the familiar riff. The whole band perform brilliantly, especially the animated Ritchie, pulling licks that only he can — I was awestruck with the dexterity and sheer technique of his playing.

"Ronnie announces that 'Tony Carey will introduce you to the 'Stargazer'.' It was a good solo which set the perfect scene for the band to reappear on stage and start what to RB lovers must be one of the all-time great songs. It was magical! A great tale was told. The solo was purely hypnotic, almost sexual as it built up to an amazing climax of slide and echo before peeling away back to the riff. An epic and stirring version greatly embellished by Ritchie's superb solo.

"No break and straight into 'Still I'm Sad'. Furious plucking by Ritchie, a short solo from Tony before Cozy set new standards in drum soloing. I always thought Ian Paice was a great technical drummer, but watching Cozy's performance set new standards in drama. His performing of the 1812 Overture weaved into the climax of the solo could perhaps have started the trend of the spectacular solo. I'll never forget the drums rising on the hydraulics, before the blinding pyrotechnic flash as the tape concluded. As the smoke cleared, the drum riser has lowered and Cozy wound up his solo. The rest of the band joined in to play out the remainder of the song, then departed the stage. A thick smoke hung over the audience as they bayed for more.

"It seemed like an absolute age before Ritchie led the band on for one more: 'Do You Close Your Eyes'; a quick flash through the verses and it was party time. Suddenly, without warning, the Fender took flight only to land back in Ritchie's arms. The next few minutes saw the Strat suffer brutal abuse as Ritchie proceeded to vent vengeance for all his frustrations of torture over the years of recording. I'll always remember the sight of Ritchie climbing atop the stage left monitors and thrash the neck of the guitar into the plaster work of this glorious hall. Chunks of plaster work rained on to the stage. This could be why there were few subsequent rock concerts at this venue. The entrails were thrown to the crowd, and that was it.

"As we filed out to the sound of Judy Garland, nobody spoke. We were just too stunned. We'd never seen anything like it. It was an event that surpassed all my expectations. As I stood on the doorstep of my home I remember my ears were absolutely ringing. I reflected on the event I'd just seen. It was to influence and change my life. I would never miss another tour. Like most people who read this, Ritchie Blackmore has had a huge influence on me, and everyone has "their event", their single reason why they love the music so much. Mine was 5th September 1976."

Harvey Goldsmith Entertertainments present
RITCHIE BLACKMORE'S
RAINBOW
+
SUPPORT
HAMMERSMITH ODEON
TUES. 7th & WED. 8th SEPTEMBER 8pm
TICKETS 3·00 2·50 1·80 1·50 inc VAT

Tuesday 7th September
Hammersmith Odeon London, England

Rainbow's London appearance over two nights attracted a lot attention from within the business. At this Tuesday show, Thin Lizzy's Scott Gorham, Don Airey and Jon Hiseman of Coliseum, and Neil Murray, bassist with National Health were all in attendance. DJ Alan 'Fluff' Freeman was also in the crowd, and during some of the quieter moments 'Fluff' — as he was nicknamed — was subjected to banter from certain sections of the crowd concerning a recent TV advert. "Brentford Nylons, special offer. Two for £3.99!"came the calls from the jokers within the audience.

Back in '76, Neil Jeffries — who became a noted journalist with a passion for quality classic rock music — was just another teenage kid, yet to tread his path of journalism. Like so many he was merely a fan, having grown up with the sounds of Deep Purple. Unsurprisingly, when Jeffries recalled his memories of seeing Rainbow for the first time, he couldn't help but pay homage to the journalists who inspired his future career move:

"*Sounds* taught me everything. The weekly told me all I needed to know about Ritchie Blackmore. The words of Geoff Barton and in particular, Pete Makowski were my lifeline. A conduit to all things Black and more. I devoured every issue, read every feature and absorbed every snippet of info, rumour and speculation.

"So on the evening of Tuesday September 7th 1976 — in the Hammersmith Odeon stalls seats rather near the back but happily on the same side as Ritchie — adrenaline was coursing through me: That and a bit of caffeine. I was sixteen and didn't drink in those days. Stone cold sober but high on expectation.

"Alongside me, my best mate Bob who then, as now, would rather listen to The Stones or The Who. Dimly aware of his scepticism I sat expectantly through the support set by Stretch with Elmer Gantry (great name, average band) singing samples of their current *You Can't Beat Your Brain For Entertainment* (great name, average songs). It didn't matter. Thanks to *Sounds*, I knew that what came next was worth the wait. And so after an agonisingly long interval as the Odeon filled, the houselights finally went out and the voice of Judy Garland drifted incongruously through the giant black PA. At last! I knew exactly what happened next, what I wasn't ready for, was the sense of disappointment.

"Prior to this I'd only seen three gigs; Nazareth supported by Snafu, Black Sabbath and something known as Bandy Legs, and most recently Uriah Heep preceded by the excellent Widowmaker, all at the Ipswich Gaumont. Tickets for each of those had cost £1.50 each but Rainbow were big league. I had to fork out a whopping £3.00. It seemed only fair, Blackmore was the master and even as an impoverished teenager I knew you only got what you paid for.

"I'd been to Oxford Street and bought Black Sabbath *Vol 4* but it would struggle to replace *Rainbow Rising* on my turntable. Well, my parents' Dixon's music centre. The album was three weeks old and I couldn't stop playing it. The other forty albums in my fast-growing collection were getting an unexpected break. It wasn't that I hadn't known about Blackmore: *24 Carat Purple*, *Made In Japan*, *Burn* and the *Ritchie Blackmore's Rainbow* debut were already firm favourites — but there was something about *Rising* that was pure. I even loved the few seconds of expectation as I impatiently lifted the stylus arm back into its rest and flipped the vinyl over, listening as the crackles gave way to Cozy's thunderous intro to 'Stargazer'. I knew that same intro would herald the replacement of the first album's guitar castle by an immense *Rising* backdrop and be even more thunderous. I was also primed to expect that although the sounds of the Munich Philharmonic would be absent, the closing bars of this epic would give way not to 'A Light In The Black' but 'Still I'm Sad'.

"On the night that combination was jaw dropping and in their full-on reworking of The Yardbirds' track the band bust a gut. But in retrospect they did so in vain because the damage had already been done. It had been done as early as 'Kill The King' when nobody rushed to the front. The relatively subdued blues of 'Mistreated' gave them an excuse to stay seated and likewise, seemingly, did Blackmore's elegantly picked intro to 'Sixteenth Century Greensleeves'. But come the riotous start of the song proper, with that riff crashing against the walls and ceiling of the Odeon almost no one took the cue to rise to their feet... the vast majority of the crowd just sat there. The bastards.

"I'd come over 130 miles to see this. I'd spent more than double my week's (paper round) wages. Did the other three-and-a-half thousand people not care? Had they just dropped by on the bus to watch just another gig at what was then London's premier rock venue? Bizarrely, this was the first night of two, the second only added after this one sold out. Surely they ought to have been keener than this? Perhaps they were hypnotised by the ever-changing patterns and colours of the stunning electronic rainbow arching over the stage. Perhaps they were annoyed that the band opened with a number they didn't know, followed it with one they hadn't recorded, and waited until after 'Catch The Rainbow' and 'Man On The Silver Mountain' — almost an hour of the set — before playing anything off, what everyone was certain was their best album. In retrospect that was a little odd — but it wasn't one of those nights when Blackmore was off form. I was in awe of the speed his hands moved over the white Stratocaster and of his ability to play while shaking his head left and right until his (obviously thinning) hair blurred before his squeezed shut eyes. I know now that he was simply pissed-off because the crowd gave him next to nothing in response. Well, apart from the odd 'Get on with it!' as he took time out to improvise.

"It was not until 'Still I'm Sad' gave way to solos by Carey and Powell, and then Blackmore, Dio and Bain returned for its stomping conclusion that the crowd finally came to life. But it was too late. An hour-and-forty-five was all we got. No encore. No 'Do You Close Your Eyes', No reject Strat demolition job.

"I wandered out in a daze. Exhilarated that I'd finally got to see Blackmore play but appalled at the complacency of the audience. I'd bought a European Tour '76 badge for 30p (with the fist, annoyingly, a mildewed green not quite like the album sleeve), the programme for 50p (a spectacularly uninspiring document that told me nothing I didn't know except technical guff and less than half what I'd read in last week's *Sounds*), and afterwards — outside, perhaps from one of the strictly unofficial hawkers — a dark and grainy live poster of the band performing beneath the electronic rainbow. Some clown had gone to the trouble of smuggling in a camera but the best for a poster was taken when the lighting was at its most subdued. I'd not been able to afford the T-shirt, but the following Saturday I sent Brockum a £2 postal order for one. I still have it and could still wear it. It's faded a little but not too much and the mud from Donington in 1980 has never washed out. But that's another story..."

Wednesday 8th September
Hammersmith Odeon London, England

The second night at Hammersmith Odeon, saw another host of celebrities in the crowd. Members of Queen (perhaps relieved that Rainbow had just withdrawn from the proposed support slot at the Cardiff Castle gig on Friday), Dave Edmunds, Ian Hunter, and most notably Blackmore's former band mates Jon Lord and Ian Paice.

This gig was also witnessed by Alan Whitman who in 2002 became sub-editor of *More Black Than Purple*: "It had been a short but steep road to reach Row M, Seat 37 of the Odeon. You see, my initiation to Blackmore had only begun some twelve months earlier when I heard *Made In Japan* on the stereo in our common room at college. To borrow some boxing analogies of the impact he was to have on me is to say that album had been a scything left hook, *Rainbow Rising* had been a devastating uppercut and tonight would prove to be the knockout blow. But wait a moment, I'm getting ahead of myself.

"*Rising,* and 'Stargazer' in particular, had held me in thrall from the moment I first heard it. I just couldn't believe that music could be so exciting and dramatic and it would be no exaggeration to say that it had a profound effect on my life. I had only attended two previous concerts (Queen, both times) and that I was sitting here at all was a bit of a fluke, as I had bought *Sounds* on a whim and this happened to be the issue in which the tour dates were announced. By the time of the tour itself I was devouring anything I could find on Rainbow and the music press tour reports only served to whet the appetite. The overwhelming consensus was that the shows were incredible, although I couldn't quite reconcile some accounts that the band were "evil" and thought this was a strange comment to make...

"The crowd on that September night were a very different bunch to those that I had previously experienced. A sea of denim, leather, dandruff and some pretty unsavoury looking individuals lent a rather intimidating (at least to this inexperienced concert-goer) atmosphere to proceedings. The place was packed as one might expect, no doubt Purple fans eager to see how Blackmore would fare without his Nemesis.

"Showtime and my eyes searched the gloom trying to pick out the top of the PA stack which seemed to stretch into eternity. The support band were Stretch, who I vaguely recall had a minor hit at the time. They were actually very good and the guitarist performed an excellent solo during the last number that earned them deserved calls for an encore, much to their bewilderment; evidently this had not happened on too many previous occasions.

"During the interval I clearly remember the "weird" music being played over the PA (it was later suggested that this may have been Blackmore/Dio's first dabblings in medieval music). The lights go down, the heart begins to pump faster, Judy Garland is clearly lost in America's Heartland and then the stage explodes into a sea of light and colour. I stand there, completely unable to absorb this assault on the senses, the electronic Rainbow pulsing crazily above the stage and pinned back by the wall of sound blasting from the PA as Ritchie's opening chords rip across the frenzied audience. The song is unfamiliar, but who cares, I have never experienced anything so exciting in my life.

"When the initial sensory overload has stabilised I'm able to focus a bit more clearly on the protagonists of this mayhem: A matter of yards away from me is this Man dressed completely in black, seemingly rooted to the spot, shock of long hair occasionally shaking to the music. He seems totally focussed on his guitar, not doing a lot, but there is this powerful aura emanating from him and I stand transfixed, unable to take my eyes from him. I really can imagine this vision in front of me being the personification of satanic wizardry. And then that report in *Sounds* flashes through my mind – this band really do have a menacing aura and the description starts to make some sense. I know it sounds crazy now, but these truly were the emotions I felt at the time.

A quiet intro to 'Mistreated', with much use of the violin effects, precedes the usual manic intro and the crowd erupts as the band launch into the song. Ritchie's solo is every bit as good as the version on *On Stage*, just gently picking away in a seemingly abstract and experimental manner. This solo highlights the thin line that the early incarnations of Rainbow tended to tread; that is, the danger of alienating some sections of the audience who were just there to shake their head and punch the air and could not comprehend these quieter moments.

An aggressive rendition of 'Sixteenth Century Greensleeves' ensues and then we are into 'Catch The Rainbow', which is greeted enthusiastically by the crowd. Ritchie really stretches out the intro again and Dio's soaring vocals echo around the auditorium as the colours on the Rainbow slowly creep across its span. The solos are excellent and the sound seems crisp, with no hint of the phaser effects reaching these ears. The quiet interlude between the two solo segments is once again extended compared to most versions I have heard and Ritchie really seems to be up for the gentler side of the music tonight.

"The start of 'Man On The Silver Mountain' is greeted with laughter as Ritchie disappears behind his amps and Dio suggests that he has gone to the toilet. Blackmore plays one line of 'Lazy' and then holds the note for ages, before playing another line and he once again holds the note, teasing the crowd, and then the band crash in to finish the excerpt.

"Ritchie's guitar blitz after the last verse of 'Man...' is unbelievable; his fingers are a blur as he blasts out some frantic runs. It seemed to go on for ages at the time and after listening to the tape it was all of three minutes in length – absolutely marvellous and the crowd go crazy at the end before he starts the 'Blues'.

"'Stargazer' is next and one of the moments I have been waiting for. I have always rated Carey and he did not disappoint tonight. I particularly liked the way he was prepared to take Ritchie on, not afraid to make his mark, although this was ultimately to cost him his job. The slide solo is of course top-notch and this is how I like Ritchie best; the band powering away behind him whilst he is left to solo over the top. The slide blitz at the end of the solo sounds like quadrophonic as it bounces around the hall. No time to pause for breath as they launch straight into 'Still I'm Sad'. Centrepiece of the song is of course Cozy's drum solo – halfway through, the drum riser was lifted into the air to a backing of the 1812 Overture. The end of the song is manic, with Ritchie bashing away and Dio trying to keep up!

"And then the band are gone and the crowd start baying for more; would they do an encore tonight as the previous night this had been absent. It takes some time, but eventually they reappear and after some frantic chord bashing and runs from Ritchie they launch straight into 'Do You Close Your Eyes'. It's not long before the Strat is off and winging its way skywards before being deftly caught again. At one point Blackmore even starts doing a jig around the guitar as it lay on the floor (yet another Blackmore innovation, as this was later picked up on by women around the world in the form of dancing around their handbags on the disco floor!). The PA and floor prove to be excellent objects in his desire to dismantle the offending instrument and the body is ceremoniously launched into the audience, closely followed by the neck which came arcing through the lights in my direction! A lunge of Olympic proportions to try and grab it was to no avail and the punter next to me emerged from the pile triumphant. But with the strings dangling temptingly I couldn't resist grabbing hold and just as the guy started to panic that I was trying to steal his neck the string gave way and I came up with a memorable souvenir

of the evening — Ritchie's E string (although my wife regards this treasure with some amusement!). At the end of the show, the experience had proved to be so exhausting that I could only stand in stunned silence staring at the stage, trying to take in what had gone before.

"It is perhaps unhealthy to focus on the past, but although Ritchie has provided some great moments over the years, I will always regard this as the pinnacle that has never been surpassed. I am sure that any of you who were privileged enough to witness one of these shows will recall the sheer excitement and spectacle. I know that it forever cemented Blackmore in my psyche and I would never be the same again.

"The only disappointment on the night was the lack of *Rising* material and the sound, which was at times so loud and distorted that it was difficult to hear what was going on. But hey, these are minor quibbles and you can never have everything!

"What would be interesting would be if I could be transported back in time to relive the concert again to see if time has romanticised and embellished my memories and whether it would have the same impact now that I'm a cynical old bastard! Until then I am happy to remember it this way. Hmmm... anybody out there who can tell me the current whereabouts of H.G. Wells?"

Thursday 9th September
Hammersmith Odeon London, England

A third night had been provisionally booked but in the end was not utilised. If they had known the gig that was due to follow would have not taken place, a third night in London may well have gone ahead.

Friday 10th September
Castle Festival, Cardiff, Wales

Rainbow was due to play at this outdoor gig as the main support to Queen. Following disagreements about the stage arrangements they pulled out of the show. Basically, Rainbow wanted to use their full stage set-up, but the logistics of erecting the rainbow for a support slot was something that the Queen entourage was clearly not going to allow. It was fortuitous in the end because the gig was marred by torrential rain. Who in their right mind would entertain an open-air gig in Wales at the tail end of the summer anyway?

Saturday 11th September
Odeon, Birmingham, England

Rainbow biographer Roy Davies was introduced to the band at this gig. He fondly recalls:

"We could all look back in the development of our musical tastes in our teens to a certain time and happening where the whole direction of said tastes suddenly undergoes a complete and radical change. So it was personally with my first experience of Ritchie Blackmore's Rainbow.

"A chance meeting in a school corridor with a friend who had a spare ticket to see "a really good band" led me to agreeing to go to Brum to see Rainbow. I was rather naively into what you might call "pop-rock" at the time — Status Quo, Slade etc. — and I had no real knowledge of Rainbow's (or Ritchie's) musical background. I was soon to be blown away.

The late lamented Birmingham Odeon was typical of the type of venue prevalent in every major town in the sixties and seventies. A converted cinema holding about 3-4,000 with real velvet seats, a commissioner in uniform and a decaying Victorian decor. (Does anyone remember the characteristic old musty smell of those places?). A moderately successful band could sell out these medium sized theatres and a UK tour could be anything up to thirty dates in those days (Happy times!).

"We got there late and missed the support (good job by all accounts!). We had seats to the right of the stage about five rows back and so had what would prove to be an excellent view of Ritchie.

"The lights went off, the *Wizard Of Oz* intro started and they were off. Despite a few sound problems, 'Kill The King' was immediately impressive and particularly forceful, with Cozy's drumming powering the song along. The overriding initial impact on me was one of sustained but barely uncontrolled power — of a band performing right on the edge, somehow keeping everything just the right side of chaos. Before I had chance to catch my breath it was straight into 'Mistreated' — for me (and most others) the highlight, the whole audience becoming transfixed with Ritchie's improvisation, taking everyone on a magic carpet ride into a musical nirvana, weaving a spell for an age before returning (eventually) to the main theme of the song. I don't think he ever played it better. In hindsight, Ronnie's performance was exceptional — he sang it far better than David Coverdale ever did. By now it was obvious to me that the focal point of the band was the guitarist — remember I had no idea of the band's history or "set-up" — with Cozy Powell a close second. Ronnie provided an able counterbalance to the instrumental side of the group.

"The rest of the show went by so quickly and all these years later is now a little blurred. But little things still stick in the memory — like Ritchie's hand signals cueing the others in and out, Tony Carey earning Ritchie's wrath when he continued playing at one point, and where Ritchie teased with a bit of 'Smoke' and the place almost erupted!

"By the end of the show my whole outlook on music had undergone a profound change. Having been used to short three-minute rock stuff, I had no idea there were musicians and groups like this with an improvisational ability to be able to sustain, stretch and deliver such strong emotions via their music. I went and bought all I could of Ritchie's work — mostly Purple at the time — and devoured all subsequent work avidly. Although my initial enthusiasm has now waned with the passing years, there has been nothing since that can match the sheer impact of that night in September."

Two fans travelling back to London after the gig had a welcome surprise when they stopped at Watford Gap Services. As Paul and Ken said at the time, "we would like to thank the man we were talking to at the Watford Gap Service Station. He proved to us that real superstars are not too big to talk to their followers. This was despite the fact that he had just finished a terrific concert — Thanks Ritchie."

Sunday 12th September
Gaumont Theatre, Southampton, England
Originally booked for this date but switched to the following day.

Monday 13th September
Capitol Theatre, Cardiff Wales
This date had been scheduled but the gig was cancelled, presumably once the open-air show had been arranged, as two shows in Cardiff in three days would have been unnecessary. With Rainbow pulling out of the gig with Queen, it deprived Welsh fans of any show at all.

Monday 13th September
Gaumont Theatre, Southampton, England
The band was actually staying in London for this show and Cozy drove the eighty miles to the venue... or at least that was the plan but unfortunately his car broke down on the way and he had to thumb a lift! Fans on the South Coast were denied an encore, much to the annoyance of many. One fan from Dorset vented his anger through the press, "I beg of you to let me use your sacred space to proclaim gross vexations towards Ritchie Blackmore's Rainbow at Southampton. That audience were bloody keen and wouldn't be denied an encore even when the house lights went on and the safety curtain was down. Thanks, Blackmore, for nothing — especially seeing as how the fuzz had to move in to force to move us after twenty minutes of bawling for more. If Ritchie and the rip offs are listening — you know where you can stick your jack plugs."

Monday 13th September
Speakeasy, London, England
Whilst technically this gig was probably on the Tuesday morning, Blackmore visited London's Speakeasy Club after the Southampton gig. It's possibly the reason for no encore. Playing at the Speakeasy that evening was The Fabulous Poodles, a band heavily influenced by The Kinks and The Who. Mott The Hoople's Ian Hunter and Blackmore joined the band on stage.

Blackmore was a particularly aggressive character at this time and it was reported that he got involved in a punch-up with one of the barmen.

Sounds erroneously listed a show at Newcastle City Hall for the same date.

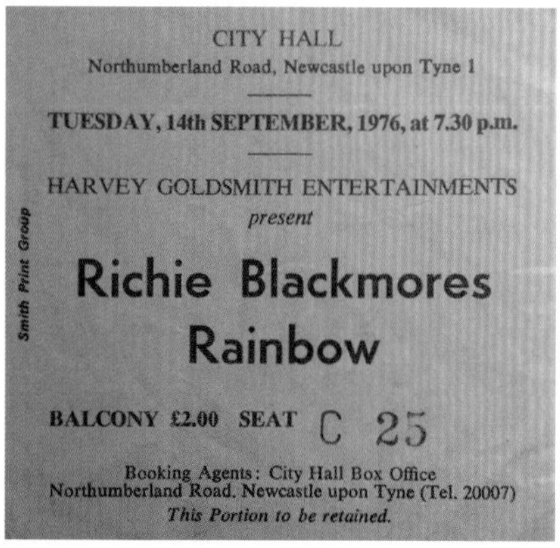

Tuesday 14th September
City Hall, Newcastle, England
Having booked in to the Holiday Inn for the last of the UK gigs, the band was forced to run for their lives when the hotel was invaded by fans. It sounds ridiculous that a band like Rainbow would be besieged by fans and in actual fact, they weren't. Although they probably wouldn't have objected to hordes of female fans throwing themselves at them, in truth the fans were

there for the Bay City Rollers, who were also checking into the hotel.

This was the last gig of the UK tour and Blackmore's growing dislike for Tony Carey culminated in a rather bizarre sacking incident. As documented in my Blackmore biography, *Black Knight*, Carey recalled the incident with some amusement: "He fired me because I was definitely playing too much. I know that now but he came over in the middle of the set and said, 'why don't you just leave then.' I was definitely not playing what he expected me to play. It was his band, he could have come over and said 'play less or stick to the rulebook' but he didn't. That's not his style. I didn't even know he was unhappy. He just kept it to himself then he came over and said 'why don't you leave then' — No warning! So after the gig I said 'okay I'm gone', took a cab back to the hotel, called the airline and they said 'oh no you can't do that in the middle of the tour', 'well he's just fired me' and I was talking to Bruce on a couch in the hotel lobby not knowing Ritchie was standing right behind me and I said, 'I think he's just jealous because I play so fast' and Ritchie of course heard this and whacked me across the back of the head but like you would hit a little kid and said to me 'you're nothing, you'll never be anything' so there was definitely an insecurity and a pride. Why should he be jealous of me? He wasn't and couldn't have been. On the one hand he's an absolute genius, he's got such magnetism about him when he walks in a room — the 'man in black' and this and that — this is one person in fifty million just from his charisma and what he's got but I wouldn't care to analyse what he is. I mean Mozart was an asshole but Ritchie is definitely an important figure, he taught me a lot. Nothing you'd ever want to teach anybody because he's way too selfish, but just observing him. The big problem I had with Rainbow was the management, they were sharks."

Thursday 16th September
Speakeasy, London, England

Blackmore returned to London before the band was due to depart to mainland Europe for stage three of the tour and once again spent the evening at the Speakeasy. This time it with his former employer from his second professional band The Savages, namely Screaming Lord Sutch who was performing that evening with his current crop of musicians. Ritchie got up on stage and joined in for a while, although nothing has been documented about this gig so it's not clear as to what Ritchie played on or how long he was on stage for.

Away from the machinations of the big gigs, Blackmore always enjoyed these low-key appearances in the company of old friends, and in more relaxed environments. It was soon back to the tour though as the band moved on to mainland Europe.

Liverpool Empire, 3rd September, 1976.

Liverpool Empire, 3rd September, 1976.

Liverpool Empire, 3rd September, 1976.

Liverpool Empire, 3rd September, 1976.

inbow

Liverpool Empire, 3rd September, 1976.

Marshall

Liverpool Empire, 3rd September, 1976.

Liverpool Empire, 3rd September, 1976.

Powell

Powell

OLYMPEN
Lund
KONSERTPROGRAM HÖSTEN 76
TED NUDGENT
Fredag 3 september kl 19.00
ROGER WHITTAKER
Måndag 6 september kl 19.30
RICHIE BLACKMORE
Lördag 18 september kl 19.00
GENTLE GIANT
Söndag 19 september kl 19.00
FLYING BURRITO BROTHERS
Fredag 1 oktober (Pireus, Malmö)
THIN LIZZY
Lördag 2 oktober kl 19.00
PATTI SMITH
Tisdag 5 oktober kl 19.00
SAILOR
Onsdag 6 oktober kl 19.00
ALEX HARVEY SENSATIONAL BAND
Torsdag 7 oktober kl 19.00
POCO
Söndag 10 oktober kl 19.00
DEMIS ROUSSOS
Fredag 26 november kl 19.00
NAZARETH
Fredag 3 december kl 19.00
MANFRED MANN
Tisdag 7 december kl 19.00
Vi jobbar på Pointer Sisters i november.
Reservation för ändringar och tillägg.
Biljettförköp: Julius Platthandel 046-14 78 88 (14—18) — SDS depeschkontor — Rollis 040-336 33 — HD-centralen 042-15 00 00 — NST-centralen 0418-125 45
Skådebanan vid vissa konserter
Information: Julius Fridtid & Nojen 046-13 52 00

Although incorrectly being billed as Ritchie Blackmore, Rainbow pulled out of this show supposedly because the electronic rainbow wouldn't fit into the arena.

6.
See How He Glides
Europe, 20th September - 18th October

"We didn't want to come over before we were really ready. Ritchie means a lot to the kids over here and we didn't want to upset them. They are what really matters. If people were going to look for Deep Purple in Rainbow they'd find it in Ritchie. He's the most awe-inspiring person in the band — there's no denying it. He deserves the credit."

Ronnie James Dio

Apparently Rainbow was originally going to play several European shows with another Thames Talent signing, Be Bop Deluxe as the supporting act, but this fell through. Ironically, given Blackmore's little run-in with AC/DC, the Aussie rockers ended up doing the support slot for the vast majority of the European dates. As had been the case in the States, there was a lot of chopping and changing of dates. In particular, the French dates remain a mystery to this day.

On a more upbeat note, by now the songs had developed through the months of touring. The most noticeable was 'Man On The Silver Mountain' where Blackmore incorporated 'Blues' — first deployed with Purple during 'You Fool No One'. The section that followed where Dio got to ad-lib sometimes saw him start singing 'Starstruck' with the rest of the band joining in.

Saturday 18th September
Olympen, Lund, Sweden
This show was cancelled with the reason given that the rainbow was too big for the hall. Very *Spinal Tap*! They could have performed without it, but hey, that's Blackmore for you!

Monday 20th September
Konserthuset, Stockholm, Sweden
So the European leg actually started in Stockholm, the same venue where Purple had been brilliantly captured for posterity six years previously by Swedish Radio in a recording that eventually saw the light of day in 1988.

The management of the concert hall had told Rainbow that they were not allowed to use the pyrotechnics that were a part of Cozy's explosive drum solo, but Blackmore being Blackmore simply ignored the demand. The show was also not well received by the press. Criticisms that the show was too "violent" and too loud were also added to by accusations that the guitar destruction was cynical; but worse, Ronnie Dio was described as a catastrophe.

Having seen Blackmore the previous year on his last tour with Purple, Mikael Wiklund relished the chance to catch Blackmore with Rainbow: "Yes, it is a long time ago but the memory lingers on... About ten of us went by train early so we had plenty of time in Stockholm before the show which was supposed to start at 21:30 according to the ticket.

"My friend had this tape recorder with him, a very large machine, and managed to get it into the venue and told me before the show... 'I forgot the microphone, I left it in my jacket! Shall I fetch it?' 'Err... yes, please...' so he did. It is a very good recording with good dynamics since it was a good quality recorder but he got nervous at the end of the show because the guards started to pay attention to him so he stopped the recording after 'Still I'm Sad'. But it was a wise choice, better to save what he got which he managed to do. Even though it is a good recording there is a lot of talk by us because we were excited!

"The show started around 22:00 around thirty minutes late. 'Kill The King' was the opening track which no one had heard at the time. A big surprise. 'Mistreated' followed which was fantastic and the intro from Ritchie was great. Other highlights were 'Man On The Silver Mountain', with 'Lazy' intro and a great improvisation in the middle. That part was different from night to night if you listen to different shows from the tour.

"And then it came. 'Stargazer'!... in all its glory. Long intro from Tony Carey and then the drum pattern and off they went. Fantastic.

"'Still I'm Sad' was next with a drum solo from Cozy Powell including pyrotechnics with a heavy flash at the end of the drum solo, which they were not allowed to do. Rainbow was not welcome back said the management after the show but they were back next year again despite this.

"Rainbow finished the show with 'Do You Close Your Eyes' and Ritchie smashed the guitar in that song. I saw Ritchie play with Deep Purple the year before in Gothenburg. Then he was not so interested, he played good but no energy. This time with Rainbow was something else. He was definitely on. Full of energy and he played fantastically.

"This was one of the greatest shows that I have seen and it had a great impact on me. Great memory. After the show we went to the stage door and walked in backstage! No guards! It was so easy back then. We met both Blackmore and Dio and they were very pleasant too. It was a great experience.

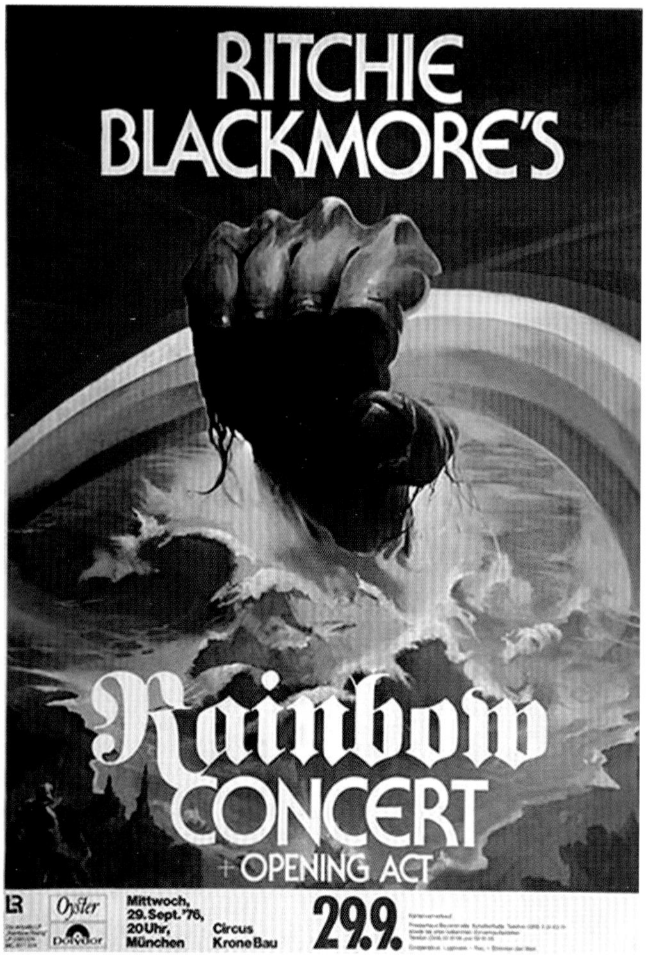

Courtesy of Mikael Wiklund

Ronnie and Ritchie backstage after the show.

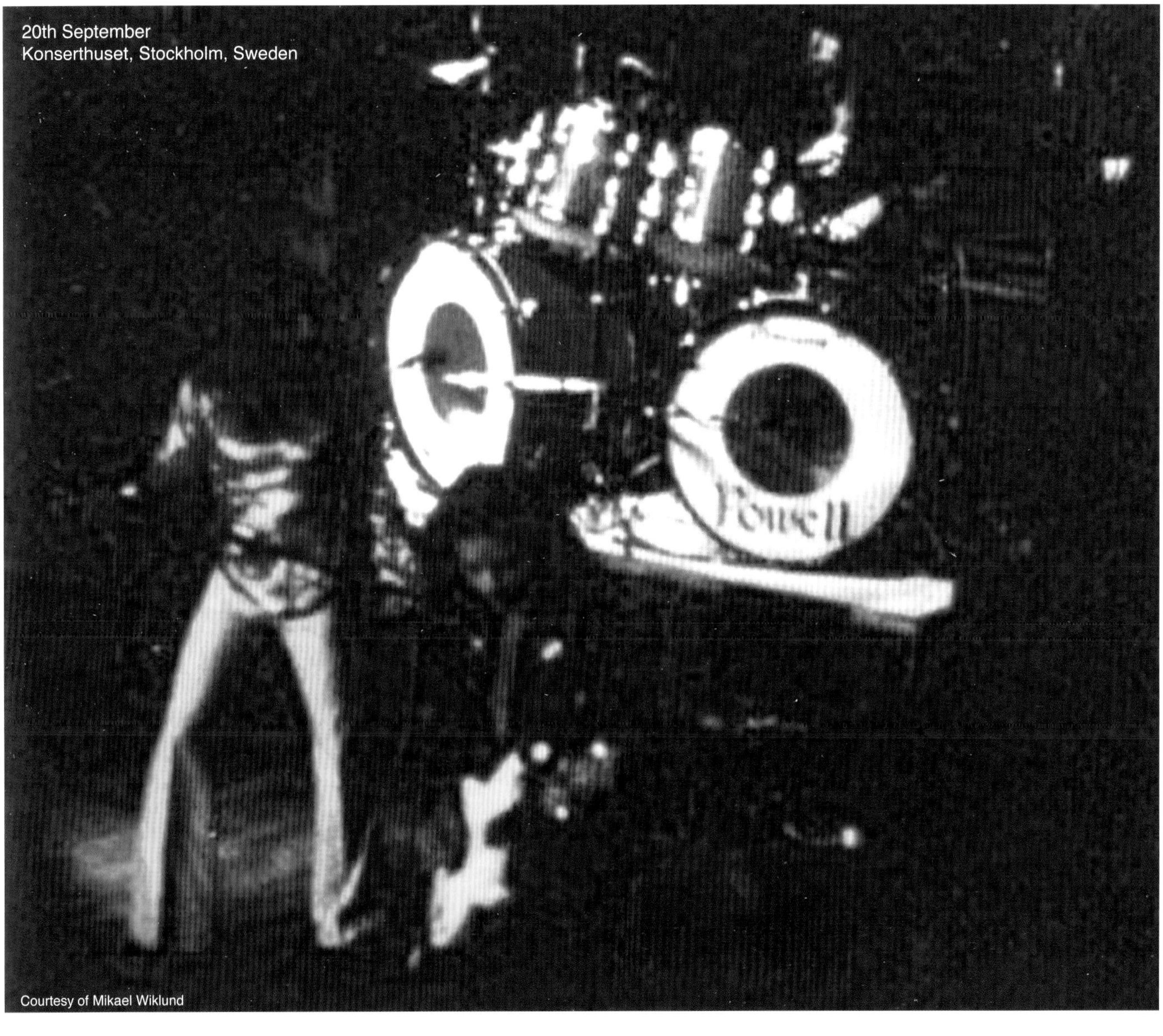

20th September
Konserthuset, Stockholm, Sweden

Courtesy of Mikael Wiklund

20th September
Konserthuset, Stockholm, Sweden

Courtesy of Mikael Wiklund

Courtesy of Mikael Wiklund

20th September
Konserthuset, Stockholm, Sweden

Courtesy of Mikael Wiklund

Cozy
Powell

23rd September, Hamburg

© Roland Guder

Philipshalle, Düsseldorf, Germany, 27th September 1976

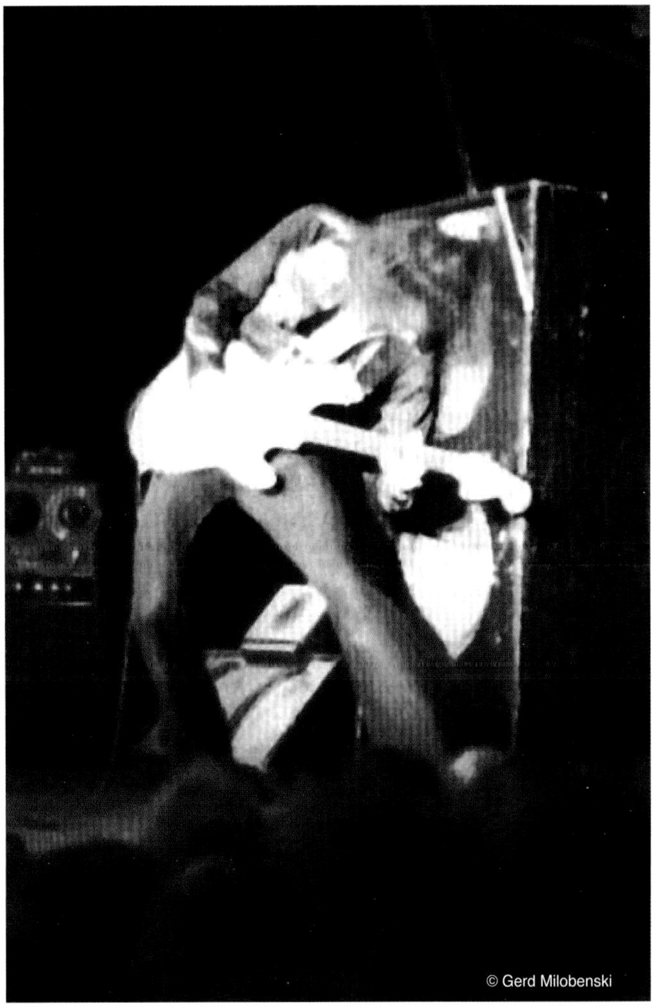

23rd September, Hamburg

23rd September, Hamburg

23rd September, Hamburg

23rd September, Hamburg

Wednesday 22nd September
Tivoli's Koncertsal, Copenhagen, Denmark

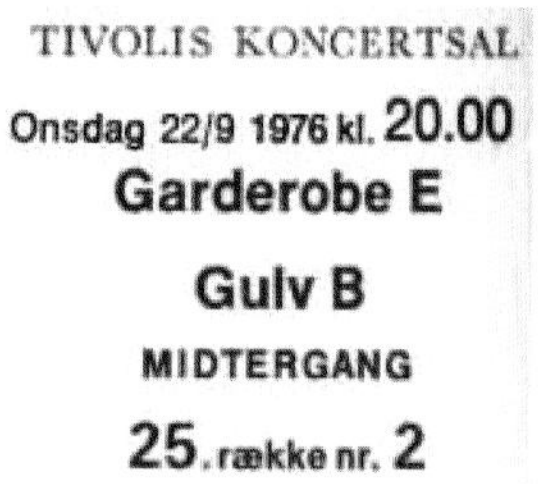

Thursday 23rd September
Musikhalle, Hamburg, Germany

Friday 24th September
Stadthalle, Bremerhaven, Germany

Saturday 25th September
Sporthalle Cologne, Germany

Plans to record a live album commenced at this gig and The Rolling Stones' mobile unit was employed for the next four shows with Martin Birch in charge of the recordings. When the *On Stage* album was released the following year, only 'Mistreated' from this show was used but the interplay between Dio and Blackmore was edited out. The full concert was released to commemorate the thirtieth anniversary in 2006.

The backing tape with 1812 Overture failed to work as can be clearly heard when Cozy does the drum roll that should be the cue for the tape to start. He continues with this for ages before realising that it was obviously one of those nights where he would have to change his solo to accommodate.

Monday 27th September
Philipshalle, Düsseldorf, Germany

No encore was performed at this gig.

Tuesday 28th September
Messezentrum Halle A, Nürnburg, Germany

Wednesday 29th September
Circus Krone, Munich, Germany

The last of the four shows recorded by Martin Birch. The encore of 'Do You Close Your Eyes' was also filmed for the TV show *Musikszene*. It's unlikely that the rest of the show was filmed.

In an article by Dolf Hartmann in *Musik Express*, he reported that David Coverdale, then living in Munich, was backstage in a dressing room with Ronnie Dio, Tony Carey and Jimmy Bain.

With Blackmore isolated in his own dressing room, Hartmann managed to secure a brief interview with Blackmore but couldn't help but comment on the note on the guitarist's dressing room door: "In this area nobody is of importance, and even if they are, he doesn't want to be disturbed by someone like you. Please take this warning seriously and — PISS OFF. Do not think, that everyone is meant except you. Also put your backstage pass in your arse and piss off outside, where you belong. And do it now!"

Blackmore told Hartmann: "Now I can do what I want. I have earned enough money with Deep Purple. With Rainbow concerts I now use the opportunity to return it somehow to the people. I would like to thank them for the affection, they brought me with Deep Purple."

Friday 1st October
Rhein Main Halle Wiesbaden, Germany

Saturday 2nd October
Grosse Westfalenhalle, Dortmund, Germany

Unlike the rest of the gigs on the tour, this was a festival show with multiple bands, thirteen acts in total. The show was billed on the poster as starting at two in the afternoon although the poster also said the opening act was on at one!

The Westfalenhallen is multiple halls within a complex so I can only assume that there must have been bands playing simultaneously on different stages in order to accommodate them all in an afternoon and evening. German guitarist Axel Rudi Pell was at this gig and recalled, "it was amazing. It was a big festival where The Scorpions also played but Rainbow easily topped them all. I remember that during a quiet solo a guy blew a trumpet and of course Ritchie was pissed off and stopped playing for a while. Ronnie went to the mic and said 'please come on stage, we're only a backing band for you!' The guy didn't show up and they carried on playing. I think it was during 'Sixteenth Century Greensleeves' but I can't remember exactly. I was sixteen years old and that's a long time ago."

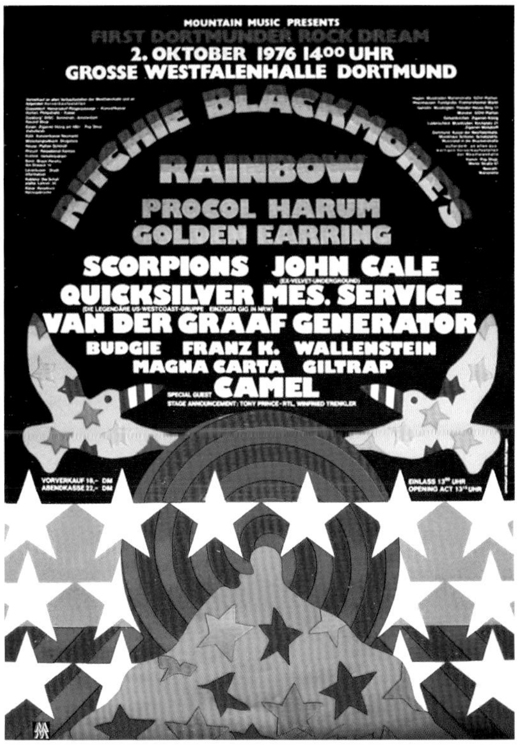

Sunday 3rd October
Palais des Expositions, Geneva, Switzerland
This was rescheduled for the 9th

Monday 4th October
Casino, Bern, Switzerland

Tuesday 5th October
Volkshaus, Zurich, Switzerland

Wednesday 6th October
Jahrhunderthalle, Frankfurt, Germany

Friday 8th October
Luxor Theatre, Hoensbroek, The Netherlands
It is unconfirmed as to whether or not this show happened.
The AC/DC tour page at ac-dc.net lists the gig, although this is possibly just copied from other sources.

Saturday 9th October
Palais des Expositions, Geneva, Switzerland

Un concert de rock

Ritchie Blackmore à Genève

Les amateurs de « Deep Purple » seront à la fête. Et ils sont nombreux puisque l'on dit que le groupe est, avec « Pink Floyd », celui qui a le plus vendu de disques en France et chez nous. Ils seront ravis puisque si le Pourpre Profond n'est plus qu'un souvenir, individuellement les musiciens poursuivent leur carrière et l'un des plus importants, le guitariste Ritchie Blackmore sera au Palais des expositions de Genève le 9 octobre.

Il sera intéressant d'aller écouter sa musique et de voir ce qu'une certaine conception du rock est devenue. Les temps ont changé, les modes aussi, que reste-t-il d'un mouvement qui faisait salle comble il y a encore quatre ans ? Peut-être qu'un peu de « fumée sur l'eau... »

P. G.

Monday 11th October
Le Mans, France

Tuesday 12th October
Le Havre, France
Both these shows were listed on the original tour schedule but are thought not to have taken place.

Tuesday 12th October
Palais des Sports, Besançon, France
It's considered that only three shows were actually done in France with this being the first. With no recordings circulating of this show or of the one in Colmar, the story that Blackmore told the author sadly cannot be corroborated. At one of these gigs, unhappy with the crowd's response, Ritchie and Cozy decided to change instruments: "I remember in France somewhere, the audience were so boring — it was about the third number — I got on drums, Cozy got on guitar, and we all started playing 'Peter Gunn.' The audience actually went crazy. They wouldn't clap because they thought we were awful. And then we did 'Peter Gunn' and they thought we were wonderful! Isn't that amazing? Only in France!"

Wednesday 13th October
Porte De Pantin Pavillon, Paris, France
The original tour schedule had Paris for the 16th.

A very lengthy version of 'Man On The Silver Mountain' starting with Blackmore teasing the audience with 'Lazy' and even a brief few notes of 'Smoke On The Water' before playing 'White Christmas' and eventually kicking into the riff. Following 'Blues', Ronnie does his ad-lib bit which goes on for ages with some tasteful accompaniment from Blackmore.

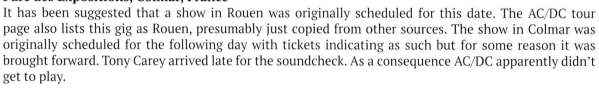

Thursday 14th October
Kings Circle, Brussels, Belgium

Friday 15th October
Rouen, France

Friday 15th October
Parc des Expositions, Colmar, France
It has been suggested that a show in Rouen was originally scheduled for this date. The AC/DC tour page also lists this gig as Rouen, presumably just copied from other sources. The show in Colmar was originally scheduled for the following day with tickets indicating as such but for some reason it was brought forward. Tony Carey arrived late for the soundcheck. As a consequence AC/DC apparently didn't get to play.

Saturday 16th October
Marseille, France
The AC/DC tour page also lists this as a gig supporting Rainbow, possibly extracted from Roy Davies' original gig list in his 2002 Rainbow biography. Roy listed it as unconfirmed based on press information from the time, but with so many alterations it is unconfirmed as to whether it took place or not.

Monday 18th October
Congressbuilding, The Hague, The Netherlands
Of all the European tour dates, the last gig of the tour was something of a surprise. Blackmore hadn't played in the Netherlands since 1973 when Purple's show in Amsterdam finished in mass destruction to the band's equipment following their early departure from the stage. Purple had called an early halt to the show after only fifty minutes, unhappy with the conditions they were expected to perform in. The Dutch press were very keen to raise the issue when interviewing Blackmore just before the gig. Dutch magazine *Muziekkrant Oor*, asked the guitarist if he would be making up for that bad show. In a typical unrepentant response, Blackmore said, "no. I play music as well as I can, but I'm not going to make up anything for anybody. If they like it, they like it; if they don't like it then they don't like it..."

Positive reviews of the gig do substantiate that even though Blackmore had indicated he was just going to walk out on stage and do his thing, that he did it very well.

Thursday 21st October
House Of Culture, Helsinki, Finland

Maanantaina 11. lokakuuta 1976

Blackmore peruuntui

Deep Purplen entisen kitaristin Ritchie Blackmoren ja hänen Rainbow -yhtyeensä Suomeen tulo on peruuntunut. Seppo Pietikäinen kertoi konsertin järjestäjien edustajana tilanteesta: "Helsinki oli suunniteltu Rainbowin Euroopan kiertueen viimeiseksi esiintymispaikaksi. Nyt kuitenkin yhtye on väsynyt pitkään kiertueeseen ja jättää viimeisenä olleen Helsingin konsertin pois."

Blackmoren ja Rainbowin oli tarkoitus konsertoida 21. 10. Lohdutukseksi kerrottakoon, että myöhemmin syksyllä on luvassa joukko hyvätasoisia konsertteja.

Blackmore cancelled
Former Deep Purple guitarist Ritchie Blackmore and his band Rainbow in Finland has been cancelled. Seppo Pieti-Käinen, the representative of the concert organisers, said of the situation: "Helsinki was planned as the last venue for the Rainbow European tour. However, the band is tired of the long tour and will leave out the last Helsinki concert."

Blackmore and Rainbow were scheduled for a concert on October 21st.
Helsingin Sanomat, 11th October 1976

7.
When The World Makes A Turn
Australia, 4th - 22nd November

"I quite like Australia, once the initial stages of jetlag are gone. Because it's so far to come, it's twenty-two hours and that was coming from Los Angeles. We had a little problem with the polarity system but apart from that the audiences have been fantastic."

Ritchie Blackmore

Rainbow arrived in Australia on 2nd November, two days before the first show in Perth, allowing themselves time to get over the jetlag. Blackmore had only previously been to Australia in '71 for a tour with Free and Manfred Mann, and the one-off show in Sunbury the year before with Deep Purple.

But this was Blackmore's biggest Australian tour by far. Perth was to be the band's base for the first week. In fact, Rainbow was in Perth for longer than the entire Deep Purple '71 tour!

After the first show, Ritchie and Ronnie were interviewed over the next few days at their hotel by DJ Trevor Smith and parts of this were used the following year, on the promo LP in conjunction with the *On Stage* album.

The tour suffered none of the endless chopping and changing of gigs or cancellations that had beset the earlier legs of the tour although there was still the odd controversy thrown in. Buffalo was the support band for the majority of the tour but due to financial constraints, they didn't play in Perth.

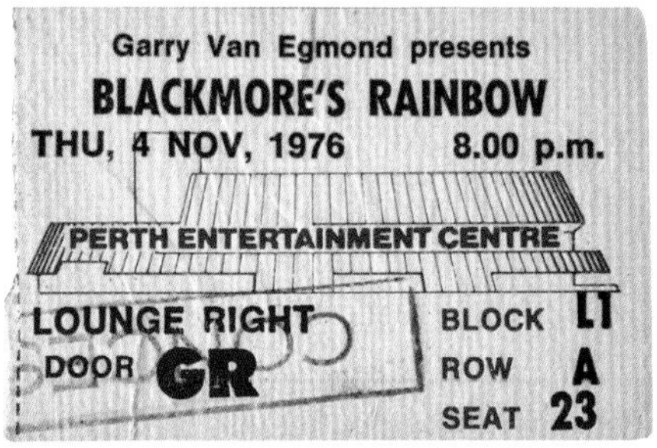

Thursday 4th November
Entertainment Centre, Perth
Support act: Fatty Lumpkin
At the opening show, no encore was performed.

Tuesday 9th November,
Festival Hall, Melbourne
This show was reviewed in the Melbourne daily newspaper, *The Age*, the following day by Christine Morris:
Is it true that good things are found at the end of the rainbow? If the audience at Festival Hall last night was a guide, then Ritchie Blackmore's Rainbow is their pot of gold.
Under the flashing lights of their huge coloured arch, Rainbow launched into what can only be described as ear-splitting heavy metal rock.
Led by Blackmore, they produced a sound with strong overtones of his former group Deep Purple, an aggressive drive broken by small brackets of old standards and blues.
A slow blues followed a short lead break from 'Lazy' which introduced 'Man On The Silver Mountain'.
Ronnie James Dio's vocals and Blackmore's guitar work provided the backbone to most of their numbers including 'Catch The Rainbow', and, believe it or not, 'Greensleeves'.
Keyboard player Tony Carey created some interesting sound using synthesiser, mellotron and organ during a solo performance of 'Stargazer'.
They will do one more concert at Festival Hall on November 22.

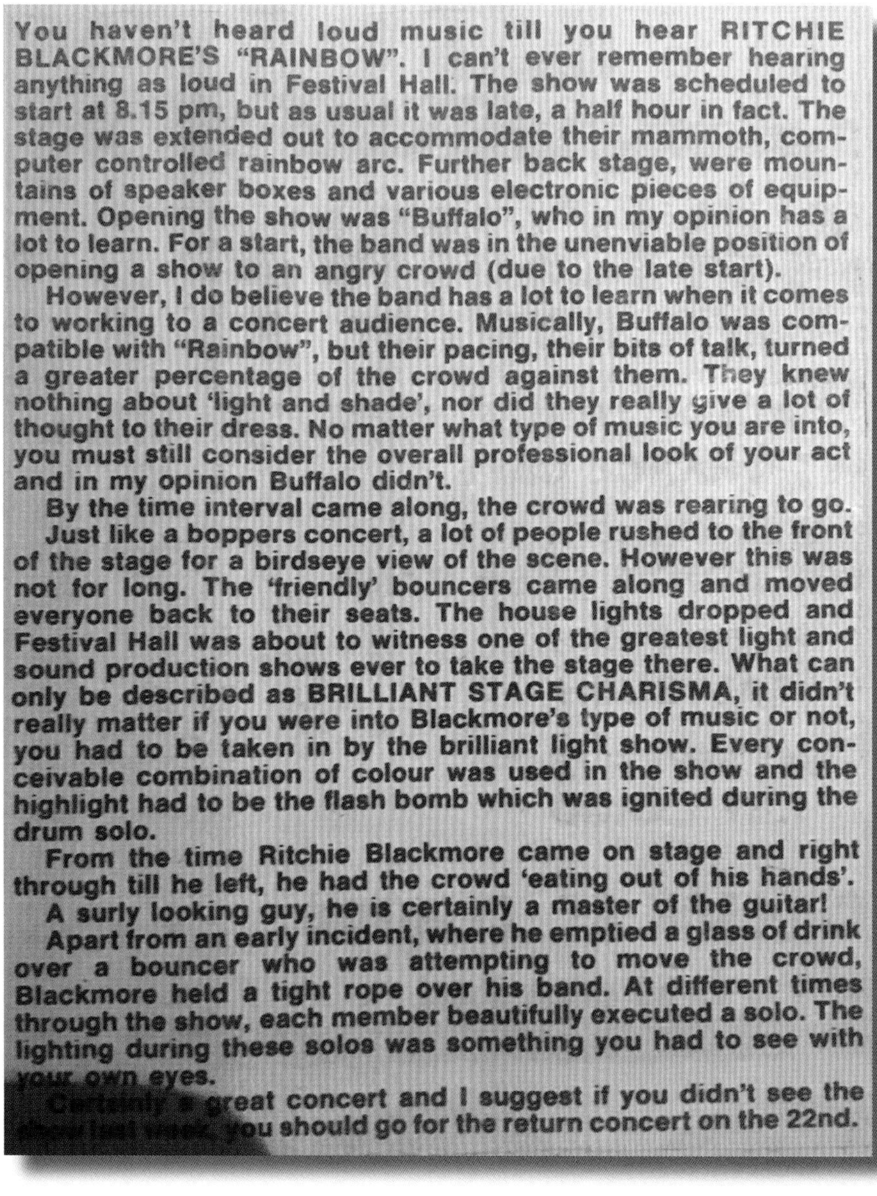

You haven't heard loud music till you hear RITCHIE BLACKMORE'S "RAINBOW". I can't ever remember hearing anything as loud in Festival Hall. The show was scheduled to start at 8.15 pm, but as usual it was late, a half hour in fact. The stage was extended out to accommodate their mammoth, computer controlled rainbow arc. Further back stage, were mountains of speaker boxes and various electronic pieces of equipment. Opening the show was "Buffalo", who in my opinion has a lot to learn. For a start, the band was in the unenviable position of opening a show to an angry crowd (due to the late start).

However, I do believe the band has a lot to learn when it comes to working to a concert audience. Musically, Buffalo was compatible with "Rainbow", but their pacing, their bits of talk, turned a greater percentage of the crowd against them. They knew nothing about 'light and shade', nor did they really give a lot of thought to their dress. No matter what type of music you are into, you must still consider the overall professional look of your act and in my opinion Buffalo didn't.

By the time interval came along, the crowd was rearing to go.

Just like a boppers concert, a lot of people rushed to the front of the stage for a birdseye view of the scene. However this was not for long. The 'friendly' bouncers came along and moved everyone back to their seats. The house lights dropped and Festival Hall was about to witness one of the greatest light and sound production shows ever to take the stage there. What can only be described as BRILLIANT STAGE CHARISMA, it didn't really matter if you were into Blackmore's type of music or not, you had to be taken in by the brilliant light show. Every conceivable combination of colour was used in the show and the highlight had to be the flash bomb which was ignited during the drum solo.

From the time Ritchie Blackmore came on stage and right through till he left, he had the crowd 'eating out of his hands'.

A surly looking guy, he is certainly a master of the guitar!

Apart from an early incident, where he emptied a glass of drink over a bouncer who was attempting to move the crowd, Blackmore held a tight rope over his band. At different times through the show, each member beautifully executed a solo. The lighting during these solos was something you had to see with your own eyes.

Certainly a great concert and I suggest if you didn't see the show last week, you should go for the return concert on the 22nd.

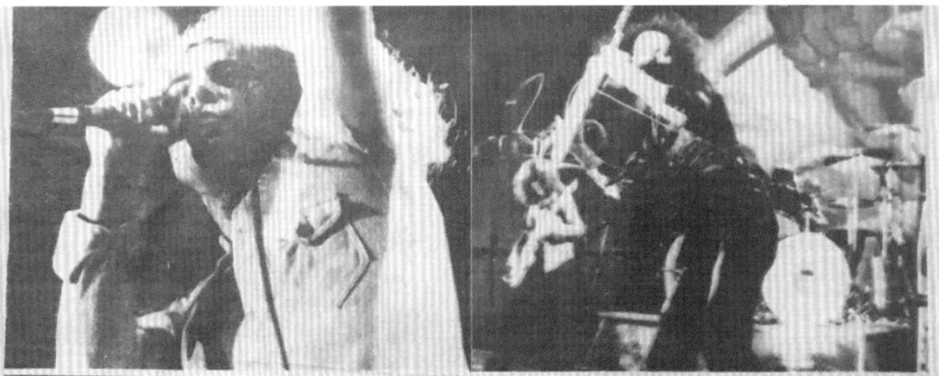

Rainbow in concert

Venue: Festival Hall, Melbourne

The concert started with the support group Buffalo, who played a reasonable bracket of material from their new album. But unfortunately the audience were keyed up to see Rainbow and therefore their reception was not what they deserved.

After an interval of half an hour Rainbow were on stage in a blaze of color and movement. Unfortunately for the first song Richie Blackmore's guitar was completely inaudible and so the concert didn't really have any impact until t the second song, the Deep Purple classic "Mistreated" in this song there is a lot of latent emotion and feeling that we only saw glimpses of in Rainbow's rendition. Rainbow has been constantly touring for eight months, so it is understandable that they don't play the song the same way at every performance they would probably become jaded and lose their enthuisiasm for performing. So instead of a relatively straight performance, there were many little additions within the songs. But it was questionable whether they actually enhanced the song, or undermined the impact.

Richie Blackmore's guitar playing was the feature of all these songs, the quiet intricate guitarist one minute, a blasting chordal guitarist the next. But it wasn't until the song "Stargazer" (about half way through the set) that the band fired in the way the audience had been anticipatring. The essence of Rainbow's second album **"Rainbow Rising** was high energy power, and from 'Stargazer' onwards they supplied it. 'Stargazer' was introduced by Tony Carey with a good keyboard/synthesizer solo, which showed that he certainly lacks no talent. Cozy Powell's drum solo in "Stargazer" was amazing. He is one of the hardest hitting drummers around, which he proved during his solo. Even though he used tried and tested rolls, he made them live, he gave them a power that no one else could give them. To finish the solo, he used the fianl part of Tchaikovsky's "1812 Overture" as a climax, a clever innovation in drum solos. Their encore, "The Light Turns Into Dark" topped the night, with Richie Blackmore smashing his guitar, and then reappearing with another one to bring the band to yet a higher peak.

The overall concept of the concert was well thought out. The backdrop during the first half of the concert was the castle from Rainbow's first album cover, and then after "Stargazer" began, it was changed to the graphic from **Rainbow Rising.**

At the end of the concert, before the encore, a neon sign descended from the roof, simply stating the band's name in a letter face similiar to their latest album. But it was the rainbow that was the most impressive effect. The electronic lighting on the rainbow was amazing. Lines of colored lighting chasing each other, changing in intensity with the music.

The concert showed that Rainbow has a well thought out performance, and that Ronnie Dio, Richie Blackmore and Cozy Powell are possibly three of the most dynamic rock musicians in the world today. Rainbow has taken high energy rock concerts one step further than anyone else, although they are perhaps the last of the great heavy metal bands.

Keith Hughes

The Doctor travelled later to the airport to meet another Master — one Ritchie Blackmore, the king of heavy metal guitar. Ritchie came off the plane at a low gait dressed in black as usual. Members of the band scurried around but Ritchie maintained an easy equilibrium — perhaps to bend notes and time on stage requires relaxed acceptance of space/time/normal the doctor looked at Ritchie's hands and marvelled that such fire could come from them — they seemed normal enough. Ronnie Dio walked by wearing a leopard skin jacket looking more heavy than Ritchie but only superficially — Ritchie carried a different kind of electricity. Perhaps it was potential energy like a lightbulb waiting to be switched on — neuter until lit it has the ability to light or incinerate the world. Scrooge was arguing with some of the roadies, Garry Van had it all together, Simon was making sure all was going well. One of the roadies carried baseball bats — seemed he was a pro player before coming a roadie — several of the band played cassette players loud in the terminal — the high accoustics caught the sound and echoed it as if through a public address system. Ritchie did not have a tape recorder — he had all the music running through his head and hands — he was ready for anything.

At Festival Hall a totally packed house — all waiting in anticipation. The Doctor presents his tickets only to be shuttled to the balcony — he is not pleased — he determines to move up at interval. Buffalo play quite a fair, heavy set although they lack any kind of colour and the audience just doesn't want to know — sporadic cries of 'we want Ritchie' are heard. Finally extremely late at 9.30 the lights go up — the doctor sashays down the front to find a seat in the third row next to Rockin' Robin and Bob Starkey. Now the show can begin. After fifteen minutes of feverish activity the lights go down — when they go up the Rainbow starts running with laser beam light and Ritchie is on stage tearing at his guitar — a whole host rushes to the front of the stage — everyone jumps up on their seat and Ronnie James Dio begins to articulate in high pitched broken notes that fly and blend with all the sound around. The sound of Rainbow mixes and coagulates in the air then falls like savage rain from heaven on the multitude below — Ritchie's first solo shoots at sulphuric speed into the ears. He waves his head from side to side, points to the sky, points to the ground, his fingers dance over the fret board, dance off the guitar as if touching the essence of the night and the light. His fingers have life of their own, he is watching them with that expression of abject wonder the doctor remembers from seeing him the past two times. Cozy Powell is laying down heartbeats and the experience of light years and Dio is wailing and bending with the tide and the power. 'Mean Mistreater' lives again, 'Man of the Silver Mountain'. Hendrix is dead, Clapton has thrown in the towel but Ritchie lives — see him coaxing the strings then tearing them apart like some mad Orpheus denied the pleasures of the underground determined to exploit the last lifefilled sounds of the wood and steel — see him coming over the top of the board, hitting the ax from underneath each movement creating, creating, creating a new music for the universe. Then come the magic runs when his hands are a blue blur and the notes that he ejaculates are in a sequence too fast for human ears. He drenches the front row with orange juice (he doesn't drink) and a hundred pairs of hands are raised up to him — he touches them all in an arc of his arm which then flies back to THE guitar. Maybe Ritchie stayed inside when all the other kids were outside playing football just so he could practice — maybe he is a solitary man — but when he plays he is on the side of the angels and they are behind his every mystical move. The lights go up and there is pandemonium — 'We want Ritchie' echoes again and again. Then the rainbow blazes to life, a single spot finds the man at the front of the stage bashing, striking, making love to the Fender around his neck — the notes cascade like a Gatling Gun and then the guitar is bounced off the floor, smashed over the amplifiers, ends its days in a screaming sacrifice to a crowd that could not get enough of it. Dio sings the words of 'Do you close your eyes when you're making love?' and the guitar in splendid pieces flies out into the lights, into the high night above all eyes and hearts — Ritchie grabs another guitar, finishes the tune and that is it. There is no way any tune can follow that and for the first time there are no further cries of 'More' for no one could be dissatisfied — orgasmic necessities have been fulfilled — Ritchie Blackmore's Rainbow is without doubt one of the worlds great groups — Ritchie has no peer on guitar in today's rock world and the show was one of the, if not **the**, most spectacular and beautiful events the doctor has ever been fortunate enough to witness and experience. When this show gets back in town if you don't go and see it you're nuts!

Thursday 11th November
Horden Pavilion, Sydney

Friday 12th November
Civic Theatre Newcastle

Saturday 13th November
Festival Hall Brisbane

POP FANS GO BERSERK

SYDNEY: Pop fans brawled and smashed seats at the Hordern Pavilion last night—because visiting pop star Ritchie Blackmore couldn't get enough petrol to set fire to his guitar.

Blackmore, formerly lead guitarist with the top group Deep Purple, always ends his stage act by smashing his guitar.

Last night Blackmore had planned to end his act by setting fire to his guitar, but was beaten by the oil strike.

The British guitarist, like thousands of Sydney motorists, couldn't buy any petrol.

The fans rioted when Blackmore and his group ended their season and walked off the stage without returning for the guitar-smashing encore.

Blackmore and his group arrive in Adelaide tomorrow night.

They are scheduled to give two near sell-out concerts at Festival Theatre [illegible] Saturday [illegible].

Last night's crowd of 4,000 hooted, catcalled and began tearing out chairs and throwing them at the stage.

As brawls broke out all over the hall, the pavilion manager, Mr. Alf Fryer, moved among the crowd explaining that the pavilion management was not responsible for Blackmore's actions.

The fans kept brawling, and Mr. Fryer was forced to call police, who dispersed the crowd. No arrests were made.

FEVER

Mr. Fryer said today the riot was the ugliest he had seen at the Hordern Pavilion.

"The crowd [illegible] angry with Blackmore and I called the police because it looked as though someone was going to get badly hurt," he said.

"If Blackmore had explained that he was not coming back for an encore, everything would probably have been okay.

"But he had built the crowd up to a fever pitch and then left them [illegible]."

Mr. Fryer estimated damage to the hall at more than $1,000.

Ritchie Blackmore

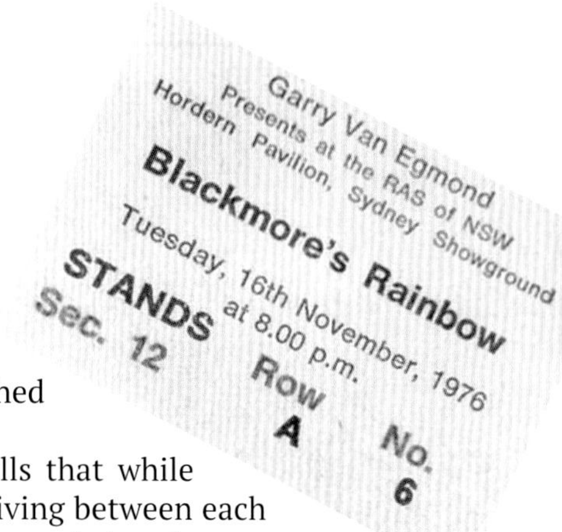
Garry Van Egmond
Presents at the RAS of NSW
Hordern Pavilion, Sydney Showground
Blackmore's Rainbow
Tuesday, 16th November, 1976
at 8.00 p.m.
STANDS
Sec. 12 Row A No. 6

Tuesday 16th November
Horden Pavilion, Sydney
Following the show at this venue the previous week, the press made great capital of Rainbow's explosive encores and Blackmore's notorious guitar demolitions. As it was, they got neither and police were called half an hour after the show finished to dispel the angered crowd, who felt short-changed.

On a separate note, Buffalo's road manager Grahame 'Yogi' Harrison recalls that while Rainbow and their crew flew everywhere, the Buffalo 'herd' were relegated to driving between each gig, even doing over-nighters all the way with virtually no sleep. Still, they had fun and played some great shows.

A major highlight for the band was this show where the disgruntled Rainbow fans had trashed several rows of the Hordern Pavilion seating after Blackmore refused to return for an encore. Blackmore had a small, private dressing room directly next to the room occupied by Buffalo. According to the Buffalo website, after the show, while Buffalo were in party-mode, Blackmore was decidedly upset. He launched a telephone book over the wall separating the two rooms and it hit Yogi on the shoulder. The irate roadie pounded on the next room's door which was opened by a surprisingly timid Blackmore. After getting his ears pinned back by a volley of abuse from Yogi, Blackmore meekly apologised and closed the door. It was only sometime later that Yogi realised that he had abused one of the world's most legendary guitarists and had gotten away with it!

Festival Theatre
Garry Van Egmond presents
BLACKMORE'S RAINBOW
Stalls door 6
row D seat 12
Saturday 20 November 5 pm
For Conditions—See back

Friday 19th November
Festival Theatre, Adelaide

Saturday 20th November
Festival Theatre, Adelaide (Two performances)

A matinee show starting at 5.00pm was added due to apparent ticket demand but actually very few turned up. Howard Kehl who attended this show wrote about it in *Stargazer*: "There couldn't have been more than two-hundred people there, of whom only half a dozen had any idea of what was going on. They didn't even recognise the 'Lazy' bit. 'Man On The Silver Mountain' was dedicated to half the audience, 'Bob Adcock's family', and Dio changed the lyrics about so that it was 'lift my rubbish higher', causing Ritchie to grin. Ritchie got the press going with stories of a grand guitar burning climax which never happened. In fact he didn't wreck a thing in three gigs in Adelaide."

Perhaps due to the low attendance, the band indulged in some levity. Kehl recalled that during Carey's solo intro to 'Stargazer' a broomstick appeared from the wings and started prodding him in the back. It transpired it was Ronnie Dio who duly appeared riding the broomstick across the stage!

Such tomfoolery was also directed at Buffalo, but it wasn't viewed as light-hearted japes as far as Buffalo frontman David Tice recalled: "That wasn't a very pleasant experience. We were treated like unwanted guests and in most instances allowed only limited use of PA and lights. In Adelaide, Mr Blackmore actually tried to sabotage our set. Pete Wells' bass amp power cord was mysteriously pulled out halfway through a song and then Jimmy (Economou) was assaulted by pieces of backstage rubbish thrown at him while he was trying to play drums. Of course, soundchecks never happened either."

Rainbow goes on rising

WANTED: For assault and battery — Blackmore's Rainbow.

Guitarist Richie Blackmore, late of heavyweight Deep Purple, and his ear-shattering Anglo-American outfit took rock-'n-roll by the seat of the pants and kicked it unmercifully around Festival Theatre for an hour and a half last night.

All, however, to the audible delight of the capacity crowd.

It was an awesome, unforgettable experience. Aboard a stage crammed with 26 tonnes of speakers and equipment was a startling new device—an enormous arc towering around and above the five-man band, and firing a frenzied fusion of cascading colored lights.

And at one end of the rainbow stood 31-year-old, black-suited, poker-faced Blackmore, unpretentiously peeling off mesmerising runs from his white guitar, which, contrary to speculation, was neither broken nor burnt by the end of the show.

Blackmore, a veteran of 20 years playing and an unlikely admirer of

ROCK

AT THE FESTIVAL THEATRE: Blackmore's Rainbow. Repeated tonight.

German Baroque music, interweaves an enormous variety of styles into his outwardly heavy metal image. Among his best were "Stargazer" and "Man on the Silver Mountain."

Another surprise was Rainbow's explosive drummer Cozy Powell, a non-stop powerhouse, underpinning every song with an unmistakable drive from his oversize drum kit.

Powell, 29, a much-lauded British drummer and sometime racing driver, smashes the senses with a mind-boggling drum solo that hits a thumping crescendo as he spars with a taped orchestra through the fiery closing stages of the "1812 Overture."

Unhappily, at the end of the Rainbow there was no encore, just the strains of Judy Garland accompanied by the boos of some understandably disappointed patrons.

Ian Meikle

RITCHIE BLACKMORE'S RAINBOW
Sydney

The P.A. stunk on dry ice, but Ritchie was real neat. No two ways about it, Blackmore's Rainbow is the sort of band about which legends are made. More than image they've got presence, more than energy they've got necromancy.

And it's not **just** Ritchie, no way. Rainbow is a band where strong personalities collide and meld. Thank god Ritchie didn't do a Paul McCartney and put together a group of jolly nice but featureless personalities. The P.A. system more often than not, sounded like a beserk concrete mixer chewing a particularly grating mixture of gravel. For one, it had too few treble horns to handle the power Rainbow's amplifiers put out. Two, the bass bins betrayed their age and clapped out condition by reducing the bottom end into a toneless boom.

Blackmore throughout the concert was throwing his arms in the air and pulling anguished faces as if to say **"Oh Jeeeeee-suuuuusss!"**

Year, but the buck has to stop somewhere Ritchie, and fairly or unfairly, it ultimately stops at the Top Name.

But even though the sound was **shithouse,** if this review concentrated on this defect, it'd be missing the main point. The main point is that it's always peculiarly thrilling and energising to see truly powerful band stretch its muscles and hammer home its magnificence. It's the feeling of been clasped by a gigantic force, there's nothing you can do to escape it and indeed, why try? Go along for the ride.

The front line of force in Rainbow is Blackmore, singer Ronnie James Dio and drummer Cozy Powell. Blackmore, judging from the times he **wasn't** showing agony over the sound, is a happier player than the cold, mean-eyed bastard that I last saw at Sunbury. Back then he was in the business of holding together a sprawling, untogether Deep Purple whose natural propensity seemed to be towards falling asleep on stage.

This time he has a wide-awake foil in the squat, gnomish form of Ronnie Dio. Ronnie is one of those very rare singers who can scream at the top of exceptionally powerful lungs and stay in absolute tune at the same time. He's so ridiculously, so easily **good,** you wonder why he wasn't a major leaguer years ago. Then you think, but what would have happened if Robert Plant had never met one James Page Esq.

The point is I guess that perfect rock marriages between singers and guitarists happen only in heaven or hell. Just like Plant/Page or Jagger/Richards, once you see a perfectly matched singer/guitarist combination you suddenly can't imagine them without each other for evermore.

The Ian Gillan/Blackmore combination from Purple was once considered a pretty nifty combination, but Dio/Blackmore seem to have some chemistry that's extra special.

And right behind them is Cozy Powell. He hits drums harder and faster than anyone who's been in Oz since John Bonham. His solo was a thunderous showpiece piece of showmanship and strength. Halfway through it, the 1812 Overture came belting through the P.A. and Powell joined in with it and just ploughed through the massed trumpets and cannon roars.

Look, there's just no space to take it much further. Rainbow presented the bulk of their two albums **Rainbow** and **Rainbow Rising** and one Deep Purple number, **Mistreated.** There was **Stargazer, Tarot Woman, Man On Silver Mountain, Catch The Rainbow, Sixteenth Century Greensleeves** and **Still I'm Sad.** The encore was **Do You Close Your Eyes** during which Blackmore did the best guitar-destructo act I've ever seen. I mean he smashed it to pieces like Jack the Ripper running amok in a brothel with a meat axe. As he did it, he keep looking up and shaking his hands in frustration at the sound. Then he'd go back to wrecking his guitar. That's the one good thing the P.A. was responsible for. It lent credibility and anger to Ritchie's guitar smashing routine.

Bassist Jimmy Bain and keyboard player Tony Carey were solid, though relatively unspectacular. And the lights and the computer electronic Rainbow? Sure they were pretty and all, although not quite as spectacular as their pre-promotion suggested they'd be.

But who wants to look at an electronic rainbow when Cozy's drumming, Ronnie's singing and Ritchie Blackmore is working his fingers over his guitar in a fashion that's half karma sutra and half karate.

Anthony O'Grady.

EXTRA CONCERT 5 P.M. TODAY

GARRY VAN EGMOND PRESENTS

BLACKMORE'S RAINBOW

Featuring

Ritchie Blackmore

Ronnie Dio Cozy Powell Jimmy Bain Tony Carey

LIVE IN CONCERT FULLY STAGED

FESTIVAL THEATRE — EXTRA CONCERT 5 P.M. TODAY!

The Festival Theatre box office will be open throughout today

GOOD SEATS AVAILABLE — $7.30 and $6.30 inc.

PLEASE NOTE, 8 P.M. CONCERT IS BOOKED OUT!

Monday 22nd November
Festival Hall, Melbourne

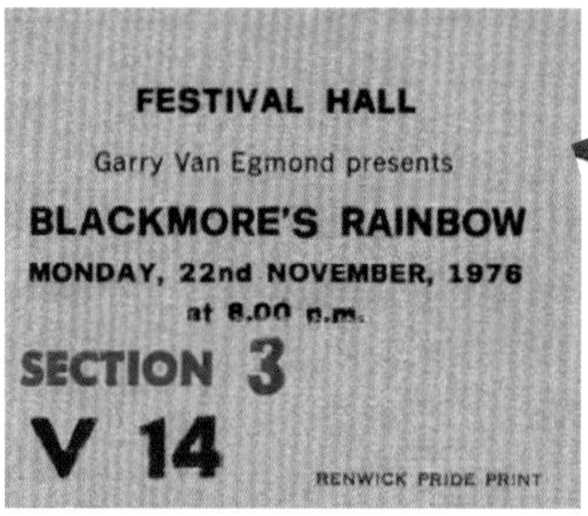
FESTIVAL HALL

Garry Van Egmond presents

BLACKMORE'S RAINBOW

MONDAY, 22nd NOVEMBER, 1976

at 8.00 p.m.

SECTION 3

V 14

RENWICK PRIDE PRINT

8. The Things That Make You Smile

Japan, 2nd - 16th December

"We have to live together, be together for so much of the year, for so much of the life of the band, that to try to take yourself seriously on every level is not only an impossibility; it just does not make for good relations. We like to try to play a joke on each other once a day if we can — go into someone's room, take all the furniture out, remove it to someone else's balcony, and the guy'll go into his room and there'll be nothing but a phone in the middle of the room. By the time ten days go by you need to relieve the boredom of the same show, the same people, the same business conversations — we start playing these jokes with each other. Nothing malicious really, 'cause there are too many strong-minded people in this band. If anything malicious happened it'd be a big punchout. The seriousness is in the music."

Ronnie James Dio

The final leg of the tour saw Blackmore returning to Japan, where he had performed with Deep Purple in '72 and '73. Rainbow flew in from Australia and touched down in Tokyo late on 30th November. "We came from the airport and there were like seven hundred people to meet us," Tony Carey recalled to me. "It was six in the morning when the flight came in from Australia and in the Tokyo Hilton we had to go in the kitchen entrance like The Beatles or whatever but we were so full or ourselves we thought we deserved it! It didn't seem like anything special, two hundred kids in front of the hotel. And they all want to give you a little present in Japan, like a pencil box. It felt like we deserved it, and at the concerts the people just exploded and stayed exploded the whole time."

Arguably some of the best performances of the entire tour were in Japan. As is typical of Japanese record companies, Polydor Japan was keen to capture some shows for a potential Japanese only album.

I have generally decided not to list bootlegs in this book for the simple reason that there are so many releases and re-releases that they would fill up a book on their own. Furthermore, the quality was often quite dire. I remember buying a tape of the Liverpool show at a record fair in the early eighties and it was so unlistenable I just threw it away.

However, it's worth mentioning one individual who used the moniker of Mr Peach. Japanese authorities had a more relaxed approach to bootlegging. Bootlegs were openly sold in stores and it appeared that a blind eye was turned to people recording shows for decades. Peach had been recording shows since a Led Zeppelin concert in 1971 and continued through until 1984. It has been documented that in that time he recorded around three-hundred gigs by a variety of different artists.

It's possible that Peach was a Rainbow fan rather than simply a bootlegger. With most artists, he generally just captured one or two shows of a tour, normally those in Tokyo where it's thought he resided. With Rainbow though, he recorded all ten of the Japanese shows. What is also astonishing is that recording every show would have required a lot of travelling and expense.

Unlike many recordings of the time, the quality he captured was quite astonishing. Apparently in 1976, Peach had upgraded to a portable Sony Cassette TC-3000SD. Japan was already developing a reputation for sophisticated electrical equipment and had come on in leaps and bounds compared to the relatively primitive equipment they produced in the sixties and this recorder would have been state of the art for the time. Whilst his recordings varied on where in the venue his ticket was allocated for, they are all streets ahead of any other recordings from the time.

With the advent of the Internet, bootlegs have in reality been bootlegged themselves and whilst decades ago they would cost you a small fortune to purchase, they are now all freely available online — another reason why I have avoided trying to catalogue them all within this book.

Sounds journalist Pete Makowski was privileged to be sent to Japan to report on the last leg of Rainbow's epic world tour. As Dio said to him, "it's been a long, hard tour and we're beginning to feel it." Perhaps it was tour fatigue after six months on the road but a good number of these shows saw a greater deal of humour thrown in to the performances, not just in Ronnie's off the cuff remarks, but in the actual music. Blackmore threw in numerous ad-libs, particularly tipping his hat in recognition to both The Shadows and Hendrix. This makes the fact that they were all captured by Mr Peach all the more remarkable. For those who spend little time on the Internet, hunting out the recordings from the Japanese tour is certainly something I would thoroughly recommend.

Thursday 2nd December
Sports Centre, Tokyo

With it having been three years since Japanese fans had a chance to see their guitar god on stage, the excitement was clearly too much for the audience at this opening show. Unusually for Japanese audiences, the fans got over excited during the interval and went wild when Rainbow appeared. After 'Kill The King' had been played, Rainbow went off stage for a few minutes to give the stewards time to calm every one down.

It's worth mentioning that the performances of 'Mistreated' were generally greeted with huge enthusiasm in Japan given that Purple MKIII had not toured there.

Saturday 5th December
Koseinenkin Hall, Osaka

The scene of Purple's 1972 triumph, this is the venue where most of *Made In Japan* had been recorded. On a website article about Mr Peach, it's said that he recorded this show from seat number 35 in row K of the second floor of the venue!

Tuesday 7th December
Shi Kokaido Nagoya
Three days earlier following a gig supporting Jeff Beck, Tommy Bolin died of a drug overdose in his Miami hotel room. This was the first show played since the news filtered through from America. Introducing 'Mistreated', Ronnie Dio said, "this is for someone who has been mistreated in the wrong way. Tommy Bolin." It was an appropriately heartfelt performance.

Wednesday 8th December
Koseinenkin Hall, Osaka
This was the first of the Japanese shows to be officially recorded. It would appear to have been a relatively last-minute decision. With Martin Birch seemingly unavailable, Musicland's resident engineer Reinhold Mack was flown in to capture this and the following evening's performances although nothing from this show was actually used. Mack was unhappy that the record company's mobile unit was already in use so he had to make do with lesser equipment put together at the last minute. The show, or at least parts of it, were also apparently recorded and broadcast by Japanese radio but despite Japanese fans claiming this to be the case I still question it.

Thursday 9th December
Koseinenkin Hall, Osaka
The second show recorded by Mack. Only a part of 'Catch The Rainbow' ended up on *On Stage*. After the second show, Mack went to Tokyo to mix the recordings. Bruce Payne took the option of capturing the final two gigs in Tokyo the following week.

Friday 10th December
Kyotokaikan, Kyoto
There was a two-minute tune up before the show started and Blackmore appeared to be having problems with his guitar as he spends time tuning again after 'Kill The King' requiring Dio to talk to the audience. Blackmore's tuning makes some of what Dio says inaudible, even though it's likely that hardly anyone in the audience would have understood what he was saying anyway. Dio then introduces Carey, Bain and Powell to the audience in a bid to give Blackmore additional time to get his guitar setting just right.

As an example of a lot of the ridiculous Monty Python-esque humour that Dio emerged himself in, after 'Mistreated' he says, "We've just had a flash announcement that the new owner of the Swiss Cottage Holiday Inn, Shish Kebab has just made room 421 — it's called now the Ian Ferguson suite — it's giving money to people who don't want to check in and pay their money in..." Ferguson of course was Blackmore's then guitar technician.

After 'Sixteenth Century Greensleeves' Dio says, "John's going to do something with a niji. Later on he's going to do something with himself — A200 I've been told." Ronnie misses his cue at the start of 'Stargazer' and one senses there is a touch of demob mode, knowing they are coming to the end of an arduous tour. In fact, the reason for Dio's apparent lapse was down to more on stage tomfoolery, this time at the expense of Tony Carey: "I'm completely involved with eleven keyboards on stage doing my intellectual thing and they're all sat there with their knees crossed like Monty Python reading newspapers and Ronnie in a gorilla mask. There was a lot of humour around the band but being an American it wasn't really humour I understood. Ronnie's American but a complete Anglophile, he was also much older than me and had been around the Deep Purple organisation. I was pretty much the outsider with the humour. I like British humour but I didn't understand it then."

After 'Stargazer' a short burst of Johnny Cash's 'I Walk The Line' is played, followed by a great version of The Shadows' 'Apache' that leads into a brief rendition of 'FBI' before kicking into 'Still I'm Sad'. During the section that leads into Carey's solo in 'Still I'm Sad' Ritchie quickly throws in the 1850 tune 'Camptown Races' that he had recorded with The Outlaws as 'Doo-Dah-Day'. Before the song reaches its conclusion there is a bit more musical humour with Blackmore ad-libbing.

This show also saw the performance of 'A Light In The Black' for the first time since the US tour. Replacing 'Do You Close Your Eyes' as the usual encore number. It starts with Tony Carey performing a wonderful three minutes of Bach, managing to get a convincing church organ sound before Ritchie takes over with a frantic barrage. Prior to kicking into the familiar riff, there is a small shredding solo as they break into 'A Light In The Black'. A very special performance.

Monday 13th December
Kyuden-Kinen-Taiikukan, Fukuoka

For one fan M. Kaminishizono, it was only his second concert experience with a rock band from abroad, the first being Deep Purple the year before at the same venue. "I threw a sickie from my high school and took the four-hour-ride train to Fukuoka from Nagasaki, my hometown. After the opening called The Anzen Band, many in the audience dashed toward the stage front abandoning their reserved seats (folding chair). I suddenly found myself standing on the second row with crowds of people. Just above my head was the rainbow arch, so I couldn't see anything of the rainbow lighting during the whole show. The band opened with 'Kill The King'. People just yelled and shouted even though they didn't know the song. I just watched every move of Ritchie, the real Ritchie. It was unbelievable."

Ronnie was up to his usual high jinx and in particular during 'Stargazer'. From the line "Hot wind..." he starts singing with completely different phrasing, in a mocking type of way and ad-libbing, so after the line "when do we leave?" he sings "oh I'd say about 10:30" and after the lines, "In the heat and the rain, with whips and chains", he throws in "Bob's yer uncle and your sister" but the overall vocal style and effect is a bit like David Byrne and Talking Heads meets Rainbow!

The familiar encore of 'Do You Close Your Eyes' returned at this show.

Tuesday 14th December
Ken Taiikukan Hiroshima

As with Kyoto, 'A Light In The Black' was performed as the encore but with no intro from Carey this time. Instead, there's a lengthy barrage of notes from Blackmore before he launches into the riff.

The following day it was back to the Tokyo Hilton which was besieged by young female fans... of The Bay City Rollers who were also staying there.

Thursday 16th December
Budokan, Tokyo, (matinee show)

Having kicked off the Japanese tour in the capital — such was the demand — Rainbow concluded the world tour back in Tokyo with two shows at the huge Budokan arena. With two gigs the same day, Mack — who was already in Tokyo — was given the task of recording both this matinee show and the later evening one. As far as Martin Birch must have been concerned, this gig was the weaker of the two as only 'Man On The Silver Mountain' was used on the resulting *On Stage* album.

This show also saw 'A Light In The Black' performed but not as an encore. It was played instead of 'Stargazer', the only time that happened, and bearing in mind a second show was to be performed in the evening, no encore was played.

Thursday 16th December
Budokan, Tokyo, (evening show)

In between the two shows, the band was presented with various awards and presentation discs in recognition of the significant sales of *Rising* since its release a few months earlier. Three years earlier, Deep Purple's MKII line-up played their last shows in Japan, likewise Rainbow's classic line-up also bowed out in the land of the rising sun and almost to the day that Purple with Bolin did likewise. As a testimony to both the band and this performance, 'Kill The King', 'Blues', 'Starstruck' and 'Sixteenth Century Greensleeves' all made their way onto *On Stage*.

Do You Close Your Eyes' concluded the performance and just as it was finishing, the road crew came on stage and pelted the band with flour and shaving foam.

9.
Can You Feel The Change Begin?

"I was fired from the band because Ritchie had something which got up his ass about me, and there was no changing his mind. The rest of the band went along with him, basically because they had no choice. He would fire them as well. He would scrap Rainbow in a minute's notice if he decided that he'd had enough."

Jimmy Bain

Whilst it had been a long tour, in the grand scheme of things, this line-up of Rainbow had only been together for barely over a year. No sooner had it begun than it was over. Blackmore's apparent inability to deal with fellow human beings saw the departure of both Bain and Carey almost as soon as the tour was completed. There was an initial change of heart though; Carey was brought back when work began on the follow up album in early '77 but he was treated with so much disdain and cruelty that of his own volition, he eventually left for good.

Initially to take over from Jimmy Bain, Craig Gruber returned but he too left soon after, dissatisfied with Blackmore's attitude. Bizarrely, Bain was then invited back again but unlike Gruber he chose not to take up the offer.

At least with eight shows having been recorded, the band's legacy has been captured for posterity for evermore. The *On Stage* album released in July '77 is a worthy souvenir of a wonderful band. The *Live In Germany 1976* album that appeared in 1990 added to the band's legacy further, and the three German shows in full released in 2006 was further evidence of what a great band this incarnation was.

But in reality — even as far back as the initial days of Deep Purple — Blackmore constantly showed a restlessness combined with a degree of self-destruction that resulted in regular band changes. Having seemingly created something quite special with Rainbow, in hindsight it was simply just another phase in his meandering, musical journey. Whilst Rainbow continued in a similar vein for one more album, the financial rewards that he had experienced with Purple weren't so forthcoming and Rainbow was proving to be costly to keep going.

Allied to his love of more commercial music, Blackmore steered the band in a new direction, helping to put them back in the black and gaining many new fans and a larger following along the way, but also leaving behind many who didn't enjoy the change.

Blackmore continued to chop and change musical direction over the next two decades and it was only with Blackmore's Night and the maturity that comes with age that he seemed to have settled on a career path that perhaps calmed his restlessness. That said, around the start of Blackmore's Night in 1997 he met up again with Cozy Powell and talks of a reunion with Ronnie Dio were discussed but soon broke down when the thorny issue of money was broached.

In the intervening years, with the passing of Powell, Dio and Bain, an attempt was made to acknowledge the past in 2016 with the re-launching of the Rainbow name for a few concerts surprised most. Choosing a singer called Ronnie, using the *Rising* imagery and deciding to play 'Stargazer' were also pointers that Blackmore had finally recognised that the 1976 Rainbow was highly regarded and justifiably so. Alas the comparisons ended there.

I am a firm believer that everything is a product of its time. The unique creation that Rainbow initially was is one perfect example of that. It can never be repeated, but there is so much audio to wallow in, we should at least be grateful for that. Hopefully, this book will help enhance your enjoyment of those recordings. For those who were lucky enough to catch the band live another chance to relive those memories. For those who missed out, there is always the hope that someday those Japanese shows will see the light of day in glorious sound quality.

SJC 31st December, 1976

R.S. Bagehot, Esq.,
Hec Enterprises Ltd.,
25 Newman Street,
London, W.1.

Dear Richard,

RAINBOW Mercedes (2)

The latest information I have about this little problem is as follows:-

1. We bought two cars, one for £7,000 and the other for £10,750 - a total of £17,750 all of which was chargeable to RAINBOW.

2. The purchases were made on the basis that, as soon as the RAINBOW Tour of Europe was over, the cars would be brought back to England and sold. The calculations were based on the assumption that it would pay to buy provided both cars could be sold for a grand total of not less than £15,750, i.e. at a loss of £2,000. On allfronts I was assured when the purchases were made that we were getting them cheap and would probably be able to sell them for what we paid for them. This would, of course, have given a nice "profit" for RAINBOW because they would have had the use of two cars for two months and would only have had to pay petrol and insurance costs.

3. You have told me of the condition in which you recently found the cars. Clearly from what you said, Cozy's friend has been playing games with us and seems to have been making little attempt to sell them but, instead, to hire them out. What progress has been made with getting them repaired and into first-class selling condition again?

Contd....

-2-

4. From your last report on selling prices on 1st December, you had been given estimates of £6,175 for one of the cars and £9,175 for the other. This only adds up to £15,350. Not only, therefore, would this represent a loss against the maximum reduction we were prepared to accept but there has been an interval of a long period during which we have also been liable for the insurance and licensing costs.

5. As you know, cash flow is most important to us. The whole deal was entered into on the basis that I would lose the use of £17,750 for not much in excess of two months. In the event, I have lost the use of this money now for getting on for four months, i.e. since 14th September, 1976.

6. Rob told me on the telephone the other day that PAL might be interested in these cars. But at whose expense, from what date and at what price? We are not in the car business - we are in the music business. Let us not dabble in things we know nothing about.

This has clearly turned out to be a very indifferent deal to say the least - certainly not the kind of deal that seems to make any money, quite apart from all the trouble it has so far caused us and will, no doubt, continue to cause us until we get rid of the beasts.

What can be done to bring this involved incident to a conclusion?

Yours,

c.c. R.J.Cooksey,
M.A.Edwards,
B. Payne

Musically Rainbow in 1976 might well have been at its peak but financially it was costing Blackmore dearly. Seeing how other bands from the late sixties and early seventies had reinvented themselves and increased their popularity, in particular Fleetwood Mac, within three years Blackmore had engineered Rainbow into a chart band and helped to secure some financial stability in the process.

With Our Flesh And Bone: In Their Own Words

Ritchie Blackmore

Connecting with Ronnie...
"Ronnie is very versatile. He used to play the trumpet in an orchestra. That's why he knows so much about scales. I like working with Ronnie, he's never out of tune, he never makes mistakes. Most vocalists I have worked with don't know what they are doing, they just hope it fits. With Ronnie you know it fits. He might be small but his voice isn't."

"When I played the songs to him, the way he interpreted them was he sings exactly where I would like to sing, if I could sing. The feeling is mutual as a guitar player. And he's got a really incredible way of getting a song across. I think his lyrics are brilliant. I think his timing is fantastic, his intonation, everything."

"'Man On The Silver Mountain', 'Sixteenth Century Greensleeves' was great. The way he sang that was perfect for what I wanted. I didn't tell him — he just sang it. 'Stargazer' too, great."

Ritchie Blackmore's Rainbow...

"At first it's gonna be called that. But, within six months, people will be coming to see the other people in the band. That's how good they are. I'm very pleased with the whole thing. The LP worked out really well."

"But it's definitely a new band, same as like Purple was. It's not me and the band. To start, I don't consider myself that good to front the band and I don't want to front the band. I'll only do my flash business on stage, which I like doing. But I just don't like being known as a leader of the band. I'd like to be a pusher, obviously, of the band. Nobody can be a leader of a band if they're really truthful. And if you're someone like Rory Gallagher, well Rory's good, but everybody else is his side band, kind of playing to back him up — this is not that kind of band."

"With Rainbow, they're all stars in their own right, especially the singer. He'll prove himself, you know. But at first, it's gonna be slanted my way because of being with Purple. But it's good in a way because people will take a listen to what else we've got to offer, whereas maybe if we were a completely unknown band, they wouldn't take time."

Practical jokes...
"Jimmy had some girl on the bed with him. I walked in and he's: 'Hey Ritchie! Do you want a drink?' 'No, I'm away to my bed, I'll see you tomorrow.' But I... let's see... I set fire to something and put it by his bed, and it started catching the bedclothes. And I thought he would see it, pick it up and put it out. But he didn't see it. So I'm there watching these flames, going: 'Er, Jimmy', 'er yeah, right, see ya later.' 'Um Jimmy?' 'Fucking hell! The bed's on fire!' And I thought, yes, that's more like it, and then I could leave. Because I couldn't leave him in a bed that was on fire without telling him! So he grabbed the bedclothes and threw them out of the window. That was all he could do by that stage. But when it hit the ground it hit the Astroturf and set that ablaze too. The hotel wasn't too happy. But the whole point was like when you set fire to someone's newspaper. They're supposed to put it out. But Jimmy was too engrossed in this girl..."

"Cozy and I together... that was really nasty! 'Cause we had a truce on each other, because that got out of control, too. It's just that Cozy would overdo it. It was like overkill. Have you ever heard this story about Cozy in Gelsenkirchen? He climbed to the thirteenth floor, went with the fire extinguisher into the wrong room, sprays this fire extinguisher, then sneaks back to his own room. (laughter) The next day, this guy's in hospital... and it wasn't even one of our crew. He'd got the wrong room! He'd got this businessman. He was in hospital for two days... and nearly died!"

Marshall

Gary Driscoll…

"Gary Driscoll had a tendency of losing the tempo, then catching up. Any drummer hearing that would think: 'Wow! That guy's so clever.' He could pull back and go forward. But Gary was going: 'Are we still playing? Oh…' He would have periods of pure genius, but I remember in the studio when we were doing that first LP, he had trouble with his headphones. We'd go: 'Okay, ready?' And we just see him (gazes off into space). 'Hello! Gary? Gary! Put your headphones on and turn them up!' 'Oh yeah, right, right, right!' So we'd start playing and I'd watch him — 'cause I'd be in the control room and his headphones would slowly slide off and he'd slowly lose the tempo. So after four takes we would have to tape them to his head. I remember once counting in: one, two… And he just went: 'Er, what? Oh… three, four, yeah!' He was so nervous. Once he counted one, two, three, four, and everybody came in — except for him! (laughs) Another time he just stopped halfway through and Martin is yelling at him: 'What are you doing? Did somebody say stop?' 'I thought I heard someone say stop.' But he was such a nice guy. I used to think, 'this is much better than The Troggs…' I've got this thing with drummers if they can't keep time. I can't understand why they should be in a band."

Equipment

"I don't use an Echoplex. I use my own thing. I made like my own tape recorder up as an echo. It gives me an echo when it's played back. It's hard to explain. I just overload the input side and I can get my sustain as well. It doesn't thin out my sound like all the echoes do. Echoes always thin the sound. The way I've got this built is to give me the exact same sound that I've had if I was actually plugged straight into an amp without all that bloody extra circuit."

"I changed to Marshalls about eight years ago. I knew Jim Marshall. He was a drum teacher, and I saw the Marshall setup and liked the way they looked. The design I liked, but the sound was awful. So I went back to the factory because I knew Jim and I said, 'Look, I want this changed and I want that changed.' And I used to play in front of all the people that were there working; there would be women there assembling things, and I had the amp boosted to 400 watts. So I would be playing away right in front of all these people and they'd be trying to work. I'd go, 'That's not right, more treble,' and they'd take out a resistor. I had to play full blast or otherwise I couldn't know what it was going to sound like. The people hated me."

"…In fact the Strat I used belonged to Eric Clapton. I used it and liked the sound of it; it was very sharp but impossible to play. The neck was so bowed, it was really bad. He just had one kicking around the house, and I picked it up and he said, 'Take it away.' It had a great sound for a wah-wah pedal because it was so sharp, but it was very difficult to play because it was so bowed. I thought it was an interesting guitar at the time, even though all the octaves were out."

"The transition was really hard. I found great difficulty in using it the first two years. With a Gibson you just race up and down, but with a Fender you have to make every note count; you have to make the note sing or otherwise it won't work. It's more rewarding because with a Gibson nobody has an identity, as I said before."

Ronnie James Dio

Connecting with Ritchie...

"Our point of reference was classical music. Bach was our point of reference, we both loved Bach. That's really where we all started from, Ritchie and I. And I had been very involved in reading this kind of material again as I say from a young boy and it was just nice to be able to be with someone who understood the same kind of feelings that I had about it. I think I'm probably much more of a collector than Ritchie is, but he collects a few things, but I think I collect a lot more than he does. That was another point of reference for us, we both loved medieval history and the attitudes of chivalry and knights and ladies in waiting and all that."

"Ritchie's the man. He's the leader, but with a bit of an exception, in that he's bright enough to know that one person in the band cannot make individual personalities — who are musicians on top of that — perform without giving them latitude. Ritchie and I have written all of the songs that we've done — on the first two LPs anyway. Basically we are the same kind of people. He's a very private person; I'm a private person. When we work together we work together, when we party together, we party together. That's it."

"We work off each other. He presents to me what he's thought about for a month or so and then I say change this, change that, and then it comes out to be a final song. We very rarely sit down to plan to write a tune. It's basically been Ritchie's riffs. Ritchie arrangements. Ritchie's chords, then my lyrics, my melody. He's a guitar player. I don't tell him how to play the guitar — he doesn't tell me how to sing. Ritchie's basically a riff writer. Once the riff is there we carry it on. Ritchie says, 'This chord, this chord, this chord. What do you think of that? After all you have to sing to it.' And I'll say, 'Change this chord just a bit.' 'Why?' 'Because I want to sing this note to it.' 'Good note, yeah'."

The rainbow...

"You must understand that the rainbow is not unlike an eighth wonder of the world. Do you know of anyone else that has a rainbow? It's not really to its point of perfection. We can't refract light through drops of water to make a rainbow. It wouldn't work out, because we'd all be electrocuted. We're always working on it, trying to make it better. We spent four tours with it. The first date we did, it was two colours, didn't work at all. It took the entire first tour to get the rainbow to work. We have great expectations for the rainbow. It will spell words out eventually. It'll give you a cup of tea."

Rainbow's influence...

"Well I am always flattered by tributes. I think it's something I never expected but anyone who attempts to do it flatters me. It's just saying thank you. So to judge it, I judge it by the thank you as opposed to what's in it but they all do a really good job of it because they all love Rainbow so much. All these kids who grew up that way, wanted to be the singer in Rainbow and probably always wanted to sing 'Kill The King' or probably always wanted to sing 'Man On The Silver Mountain'. Just as I always wanted to sing 'Smoke On The Water' or the things that you grew up with, that's what you want to do at some point in your life. So they do it with care and they imitate very well I think. But you know there is only one original. And like I said before, and especially in Europe, it's had an incredible effect on so many people. I've spoken to a lot of people in my life who were stunned by the first time they saw Rainbow and went on to become what they became, not because of Rainbow but because they wanted to be like that. I know Lars Ulrich is one of them and Yngwie Malmsteen is another. I just know so many people who I've spoken to who are in bands and even bands you'd know very well go 'ohh I saw Rainbow and for me that was ohhhh'. It's just amazing how that band, and we were always huge in Europe but we weren't that massive in America, at least the Rainbow I was in at the beginning of the band. I think we were more of an underground band at that time, I don't know why. I remember playing in, I think it was Toronto, at the Maple Leaf Gardens. They had to cut the place back pretty drastically but I think we only drew like 1,500 people or so. I thought, 'Well this isn't going to work.' Then we started to do a little better here and there but we were smart enough not to play massive places like that. Then twenty-five years later it has become this band that everyone saw at Maple Leaf Gardens. There must have been 150,000 people there and I didn't see them. That's what happens but it's been a very important thing especially from the "duo" combination, which works so well all the time. From Mick Jagger and Keith Richards to Perry and Tyler, there are many more of them... I don't say we were on that level, Ritchie and I, but we created something very unique just as Tony and I did in Sabbath as well. You connect as two musicians who are necessary to make it happen and it's a magical thing. Rainbow just had impact on everyone because they hadn't heard anything like that before."

Cozy Powell

Influences...
"When I started. Buddy Rich, Louis Bellson really more than anybody else because he used to use two bass drums. Cozy Cole, that's where the name came from. Then I used to listen to a guy from The Hollies, Bobby Elliot and Brian Bennett from The Shadows. Bobby's a really good guy, a typically English player, he's also one of my good friends now and we kind of got to know each other over the years. He's great. John Bonham obviously."

"I'm not really impressed by a lot these days but, personally, I like John Bonham. There's a long gap between him and all the others as far as I'm concerned. Some people may like Carl Palmer and some may like Billy Cobham but I'm talking about rock and roll drummers and he's the best. It's not that he does much that's particularly flash, he's just always there keeping the whole thing going. John and I are good friends anyway but I'm after his crown!"

Joining Rainbow...
"I got this phone call out of the blue really saying can you come to the States. Would you like to come and audition for Ritchie's band. Simple as that. I wasn't doing anything at the time. I was just in the middle of doing some motor racing actually. I thought, yeah okay. Literally got on the next plane the next day. Flew to Los Angeles went to where the auditions were being held. There were like hundreds of people in there, and the band and like goodness knows half of Hollywood

seemed to be there. Got the drum kit together and just started playing. Ritchie said, 'can you play a shuffle?' so I said 'you want a shuffle?' Bang! I played this shuffle and about twenty minutes later he said 'you've got the job'."

"I think I'd met him a couple of times before. He'd come to see me when I was with Jeff Beck at the Roundhouse. Which is what kind of alerted him to what I could do, and he's a big fan of Jeff's. He said to me afterwards 'I remember you from the Roundhouse show' and I think he had auditioned so many people and not really got the kind of playing that he wanted from any of the Americans. Most of them were American drummers I think. I think Ritchie, maybe not now but obviously with Ian Paice and various other people, he liked the English style of drumming so that's probably why I got the call."

"I'm now giving the drums all the power I should have two years ago. With Jeff Beck it was impossible to whack hell out of the drums because it wasn't that sort of a band. Now I'm in a band where I can do what I want to do, and unleash the power! In the past I must have played as much different music as most drummers have done. But this is the sort of music I most enjoy and I'm best at. I'm not really a jazzer, I'm just a straightforward rock drummer, but I listen to everything that's going on. I'd never played with Ritch before, but going back fifteen years I was in a support band to his group, The Outlaws, and that was the last time I saw him. He's from the West Country, same as me, and we did the same round of clubs and bars."

Beck and Blackmore...
"They say Ritchie is a difficult man to work with, and he is at times. But he leaves me alone and lets me get on with it, which suits me. He's very demanding – he knows exactly what he wants and won't settle for anything less. Jeff on the other hand – brilliant guitar player – very difficult to know what he's thinking. You can't expect to know what's going on in a guy's head, so consequently it's very difficult to play with him. Some nights would be great and other nights he'd just go off on a tangent and it was very hard to keep up. All guitar players are prone to that."

"Personally, we've got on very well since the band started. But I hate to think what will happen when we do have an argument... no, he's been very good. He more or less lets me have a free hand. I like it this way. With my own band I had before, all the responsibility was on my shoulders and it was so difficult for me to tell a guitarist what to do, what notes and chords to play. Ritchie has got it all pat. All I've got to do is give him the foundation he wants."

"It's nice to work with someone as good as Ritchie and good for me to get back into it again after having been laid off for a while. I didn't feel rusty. After ten minutes it all came back. I'd built up so much energy and aggression in that nine months off, that when I got to the rehearsal room in LA I went bananas. We just blasted away for two hours. And then it all fell into place. Ritchie had tried some English and American guys and basically they were all frightened of him. I'm not frightened of anybody and just went and steamed in. Exactly the same story with Jeff. I went down to the audition, and there were literally twenty-five drummers all there with the kit that was supplied... 'Is it my turn now?... tapping away very lightly. I thought 'sod all this, slung the kit out, got mine in and sat right in front and said 'right, you wanna play? Let's play.' You've gotta be a bit arrogant if you're a drummer. You've gotta give 'em a kick up the ass."

"Ritchie is very much into classical music and the medieval period, and he's into the technique of the guitar. He likes to be a complete guitarist. Ritchie plays from the head and I really like the challenge of working with somebody who is that good on guitar. Jeff Beck was always a complete maniac. You never knew what he was going to do or say, but I'm privileged to be able to work with such good players as Jeff and Ritchie."

Giving his all...
"Tonight I didn't play a good performance and was really pissed off with myself. The night before I played really well. Jon Hiseman was in the audience and I knew I had to play well! When you get someone that good, it inspires you to play well. Last night I just drained myself completely and didn't have enough energy left for the drum solo. It's nice to bring the volume down on some numbers. Like the quiet part of 'Catch The Rainbow'. Then I did a sudden fill-in...

bam! And you see the kids jump. Things like that make rock 'n' roll. There's lots of time and tempo changes, which took a while to get off, but they become second nature. It's no big deal. With my drum solo — well, I've seen hundreds of them, and I know you have. They may be technically brilliant, and everybody gets up at the end and claps. But to the average punter — what do they know?"

"So I say just give them a little bit of rhythm, a little bit of this and that thrown in, then give them something completely different, like the 1812 Overture! Blow 'em all up at the end, and they'll go 'oh!' 'cause they're not ready for it. I'm just trying to make the drum solo entertaining, something people can watch as well as listen. In the old days you could get away with it, like Ginger with Cream, bashing away for ten minutes. Great. That was the accepted thing. But we've gone a long way since Cream, and there have been a lot of different drummers coming up, and if you're going to do a solo these days you've gotta make it a little bit special. I don't want to go on for too long. You'll notice it was pretty short. You can say what you wanna say in two or three minutes. I put one hundred per cent into the whole show, so come the drum solo, sometimes I haven't got any energy left. You have to pace yourself, which is very difficult in our show as you may have noticed. It's an hour and a half of torture! Yeah, it's painful all right. My hands are really suffering. I've drawn blood many times. I usually cut my hands up on the cymbals and now wear tape on my fingers, which gets cut to shreds because of the sticks I use. I'm using extra heavy military sticks, but I'm going through them at a furious rate. Trouble is I can't afford to have my hands bleeding, which they did at the start of the tour. I could play, but not hard."

"John Bonham is of the same ilk and I lived in Birmingham for a while and met my wife there. John and I are probably the only two drummers in England who play in that style. I like him because he doesn't play too many fills but when he does, it means something."

On Stage...

"I'd just like to say that the thing I like about the live LP, for Ritchie's sake, is that it's the best guitar playing he's ever done on stage. Deep Purple fans may disagree, but it blows both *Made In Japan* and *Made In Europe* into the weeds. For people who like guitarists, this is a winner. Really. I just don't know if it's right to put out a live album so early in a band's career. There's a lot going against it."

Jimmy Bain

On joining Rainbow...
"It's actually a crazy story. When I was living in London I was living with a couple of roadies who were also Scottish. One of them, named Fergie, worked with Jethro Tull and the other one worked with Ritchie. He was with a band called Badfinger before that. Ritchie decided to leave Deep Purple and planned to put the Rainbow together, and he did it with Ronnie and the guys from Elf. But he didn't really like the bass player at all so he was going to be the first to get replaced. So I got a call from this guy Fergie, from L.A., and I was in London, it was about 3:00 in the morning on a Wednesday. And he said 'Ritchie's looking for a bass player blah blah blah,' and the next minute he hands the phone to Ritchie and he talks to me for about an hour. And he basically asked me when I was playing next. And I said, at the weekend. We had a residency at the Marquee for about six Sunday nights. So he said, 'well, I'll come over and check you out.' And I was going, 'yeah, sure, sure.' You think there's no way that's going to happen. On the Sunday when I went down to the bar, just down from the Marquee, I walked in and there was Blackmore and Ronnie Dio, and their manager and Fergie, and a couple of other people that had flown over from L.A. to check me out. So with my band unfortunately, the two guitar players couldn't play a note, and the drummer, you know, he just drank too much Guinness or something like that. The band just completely sucked. I thought, 'oh, there we go, there's my big chance to get into something good.' But then Ritchie took me aside after. I was apologising because the band really didn't play very well, and he said, 'well, they made you look really good.' And a couple of weeks later I was in L.A. and I had gotten the gig with Rainbow. And then later he threw out most of the other guys in the band and replaced them with Cozy and Tony Carey, and then we went and did *Rainbow Rising*."

The chemistry between Ritchie and Ronnie...
"At that point I think they were pretty happy with each other. Ritchie was definitely happy with Ronnie's vocals and the fact that Ronnie had a really down to earth personality. And Ronnie could handle doing a bunch of interviews, which Ritchie didn't really like doing. He had this image of not talking to the press, and he worked on that really hard. Ronnie's lyrics were also important. Absolutely! In essence, that is probably what he loved as much as anything about Ronnie. Because that medieval thing was really where Ritchie was at also."

Ritchie Blackmore's Rainbow and *Rainbow Rising...*
"I like the first album, but I think *Rainbow Rising* was more of a band effort. I mean, the first album sounds like it gelled and everything, and the songs are good. I thought *Rainbow Rising* was a little bit short in terms of tracks. We always did the absolute minimum, never anything left over. But I really liked being involved with it. It had great potential and I would have liked to have been around a little longer because I had just started getting into writing with them on a couple of songs that didn't make it until the album after that, 'Kill The King' for one. I was involved with the writing of that with Cozy. That was the first band thing that we did. But by the time that came out, it was just Powell, Blackmore and Dio. If I had been in the band I think, I would have gotten credit for it. But we were starting to do things like that. But unfortunately Ritchie would wake up one day and he wouldn't hear Rainbow on the radio, because they weren't playing anything as hard as that, and he would decide to change one of the musicians. When I got fired, I was in shock. I went over to see him and he really couldn't give me a reason why he got rid of me. He just sort of looked every which way but at me. I had gathered from that that he had made a decision and he had to stick by it. Because, you know, the management had got hold of me and fired me, and then I went to see him. I don't know if he had second thoughts about it. I know they had a bit of difficulty replacing me because the guy that they got, Mark Clarke, didn't work out. They gave me a call, and I said, 'I don't really think so. After you got rid of me once, it would be quite easy to get rid of me again, so why should I bother?' So I went on to do Wild Horses with Robbo."

Rainbow on tour and *On Stage...*
"Pretty well everything that was in the live show went on *On Stage*. I don't think there was any doctoring at all either. I don't think Ritchie would ever consider going in and overdubbing or anything like that. It's quite a long record. It was just a lot of fun to do. That came out after I was out of the band, so that was kind of a bonus for me. In terms of touring, it was all funny at the time, because Ritchie, at the best of times, was pretty neurotic to say the least. All kinds of stuff went on, but not on stage. You'd come back and your room would be completely gone. You'd come back to the hotel and there would be nothing there, just a light bulb, no dresser or anything and it was all in the bathroom. They would spend hours and hours and hours trying to keep you away from your room so they could do all this stuff to you. And there were a couple of instances where we got kicked out of hotels in the middle of the night because of something one of the guys had done. I remember Cozy at one time scaled up the side of this hotel in Germany. I think he was on some kind of medication at the time (laughs) and he had a fire extinguisher and he let it go. But unfortunately he had gotten the floors mixed up. He was supposed to be letting it off in Ian Broad's room, Ritchie's roadie at the time, but he misjudged the floors and he let it off in some German salesman's room. Then we were all woken up and ejected from the hotel. It was a lot of crazy stuff. You'd wake up to somebody axing your door down. It was crazy, but it never really affected your performance or the records. It was always done on the side."

Leaving Rainbow…

"I got fired. I came home on January 3rd and got a phone call from the manager in New York saying, 'your services are no longer required.' There were no reasons given which was the surprising thing. It was a bit of a shock after being in the band for a year and a half. I joined Rainbow, or rather I was asked to join Rainbow for several reasons. First was because I could play bass; second, because I had a good stage presence; and third, which was the most important, because I could write songs. In Rainbow, the only people that ever got their songs recorded were Ritchie and Ronnie Dio, although everyone else in the band could write. Cozy Powell used to say to me whenever I got uptight, to cool it you're only a side man and it really got on my case that he would say that. When I was on stage or when I was recording, I was putting out one hundred per cent effort and I felt I was one-fifth of Rainbow. It was really silly, but that is a little bit why I didn't obey all the commands per se as they were given."

"You see, Rainbow was like a dynasty. Ritchie was number one; Cozy and Ronnie fought for number two, but I think Cozy likely came off second; Ronnie was number three; I was number four; and Tony was five. That was the way you were related to by anyone concerned with the band in so far as your needs went. I told Ritchie when I joined, it would be a stepping stone. I would have liked it to have lasted a bit longer than it did because I thought Rainbow was just on the verge of being one of the top five bands in the world. I think with the *On Stage* album doing so well here and in America."

"I'm a lot happier now. I'm not working for Ritchie, I'm not working for Purple. I'm working to get my music across to as many people as I can. Rainbow was good for me because it got me out of the level I had been at for a few years, it paid off because I always believed in myself. I got the break and it lasted one and a half years. It was great, I enjoyed every minute of it."

Tony Carey

The Blackmore/Dio writing partnership...
"There was a vibe in the air, once again there wasn't much said but there was a lot done. The melody and the track would be in the air for a couple of days and all of a sudden Ronnie would be gone with his paper and he'd come down and basically just sing the motherfucker, not spend hours doing it either. He'd just do it as if it had always been th-ere, which is the mark of an acceptable song. It's got to sound non-contrived and I thought they had a great writing chemistry."

On why the bass is lacking on *Rising*...
"There is a physical law, turn everything up and the bass gets louder. If you listen to it really loud, you can hear the bass. Who knows what the monitors were like in Musicland really. There was a huge wall of speakers but nobody missed the bass until the record came out so I guess it was done in mastering. It's not the volume of the instrument because if the frequency was there you would hear it. The instrument is there but it's like everything from 100hz down is gone. Maybe they mastered it so it would be louder. If the record has too much bass on it, a vinyl record, the needle would jump out of the groove, so maybe that was the reason for maximum volume, before we get too deep into Ritchie's problems with bass players. Ritchie's problems would extend to most of the human race I think! Without saying bass players, or trumpet players, or flute players or whatever."

Ritchie the cellist...
"Oh he carried this stupid cello around with him. I wonder if he can play it? Because he couldn't play it then! Before he became Robin Hood, which he now is, he had a little witch's hat he put on sometimes and he had his cello. We were all into classical music, Cozy did his solo to 1812 Overture, and we were very much into the 'Planets Suite' by Gustav Holst. In fact, Ritchie gave me a tape of that I had for twenty-five years. We were all into this... 'we're better than Kiss'. Not that anybody had anything against Kiss but we were the intellectual end of the scale here 'although we are as loud as fuck and we'll blow you out of your socks!'"

"He just lugged it around and posed with it. I never heard him play a note. My quote to Ritchie Blackmore is he still can't play the fucking cello. One thing that RB taught me... he used to check in an acoustic guitar, a nylon string Spanish guitar, into airlines without a case. Just like the most fragile thing you ever saw but it always came back whole because no one would ever throw it and all this equipment in flight cases would come back smashed and scratched. So if you want to send your Stratovarius in the mail don't wrap it. It always came back perfect that guitar."

On leaving the band...
I'm not sure how aware Ritchie was of everything either. In his defence actually, you will notice with the Deep Purple song writing credits they were all split five ways and how much did Ian Paice write of 'Smoke On The Water'? I would say that's Ritchie's financial advisor, Bruce Payne. I tried to sue them — to litigate just about a year after I left the band because of these live recordings and everything. When we were in Australia and Japan I noticed more microphones on the stage than should have been there. I said, 'We're not recording this are we?' 'Oh yeah we're recording.' I said, 'Well I want a piece of it', 'okay of course kid, you will get your contract'. I never got a penny from all these Rainbow bootlegs or the official stuff that is around now."

"By the way, on that *Long Live Rock 'n' Roll* album those keyboards are mine but I didn't get credited or anything. I wanted to get something on paper. And the biggest hurdle in suing Ritchie Blackmore or Rainbow is he didn't exist as an entity on paper in the seventies. Everything was so touchy. I tried to have a lawyer serve Bruce Payne. It would have cost two years in court just to find out who was pulling the strings and it was Bruce Payne. I wish him well."

"It was also completely normal business practice in the seventies. But what I have to say about Rainbow is we could have been one of the great progressive rock bands. We started off with a real bang with *Rainbow Rising* and the live recording but on a personal level, Ritchie tends to fire everybody after about five minutes and he can't get along with anybody and never gave the band chance to grow. We raged into *Rainbow Rising* after a couple of concerts and a couple of rehearsals and imagine how good the band would have been three years later?"

RITCHIE BLACKMORE'S
R-A-I-N-B-O-W
Rainbow
Rising
On Stage
Rainbow
On Stage
SPECIAL EDITED VERSIONS
FROM THE LIVE DOUBLE ALBUM
WITH
SPECIAL RADIO PROMOTION RECORD
Rainbow
DEUTSCHLAND TOURNEE 1976
On Stage
Rainbow
On Stage

Recording Guide

This section documents all the officially recorded and released Rainbow material from 1975-1976. Listed chronologically are all the major releases, promotional records and media broadcasts that make up the full body of recordings.

It doesn't list numerous variants of each release. In fact, it centres on the UK and USA releases, which are arguably the major markets. That said, it is also worth pointing out that invariably most European countries releases mirrored those of the UK, and likewise Canadian and Japanese releases did so with the USA. Some non UK / USA releases are listed, where they are of particular interest, most notably if they contain material that was not available on UK or USA releases at the time, even though it may have appeared in these territories in subsequent years, either in part or full.

With that declaration in mind, some may question the need for this, especially with so much information available on the Internet. But this goes way beyond anything you may find on Wikipedia or fan sites. The objective is to comprehensively guide you through the recordings with detailed information about them, and to provide more context on what happened and when.

RELEASE INFORMATION

The type of release is denoted in brackets after the title of it. The key for these is as follows:

LP = long play album vinyl
EP = extended play vinyl
SP = single play vinyl
FM = Frequency modulation radio broadcast
AM = Amplitude modulation radio broadcast
VHS = video home system, analogue videotape.
CD = compact disc album
CDs = compact disc single
DVD = digital versatile disc video

RECORDING INFORMATION

As this only lists official recordings, you might be wondering why it would be necessary to list recording details. This has been done to differentiate between the standard multi-track recordings, which are then mixed down to stereo, and those that were recorded directly from a soundboard. In the case of the latter these are invariably recordings made in concert by the front of house engineer, and in most cases recorded directly on to audiocassettes as a stereo mix. This documents the mix that the audience would have heard — often just recorded for the band and engineer's monitoring purposes. Engineers have been known to re-use the same cassettes once they have been listened back to, so whilst more concerts would probably have been recorded this way than are documented here, sadly many such recordings are probably lost forever. The other notable thing with these recordings is that there is a very unnatural sound to them because unlike other concert recordings made for the intention of commercial release, they do not have ambient microphones placed around the venue to record the audience.

Those who bemoan the omission of bootleg recordings are advised to read about them online. Frans van Arkel's Rainbow Fanclan Legacy website has a comprehensive list but in theory every concert could have been recorded.

INFORMATION SOURCES

Whilst much of the material in this book has been officially released, the archives of both Deep Purple (Overseas) Ltd. and Universal Music have been invaluable for filling in various gaps regarding recording dates and details concerning unreleased material.

THE RELEASES

RITCHIE BLACKMORE'S RAINBOW (LP)
UK Release: Oyster, OYA2001, 4th August 1975
US Release: Oyster, PD 1-6049, 1975
Recording data: Musicland Studios, Munich, Germany, 20th February - 14th March and May. Dynamic Sound, Kingston, Jamaica, April 1975
Producers: Ritchie Blackmore, Martin Birch & Ronnie Dio
Tracks: Man On The Silver Mountain / Self Portrait / Black Sheep Of The Family / Catch The Rainbow / Snake Charmer / Temple Of The King / If You Don't Like Rock `N' Roll / Sixteenth Century Greensleeves / Still I'm Sad //

As detailed elsewhere in this book, despite the album sleeve claiming it was recorded in Munich between 20th February and 14th March, a slight amount of additional work was done in Jamaica and finished off in Munich in May.

MAN ON THE SILVER MOUNTAIN / SNAKE CHARMER (SP)
UK Release: Oyster, OYR 103, 10th October 1975
US Release: Polydor PD 14290, September 1975
Producers: Ritchie Blackmore, Martin Birch & Ronnie Dio

THE RITCHIE BLACKMORE'S RAINBOW RADIO SPECIAL (LP)
US Release: Polydor SA-013, October or November 1975
Recording data: See Ritchie Blackmore's Rainbow
Producer: Fred Robbins
Tracks: Man On The Silver Mountain / Catch The Rainbow / Still I'm Sad / Sixteenth Century Greensleeves //

This promotional album includes four tracks from the debut release and came with an insert describing the radio show. The tracks are interspersed with commentary from Blackmore and Dio about the songs and the formation of the band.
Although logic would dictate that this came out to promote the album release in August, the accompanying press sheet lists the band including Carey; it was possibly done to give the record an extra push and/or to promote the tour.

RISING (LP)
UK Release: Polydor, 2490 137, 21st May 1976
US Release: Oyster, OY 1-1601, May 1976
Recording data: Musicland Studios, Munich, Germany, February 1976
Producer: Martin Birch
Tracks: Tarot Woman / Run With The Wolf / Starstruck / Do You Close Your Eyes / Stargazer / Light In The Black //

STARSTRUCK / RUN WITH THE WOLF (SP)
US Release: Oyster, OY 701, 26th July 1976
Recording data: Musicland Studios, Munich, Germany, February 1976
Producer: Martin Birch

It had been reported in the UK press that 'Tarot Woman' was to be released as the single. In the end Polydor UK did not release a single at all. However, its American counterparts selected the two shortest tracks from *Rising* as a coupling for the US market. 'Starstruck' was the logical choice but releasing it several weeks after the album clearly didn't help its sales potential and it made little impression on the American public. Several European countries and Japan also released this coupling.

MUSIKSZENE (TV)
German release: WDR, 1976
Recording data: Circus Krone, Munich, Germany, 29th September 1976
Tracks: Do You Close Your Eyes

This encore number was probably originally filmed and broadcast by this German broadcaster although if so the broadcast date is unknown. It was also aired on 13th April 1977 on the French TV show *JukeBox - Un Sur Cinq*. The

whole program lasts for twenty-two minutes and contains some clips of Purple, P.A.L and David Coverdale who is interviewed and mimes to the song 'White Snake'. Poor quality black and white versions of this Rainbow performance had circulated for years, probably taken from the French broadcast. Vision converted from the French Secam system to the PAL system — more widely used throughout Europe — results in colour converting to black and white.
On 12th January 2012 a very good quality full colour version of the French broadcast was uploaded to YouTube, hence David Coverdale's appearance at the very beginning of the clip.

NIGHTMOVES (TV)
Australian release: Channel 10, TV broadcast, November 1976
Recording data: Houston Music Hall Texas, USA, 10th July 1976
Tracks: Man On The Silver Mountain / Stargazer / A Light In The Black / Cozy Powell drum solo / Do You Close Your Eyes

This is one release where I am not one hundred per cent certain about the actual broadcast date. *Nightmoves* was claimed to be Australia's first late-night music TV programme for adults. It was an Australian Channel 10 production, hosted by Lee Simon. Although the Internet Movie Database indicates that the show was first aired in 1976, it would appear that Simon didn't start hosting it until 1977. It is conceivable that the first few shows may have had a different host or have been in a slightly different format. But most other sources tend to indicate that the show only started in 1977. However, the owners of this footage have the date listed in their archive as November '76. Therefore the broadcast date as listed would be perfectly logical. Furthermore, the Jan/Feb 1977 issue of *Stargazer* magazine reported that a broadcast of Rainbow material had been aired on Australian TV, which would help to support this supposition.

Oyster Records made this ten-minute film for promotional purposes and it's not inconceivable that it was done solely for the purpose of promoting the Australian tour that ran between the 4th-22nd November. The film starts with the 'Over The Rainbow' intro. It shows the crew erecting the electronic rainbow. This is followed by a brief snippet of 'Man On The Silver Mountain', and then cuts to 'Stargazer'. This is interspersed with a brief comment from Dio on how they want to stop calling it Ritchie Blackmore's Rainbow and eventually just call the band Rainbow "because everyone contributes". The footage switches back to the guitar solo from 'Stargazer' and once again is cut as more interview footage is interspersed. Blackmore talks for a few seconds about the electronic rainbow, before encouraging Dio to explain about it in more detail. A brief section of 'A Light In The Black' is then shown, which cuts to Blackmore briefly talking again, followed by part of Powell's drum solo. This segues into Blackmore's guitar demolition during 'Do You Close Your Eyes'.

In the days before video machines were standard household items, there would have been a limited commercial outlet for such a film. *Stargazer* magazine reported in its March/April 1977 issue that it was shown on Pat Travers' tour during the interval, which seems very odd. The likelihood that venues would have been set up to show films seems highly improbable. Where would they have erected the screens? Where would the film projectors have been placed? It sounds like a potentially logistical nightmare. However, I suppose the odd venue may have been able to cater for such a thing. Rainbow and Travers were on the same label and Polydor could have been keen to promote Rainbow through the channel of their other rock acts.

Needless to say that many fans assume that the whole concert must still exist although it is highly unlikely the "rushes"— that is, the unedited footage, is still around. In the days when film reels were very expensive, it was a common policy to re-use them once the required edit had been made.

JAPANESE RADIO BROADCAST, OSAKA (AM) (Unconfirmed)
Release date: unknown
Recording data: Osaka Koseinenkin Kaikan, Japan, 8th December 1976
Tracks: Purple Haze / Man On The Silver Mountain / Still I'm Sad / Stargazer

These tracks were reportedly broadcast on Japanese radio, but as to when, or what station is unclear. The recording was subsequently bootlegged on *Time Standing Still*. 'Mistreated' is dedicated to Tommy Bolin.

JAPANESE RADIO BROADCAST, OSAKA (AM) (Unconfirmed)
Release date: unknown
Recording data: Osaka Koseinenkin Kaikan, Japan, 9th December 1976
Tracks: Kill The King / Mistreated / Purple Haze / Lazy / Man On The Silver Mountain

As with the previous recording, these tracks were also reportedly broadcast on Japanese radio. Although this information has come via collectors in Japan, both shows were officially recorded by Martin Birch for the prospective live album release *On Stage*. It is therefore odd that recordings earmarked for an official album would have been supplied to a radio station, even if it were after July 1977. When the album was released as *On Stage*, it only contained one song recorded in Osaka — 'Catch The Rainbow'.

ON STAGE SPECIAL EDITION (LP)
German release: Polydor/Oyster 2808 010, June 1977
Recording data: Perth, Australia, 4th-8th November 1976 (interviews)*. See next entry for concert info.
Tracks: Ritchie: Rainbow And Ronnie Dio / Man On The Silver Mountain / Ritchie & Ronnie: Greensleeves & Rainbow / Sixteenth Century Greensleeves / Ronnie & Ritchie: 'Starstruck' Muriel / Starstruck / Ritchie: Mistreated / Ritchie: His departure from Deep Purple / Kill The King / Ritchie: Rainbow and their audience / Catch The Rainbow / Ritchie & Ronnie (And Cozy): A Title? / Still I'm Sad //
*The interviews were conducted by Australian DJ Trevor Smith over three days in a Perth Hotel. The band played in Perth on the 4th and had several days off before the next show in Melbourne on the 9th. The exact three days are therefore not certain, but they are most likely to have been the 5th-7th, as the band may well have flown to Melbourne on the 8th, rather than on the day of the gig.

This promotional release — of which probably no more than a few dozen were pressed up — came in a red plastic wallet housing the press pack and with space for the company reps' business card. The album is in the same inner sleeve that record one of the commercial double album is in. Some tracks are short edits.

ON STAGE (2LP)
UK Release: Polydor, 2657 142, July 1977
US Release: Polydor, OY-2-1801, 1977
Producer: Martin Birch
Tracks: (Disc 1) Kill The King / Man On The Silver Mountain / Blues / Starstruck //
(Disc 2): Catch The Rainbow //
(Disc 3): Mistreated //
(Disc 4): Sixteenth Century Greensleeves / Still I'm Sad //
Recording data: Sporthalle, Cologne, 25th September, Messezentrum Halle, Nuremberg, 28th September, Circus Krone, Munich 29th, Osaka 9th December, Tokyo 16th December 1976 (matinee and evening shows).

The album is thought to have been compiled as follows:
Kill The King: Tokyo 16th December (evening show) and Munich 29th September.
Man On The Silver Mountain: Tokyo 16th December (afternoon show).
Blues/Starstruck: Tokyo 16th December (evening show, edited).
Catch The Rainbow Osaka 9th December and Tokyo 16th December (evening show).
Mistreated: Cologne 25th September.
Sixteenth Century Greensleeves: Tokyo 16th December (evening show).
Still I'm Sad: Nuremberg 28th September.

Not many bands release a double live album after just two studio releases, but such was the musical chemistry with the line-up responsible for *Rising*, it was a highly logical move to make. Even after all the years that have passed, the *Rising* tour is considered by most aficionados of the band to be the pinnacle of Rainbow's career. It would appear that those within the fold were also aware of the fantastic music they were making, hence the desire to capture some of the gigs on tape.

The ever-present Martin Birch, who had worked with Deep Purple from 1969, and also produced the first two Rainbow albums, was largely responsible for putting the live recordings together. The album comprised of recordings done at four German and four Japanese concerts but as no recording data was listed on the album it's speculative as to exactly where the tracks were recorded. In fact, some tracks were spliced together from different shows, and there was some heavy editing as well.

The previous year Birch had put together *Made In Europe*, a posthumous Deep Purple release of the last recordings Ritchie Blackmore made with the band. Birch was a master engineer and producer and had the knack of not only producing a great, recorded sound but also separating the wheat from the chaff. Having already done that with *Made In Europe*, he was well equipped to produce Rainbow's live document. Despite criticism on the length of the album, by and large Birch knew what to leave out, such as Cozy Powell's lengthy drum solo, and the encore number of 'Do You Close Your Eyes' that included Blackmore's guitar demolition. Whilst visually both pieces were fantastic, the same effect doesn't always come across on record. Also, in order to accommodate the four sides of vinyl, the original concert running order was changed but fundamentally it didn't diminish the end result and clearly showed what a superb live act Rainbow was.

On the downside, the major criticism is the baffling exclusion of 'Stargazer' and 'A Light In The Black'. In fairness, only one of the eight shows recorded captured the latter but 'Stargazer' was played at virtually every gig and for many was the highlight of the show.

But what Birch did capture was brilliantly recorded, engineered and mixed, and is testimony to his skills. Birch mixed the recording at Kingsway Recorders in March 1977. At the time, Rainbow was starting to record the follow up to *Rising* but recording was put on hold in May. With no indication of when the next studio album was going to be released, *On Stage* was a much welcomed release.

LIVE EP
UK Release: Polydor, 2066 845, August 1977
Recording data: Cologne 25th September 1976, Munich 29th September 1976, Tokyo 16th December 1976 (matinee and evening shows)
Tracks: Kill The King / Man On The Silver Mountain / Mistreated //

Edited versions from the album. This was only released in the UK and Ireland.

LIVE IN GERMANY 1976 (LIVE IN EUROPE) (LP / CD)
UK Release: Connoisseur Collection DP VSOP LP 155, November 1990
US Release: Mausoleum Classix/BMG 71278-60024-2, USA, March 26th, 1996
Recording data: Sportshalle, Cologne, 25th September[1], Philipshalle, Düsseldorf, 27th September[2], Messezentrum Halle, Nuremberg, 28th September[3] & Circus Krone, Munich, 29th September 1976[4]
Tracks: Kill The King[4] / Mistreated[4] / Sixteenth Century Greensleeves[1] / Catch The Rainbow[2] / Man On The Silver Mountain[3] / Stargazer[1] / Still I'm Sad[1] / Do You Close Your Eyes[4] //

With continued interest in this period of Rainbow, the advent of the compact disc and encouragement from Simon Robinson of the Deep Purple Appreciation Society, Tony Edwards' label compiled a full show from the tapes of the four German gigs. At the time, one of the tape boxes was incorrectly marked up and the release listed the show of the 28th as being from Mannheim when it was in fact Nuremberg.

The vinyl release also managed to squeeze an entire show across all four sides even though side four ran to over half an hour. No one is credited with the mix and although not quite to the same high standard that *On Stage* had been produced by Birch, soundwise it was more than acceptable and presented a full '76 show for the first time, complete with 'Stargazer'.

RITCHIE BLACKMORE - ROCK PROFILE VOLUME 2 (LP / CD)
UK Release: Connoisseur Collection RP VSOP LP 157 / RP VSOP CD 157, 15th April 1991 (2LPs / 1CD)
Tracks: Still I'm Sad / Man On The Silver Mountain[1] / Sixteenth Century Greensleeves[2] / Lady Of The Lake
Recording data: Musicland Studios, Munich, Germany, 20 February-14 March 1975, Sporthalle, Cologne, 25th September[1] & Circus Krone, Munich, 29th September 1976[2]

The previous year Tony Edwards' Connoisseur label had issued a Ritchie Blackmore compilation that covered his Deep Purple work, alongside some early sixties sessions. The second volume focused on his Rainbow period alongside further session recordings. Due to licensing constraints, the two volumes could not run chronologically and this second volume also included Blackmore's 1965 solo single, another sixties session, plus some earlier seventies sessions, as well as some eighties recordings — a Deep Purple track and 'I Call, No Answer', a session he did for Jack Green's album *Humanesque* in 1980. Four Rainbow tracks were included. Two studio recordings, 'Still I'm Sad' from the first album, and 'Lady Of The Lake' from *Long Live Rock 'n' Roll*, and two unreleased live tracks from Germany 1976. 'Man On The Silver Mountain' was from the Cologne show and 'Sixteenth Century Greensleeves' was recorded in Munich. The former has subsequently been released on *Live In Köln 1976*, but the latter is unique to this release, and aside from the three other tracks from Munich that had been released on *Live In Germany 1976*, the rest of that particular show remains unreleased.

RAINBOW FAMILY ALBUM (CD)
UK Release: Connoisseur Collection VSOP CD 195, 1994
Tracks include: Kill The King / Sixteenth Century Greensleeves

Both tracks are from *Live In Germany 1976.*

THE LIVE EP (CDs)
UK Release: The Sweet, PR001, 1996
Recording data: Santa Monica Auditorium, California, 24th March 1976.
Tracks: Alright Now[1] / Hellraiser / Restless //
Twenty years after the event, the Sweet Fan Club released this three track CD EP that contains two tracks from their March concert in Santa Monica. ('Hellraiser' is from a different show at Masonic Hall Detroit 27 February 1976).

[1] 'Alright Now' was the encore number and a tribute to Paul Kossoff who had died on the 19th. Blackmore joined the band for this tribute, which was documented in the music press at the time.

DEUTSCHLAND TOURNEE 1976 (CD)
Japanese Release: VAP, VPCK85354, 24th May 2006, (6 CD box set)
Recording data: Sporthalle, Köln, Germany 25th September 1976, Philipshalle, Düsseldorf, Germany 27th September 1976 & Messezentrum Halle, Nuremberg, Germany, 28th September 1976
Tracks (Disc 1): Intro (Over The Rainbow)/ Kill The King / Mistreated / Sixteenth Century Greensleeves / Catch The Rainbow / Man On The Silver Mountain //
(Disc 2): Stargazer / Still I'm Sad / Do You Close Your Eyes //
(Disc 3): Intro (Over The Rainbow)/ Kill The King / Mistreated / Sixteenth Century Greensleeves / Catch The Rainbow / Man On The Silver Mountain //
(Disc 4): Stargazer / Still I'm Sad //
(Disc 5): Intro (Over The Rainbow)/ Kill The King / Mistreated / Sixteenth Century Greensleeves / Catch The Rainbow / Man On The Silver Mountain //
(Disc 6): Stargazer / Still I'm Sad / Do You Close Your Eyes //

Three of the four complete concerts from the German tour recorded by Martin Birch, parts of which were originally released on *Live In Germany 1976*.

LIVE IN KÖLN 1976 (2CD)
UK Release: AFM Records T2CD0105, 10th July 2006
Tracks (Disc 1): Intro (Over The Rainbow)/ Kill The King / Mistreated / Sixteenth Century Greensleeves / Catch The Rainbow / Man On The Silver Mountain //
(Disc 2): Stargazer / Still I'm Sad / Do You Close Your Eyes //
Recording data: Sporthalle, Köln, Germany 25th September 1976
The first two discs from the *Deutschland Tournee 1976* Japanese box set. The other two followed over the next fifteen months as detailed below.

LIVE IN DÜSSELDORF 1976 (2CD)
UK Release: AFM Records, T2CD0110, 12th February 2007
Tracks (CD1): Kill The King / Mistreated / Sixteenth Century Greensleeves / Man On The Silver Mountain / Catch The Rainbow // (CD2): Stargazer / Still I'm Sad //
Recording data: Philipshalle, Düsseldorf, Germany 27th September 1976

LIVE IN NUREMBERG 1976 (2CD)
UK Release: AFM Records, T2CD0111, 29th October 2007
Tracks (Disc 1): Kill The King / Mistreated / Sixteenth Century Greensleeves / Man On The Silver Mountain / Catch The Rainbow //
(Disc 2): Stargazer / Still I'm Sad / Do You Close Your Eyes //
Recording data: Messezentrum Halle, Nuremberg, Germany, 28th September 1976

THE VERY BEST OF RAINBOW 1997 (CD)
Tracks: Man On The Silver Mountain / Catch The Rainbow / Starstruck / Stargazer / Kill The King / Long Live Rock 'n' Roll / Gates Of Babylon/ Since You Been Gone / All Night Long / I Surrender / Can't Happen Here / Jealous Lover / Stone Cold / Power / Can't Let You Go / Street Of Dreams //

20TH CENTURY MASTERS: THE MILLENNIUM COLLECTION: THE BEST OF RAINBOW (CD)
US Release: Polydor 314 549 138-2, 3rd October 2000
Tracks: Man On The Silver Mountain / Catch The Rainbow / Stargazer / Mistreated (Live) / Kill The King / Rainbow Eyes / Since You Been Gone / I Surrender / Stone Cold / Power / Street Of Dreams

POT OF GOLD (CD)
UK Release: Polydor 44 651-2, 5th February 2002
Tracks: Still I'm Sad / Stargazer / Kill The King / L.A. Connection / Rainbow Eyes / Since You Been Gone / Makin' Love / Danger Zone / Vielleicht Das Nachste Mal (Maybe Next Time) / Eyes Of Fire / Stone Cold / Fire Dance / Fool For The Night //

ALL NIGHT LONG: AN INTRODUCTION (CD)
UK Release: Polydor 589 652-2, 7th May 2002
Tracks: Temple Of The King / Tarot Woman / Stargazer / Lady Of The Lake / Eyes Of The World / All Night Long (live) / Love's No Friend / Spotlight Kid / Stone Cold / Fire Dance / Weiss Heim //

CATCH THE RAINBOW: THE ANTHOLOGY (CD)
UK Release: Polydor 18th March 2003
Tracks (Disc 1): Man On The Silver Mountain / Sixteenth Century Greensleeves / Catch The Rainbow / Tarot Woman / Starstruck / Stargazer / A Light In The Black / Mistreated (Live) / Long Live Rock 'n' Roll / Gates Of Babylon / Kill The King / Rainbow Eyes
(Disc 2): Eyes Of The World / Since You Been Gone / All Night Long / Weiss Heim / I Surrender / Spotlight Kid / Can't Happen Here / Jealous Lover / Death Alley Driver / Stone Cold / Tearin' Out My Heart / Power / Can't Let You Go / Desperate Heart / Street Of Dreams / Difficult To Cure (Live) /

RAINBOW COLOUR COLLECTION 2006 (CD)
UK Release: Polydor 060249839687, 16th February 2009
Tracks: All Night Long / Catch The Rainbow / Since You Been Gone / I Surrender / Stone Cold / Kill The King / Stargazer / Starstruck / Sixteenth Century Greensleeves (live) / Man On The Silver Mountain / Long Live Rock 'n' Roll / Run With The Wolf / Lost In Hollywood / If You Don't Like Rock 'n' Roll / Miss Mistreated / Death Alley Driver
Another re-issue of Classic Rainbow: The Universal Master Collection. 'Greensleeves' is from *On Stage*.

STARGAZER - THE BEST OF RAINBOW (CD)
UK Release: United UTD059, 27th March 2006
Tracks: Still I'm Sad / Stargazer / Kill The King - Album Version / Rainbow Eyes - Album Version / Since You Been Gone - Album Version / Makin' Love / Danger Zone / Vielleicht Das Nächster Mal / Eyes Of Fire / Fire Dance / Fool For The Night - Album Version

CLASSIC: MASTERS COLLECTION (CD)
UK Release: Polydor, 7858781, 9th February 2009
Re-issued in 2009 as Classic Rainbow with completely new artwork that includes a great off-stage colour image of the MKIII Daisley / Stone line-up. The back cover includes another publicity shot of the same line-up, while the booklet includes a '76 era shot of Blackmore and a Dio / Blackmore photo from the first publicity photo shoot with Fin Costello in 1975.

ANTHOLOGY 1975 - 1984 (CD)
UK release: Polydor, 5319273, 2009
Tracks (Disc 1): Sixteenth Century Greensleeves / Temple Of The King / Man On The Silver Mountain / Still I'm Sad / Tarot Woman / A Light In The Black / Stargazer / Catch The Rainbow (live)/ Kill The King (live) / Gates Of Babylon / Lady Of The Lake / L.A Connection //
(Disc 2): Eyes Of The World / Since You Been Gone / Lost In Hollywood / Weiss Heim / Will You Love Me Tomorrow / I Surrender / Maybe Next Time / Jealous Lover / Stone Cold / Death Alley Driver / Eyes Of Fire / Can't Let You Go / Street Of Dreams / Snowman / Stranded (live) / All Night Long (live) //

RAINBOW RISING DELUXE EDITION (2CD)
UK release: Polydor, 5332266, 2011
Tracks: Tarot Woman / Run With The Wolf / Starstruck / Do You Close Your Eyes / Stargazer / A Light In The Black (New York Mix / Los Angeles Mix / Rough Mix) / Stargazer (Pirate Sound Rehearsal) //
In 2009 Universal started a plan to release remastered and expanded double CD versions of Rainbow's back catalogue. The multi-track masters could not be located and therefore the possibility of tracks without fadeouts, or even alternative versions resulted instead in three different mixes of *Rising* being deployed, plus one extra track taken from the tour rehearsals and lifted from the bootleg *Tower Of Babel*.

When the album was first transferred to CD in the late eighties, it was re-mixed and mastered in Los Angeles but this mix was rejected and it was done again in New York the following month. Somehow the LA mix — despite being rejected for the US and European markets — had been used by Polydor in Japan but elsewhere the New York mix was used.

With noticeable differences, it was decided to include both. As I was involved with this release and wrote the sleeve notes which referred to this, for some strange reason, when reviewing the album Peter Makowski was under the impression that I had remixed the album!

The third mix on this deluxe edition was Martin Birch's initial mix done at Kingsway and included a keyboard intro to 'Stargazer' that was abandoned for the actual release.

As for the extra version of 'Stargazer' from the May '76 rehearsals, along with other tracks from this recording, these had been sent to Blackmore for approval to include but he rejected them simply on the grounds that the audio quality was below par. For some reason, it was still decided to include this extra track.

ON STAGE DELUXE EDITION (2CD)
UK Release: Polydor 3716816, 2012
Tracks (Disc 1): Over The Rainbow - Kill The King / Medley: Man On The Silver Mountain / Catch The Rainbow / Mistreated Rainbow / Sixteenth Century Greensleeves / Still I'm Sad //
(Disc 2): Kill The King / Mistreated / Sixteenth Century Greensleeves / Catch The Rainbow / Medley: Man On The Silver Mountain – Blues - Starstruck / Do You Close Your Eyes //

This release was initially to be a triple, with a complete Japanese show from either Osaka with 'A Light In The Black' from the matinee Tokyo show dropped in, or alternatively the matinee Tokyo show, which excluded 'Stargazer', with the intention of dropping particular song in from another show. Problems arose when the individual who had been entrusted with the archive material took about a year to arrange for the tapes to be transferred. Universal were also told that no full shows existed and some of the reels were missing, including all those that included any versions of 'Stargazer'. More worryingly, the whereabouts of the entire matinee show were — and still are — unknown. Universal had been told that most of the Osaka show from the 8th was amongst the archives, so it was decided to use this as the bonus material. Everything had been set up for this, but when the tapes were finally delivered they included just some of the songs from the evening Tokyo show, which were then used for the bonus disc, although parts of it duplicated the original release. Sadly the sleeve notes were not changed to reflect this, as Universal, over a year behind schedule with the project were keen to release it as soon as possible.

Since this release, all the tapes that had previously been archived by the said individual have now been transferred to Abbey Road's archive. Frustratingly they do include the full show for Osaka (8th) although some reels for the other shows are still missing.

A LIGHT IN THE BLACK 1975-1984 (6CD)
UK Release: Polydor 5348722, 23rd January 2015
Tracks (Disc 1 1975-1976): Black Sheep Of The Family / Sixteenth Century Greensleeves / Snake Charmer / Temple Of The King /
Tarot Woman (Rough Mix) / Stargazer (Rough Mix) / Run With The Wolf (Rough Mix) / Mistreated (Live In Osaka, Japan, 1976) /
Purple Haze-White Christmas-Lazy-Man On The Silver Mountain-Blues-Man On The Silver Mountain (Reprise) (Live In Osaka, Japan, 1976) //
Disc 2 (1977-1978)
Disc 3 (1979-1980)
Disc 4 (1981-1982)
Disc 5 (1983-1984)
Disc 6 (Live At Monsters Of Rock, Castle Donington, UK, 16 August 1980)

As with all good intentions, this career retrospective box set didn't materialise exactly as nature intended. Whilst it was extremely wishful thinking, the original plan was for it to actually start with the 1974 recordings of 'Black Sheep Of The Family' and 'Sixteenth Century Greensleeves', assuming that Blackmore still has them, as Universal was liaising with him on the project but nothing came of it. It was also hoped that something live from 1975 could be included, particularly 'Self Portrait'. Once the tapes for that were sold on though, that idea was also scrapped.

With the cock-up over the extra tracks for the deluxe edition of *On Stage*, at least this was compensated for to a degree with the inclusion of some tracks from the third Osaka show.

The Recordings: Track By Track

This section lists all the known studio sessions and officially recorded concert performances laid out in a simple chronological format. The releases that each version appears on are indicated alongside the tracks. This is essentially designed to function as an index.

Reading of the many unreleased recordings detailed here fans will inevitably be wondering "when will some of this stuff get released?" It should be pointed out that there are many legal issues regarding ownership of the recordings etc. Basically, recordings from 1975 and 1976 came under the auspices of Deep Purple (Overseas) Ltd. Both Blackmore and his former Deep Purple colleagues took separate legal actions against the company over several years. Eventually DPO accountant Dipak Rao was sentenced to six years and four months in prison in 2019 for stealing £2.2million from the company, which has since been dissolved.

Because the musicians had little in the way of control over Deep Purple (Overseas) Ltd., a new company Purpletuity Ltd. was formed in 2005. The offspring of the original managers Edwards and Coletta are still actively involved and remain company directors to this day, as does Blackmore's manager (Carole Stevens), as well as Ian Paice and Ian Gillan.

Away from the business shenanigans, sadly, the whereabouts of many of the multi-track masters are unknown. According to Universal's archive — regarding this period of Rainbow — they do not reside with them. Whilst theoretically these tapes were retained by either Deep Purple (Overseas) Ltd. or Thames Talent Ltd. at the time, some tapes are still not accounted for. For example, the multi-tracks for both the first two albums have not been located, despite extensive searching from various people, none more so than Drew Thompson who has worked tirelessly for years trying to unearth as much stuff us possible.

As an example of how convoluted this has been over the decades, when Musicland Studios closed in the early nineties, the multi-track tapes of Deep Purple (Overseas) Ltd. recordings were sent to Deep Purple's then manager Bruce Payne at Thames Talent. These included Deep Purple albums *Stormbringer* and *Come Taste The Band*, neither of which had anything to do with Thames Talent. No tapes from either of the first two Rainbow albums were amongst the shipment. The tapes that Payne received were later passed on to DPO.

Regarding the live shows, the tapes for the matinee show from Tokyo 16th December 1976 cannot be located. Most of the recordings from the German and Japanese shows are now archived at Abbey Road Studios, London. The majority of stereo master tapes are in Universal's archives in different locations in New York, London and Germany. Thames Talent Ltd. has an archive at a place called Westside, New York, but the author has not had access to the full list of tapes, so is unsure what (if any) tapes pertaining to this period of Rainbow's career might be stored there.

Finally, it's worth pointing out that many shows were recorded via the soundboard and Cozy Powell had a collection of them on cassettes. In fact, when I interviewed him in 1997, he said, "I've got quite a lot of stuff. I've got tapes of virtually every live show we've done." After his death, his former band mate Denny Ball acquired the collection. Universal wanted to purchase them, particularly as they apparently included 1975 shows with 'Self Portrait'. Drew Thompson visited Ball with the view to doing the deal on behalf of Universal, and had received a tape with some brief snippets to give an indication of content and quality. However, before any deal could be struck, Ball claims to have sold them to a private collector. For that reason it hasn't been possible to document which shows actually exist.

All hope should not be lost though. Cozy's tapes are thought to be copies that Rainbow's sound engineer at the time, Davy Kirkwood, had made. Kirkwood died in 2011 but his estate is thought to be in possession of a large number of tapes but as yet nothing appears to have been catalogued.

(Blackmore, Dio, Soule, Gruber, Driscoll)

Kingsway Recorders, London, 1974

Black Sheep Of The Family	unreleased

According to correspondence at the time, detailed elsewhere in this book, a session with Ronnie Dio was done at Ian Gillan's studio sometime in 1974. No more information is available so it is purely speculative, although it is logical to suggest that 'Black Sheep Of The Family' would have been worked on. In an interview with Steve Rosen in the summer of 1975, Dio might well have referred to this session when he said, "I had been in England for about four or five months doing other sessions for other people. When we started the rehearsals for it, it was interesting because it was something new. It was working with different people but it was still very doubtful. You know what I mean? It was like when you're used to working in a structure where you're really confident because you've worked with the people so many times. One guy's pants come full off and the other guy covers up by pulling his higher up to his chest. You know, that kind of a thing. It was new but interesting and exciting but completely different. The session was good and it went well except for a little foul up with one of the musicians but that wasn't Ritchie's fault. We were very pleased with the product. We were very tired that night and we probably thought it was better than it was. We did the track again eventually. I think it turned out quite a bit better and we were much more pleased with it."

Dio had certainly spent some considerable time in England in 1974. The second Elf album was recorded in England between January through to March, and he also did Glover's session for the *Butterfly Ball*. In April and May, Elf toured the UK supporting Purple. June was a period of relative inactivity for Purple. Jon Lord spent a few days in Munich for his *Windows* concert but Purple had no activity (apart from one rearranged gig on 27th June) until August, so it's feasible that a session could have happened sometime in June or July.

Unknown studio, Minneapolis, 7th and / or 8th December 1974

Black Sheep Of The Family	unreleased
Sixteenth Century Greensleeves	unreleased

Prior to his death, I had some correspondence with Craig Gruber via social media and he didn't recall doing 'Black Sheep Of The Family' but of 'Sixteenth Century Greensleeves' he said, "We did however write and record 'Sixteenth Century Greensleeves' in one day in a little tiny studio near Minneapolis."

Some suggestions are that Blackmore originally entered the studio with just Dio and Driscoll. It's possible that if this is the case, they laid down some basic structure for 'Black Sheep Of The Family' with the plan to do additional work at the next opportunity.

Unknown studio, Tampa Bay, Florida, 12th December 1974 (session also included Hugh McDowell on cello)

Sixteenth Century Greensleeves	unreleased

"Well as far as the session in Tampa... not much was done. We ran over a few riffs with Ritchie, that's all. Nothing laid down," recalls Gruber.

However, his recollection did come thirty-eight years after the event! Cameron Crowe for *Rolling Stone* portrayed what is probably a more accurate picture of this session. Crowe was with Blackmore in Jacksonville covering the Purple tour and on 14th December his report stated, "two nights before, on an off night, Blackmore completed a long promised solo project — a single — at a Tampa studio. His backup includes Ronnie Dio and Gary Driscoll and cellist Hugh McDowell."

McDowell was cellist with the Electric Light Orchestra; who as well as Elf was a supporting act on Purple's US tour. It's probable that this session was just to add a few overdubs such as McDowell's cello, but until Blackmore digs out the tapes and lets the world hear them, we will never know. It has widely been reported over the years that former Procul Harum organist Matthew Fisher was involved with these sessions, but Gruber is adamant he wasn't. The author has also quizzed Fisher about this, and he had no recollection of any involvement, which should be pretty comprehensive evidence that he was never a part of it.

In an interview with Steve Rosen for *Guitar International* the following year, Blackmore was talking about the album and said, "Hugh McDowell, he played on one of the tracks. And a good friend of mine — is teaching me cello. I think unfortunately the track that he was on got wiped off because he was playing in America. But we have to do it again. He is brilliant and if I ever got a cellist in the band it would be him, if he was available."

It is unclear exactly what Blackmore meant by the track being "wiped off because he was playing in America." It's possible that McDowell's work could not be used for contractual or tax reasons, but as nothing from these sessions has been released anyway, the speculation is somewhat academic.

Musicland Studios, Munich, Germany, 21st February - 14th March 1975 (session also includes Judith Feinstein on vocals*, aka Shoshana)

Man On The Silver Mountain	*Ritchie Blackmore's Rainbow; The Best Of Rainbow; The Very Best Of Rainbow; 20th Century Masters: The Millennium Collection: The Best Of Rainbow; Catch The Rainbow: The Anthology; Anthology 1975 - 1984*
Self Portrait	*Ritchie Blackmore's Rainbow*
Black Sheep Of The Family	*Ritchie Blackmore's Rainbow*
Catch The Rainbow*	*Ritchie Blackmore's Rainbow; The Best Of Rainbow; The Very Best Of Rainbow; 20th Century Masters: The Millennium Collection: The Best Of Rainbow; Catch The Rainbow: The Anthology*
Snake Charmer	*Ritchie Blackmore's Rainbow*
Temple Of The King	*Ritchie Blackmore's Rainbow; All Night Long: An Introduction; The Anthology; Anthology 1975 - 1984*
If You Don't Like Rock 'n' Roll	*Ritchie Blackmore's Rainbow*
Sixteenth Century Greensleeves	*Ritchie Blackmore's Rainbow; The Best Of Rainbow; Catch The Rainbow: The Anthology; Anthology 1975 - 1984*
Still I'm Sad*	*Ritchie Blackmore's Rainbow; Ritchie Blackmore Rock Profile Vol 2; Pot Of Gold; Anthology 1975 - 1984*

Dynamic Sound, Kingston, Jamaica, late April 1975

Man On The Silver Mountain (overdubs)	*Ritchie Blackmore's Rainbow*
Catch The Rainbow (overdubs)	*Ritchie Blackmore's Rainbow*

This session was just Blackmore and Dio adding some additional work to the tracks. It was probably an excuse for a holiday more than anything else, following the completion of Blackmore's last tour with Purple.

Musicland Studios, Munich, Germany, May 1975

Man On The Silver Mountain	*Ritchie Blackmore's Rainbow*
Catch The Rainbow	*Ritchie Blackmore's Rainbow*

This session is less clear. It may have been additional overdubs, or possibly just final mixing.

(Blackmore, Dio, Powell, Bain, Carey)

Pirate Sound, Los Angeles, California, late October / early November 1975 (Two recordings)
Robert Simon recorded six Rainbow rehearsals at his Pirate Sound including two just before the first gigs. There is no more information as to which songs were recorded. Apparently John Bonham was present at the first recording with his nine-year-old son Jason. The young Bonham had been playing drums since the age of five and according to Simon plays on a version of 'Man On The Silver Mountain' which he dedicates to his dad.

Musicland Studios, Munich, Germany, February 1976 (session also includes the Munich Philharmonic Orchestra conducted by Rainer Pietsch*)

Tarot Woman	*Rising; All Night Long: An Introduction; Catch The Rainbow: The Anthology; Anthology 1975 – 1984; Rising Deluxe Edition; A Light In The Black 1975-84*
Run With The Wolf	*Rising; Rising Deluxe Edition; A Light In The Black 1975-84*
Starstruck	*Rising; The Very Best Of Rainbow; Catch The Rainbow: The Anthology; Rising Deluxe edition; A Light In The Black 1975-84*
Do You Close Your Eyes	*Rising; Rising Deluxe Edition; A Light In The Black 1975-84*
Stargazer*	*Rising; The Best Of Rainbow; The Very Best Of Rainbow; 20th Century Masters: The Millennium Collection: The Best Of Rainbow; Pot Of Gold; All Night Long: An Introduction; Catch The Rainbow: The Anthology; Anthology 1975 – 1984; Rising Deluxe Edition; A Light In The Black 1975-84*
A Light In The Black	*Rising; The Best Of Rainbow; Catch The Rainbow: The Anthology; Anthology 1975 – 1984; Rising Deluxe Edition; A Light In The Black 1975-84*
Tarot Woman (rough mix)	*Rising Deluxe Edition; A Light In The Black 1975-84*
Run With The Wolf (rough mix)	*Rising Deluxe Edition; A Light In The Black 1975-84*
Starstruck (rough mix)	*Rising Deluxe Edition*
Do You Close Your Eyes (rough mix)	*Rising Deluxe Edition*
Stargazer (rough mix)	*Rising Deluxe Edition; A Light In The Black 1975-84*
A Light In The Black (rough mix)	*Rising Deluxe Edition*

Blackmore has previously stated in interviews that 'Stargazer' was longer than the documented version and ended with a violin solo from one of the orchestra members, but the tape ran out and it wasn't captured for posterity. Although he is prone to winding journalists up with fanciful stories, it is perfectly logical, and might well explain why 'Gates Of Babylon' on the follow-up album finished that way creating the desired affect intended for 'Stargazer'. In 2014 the author spoke to Reinhold Mack (Musicland engineer) about this story. Whilst he could not remember, he did point out that if that had happened, he thought that logically they would have got the violinist to play it again and spliced it in later.

Tony Carey recalls doing two solos for 'A Light In The Black', but whether or not the tape has survived is unclear as the multitrack masters could not be located when the 2011 remastered edition was released.

There is a ¼" master from the Record Plant - where the album was mastered - that contains ten mixes of 'Tarot Woman': nine incomplete and one complete. The complete mix with different balances, effects etc. was used on the *A Light In The Black* box set.

The initial "rough" mixes done by Martin Birch included a keyboard solo intro to 'Stargazer'.

Santa Monica Auditorium, California, 24th March 1976 (The Sweet with Ritchie Blackmore)

Alright Now	*The Live EP*

Pirate Sound, Los Angeles, California, May 1976 +

Kill The King take 1	*unreleased*
Kill The King take 2	*unreleased*
Kill The King take 3	*unreleased*
Kill The King take 4	*unreleased*
Kill The King take 5	*unreleased*
Kill The King take 6	*unreleased*
Kill The King take 7	*unreleased*
Man On The Silver Mountain	*unreleased*
Mistreated take 1	*unreleased*
Mistreated take 2	*unreleased*
Mistreated take 3	*unreleased*
Mistreated take 4	*unreleased*
Mistreated take 5	*unreleased*
Keyboard Solo	*unreleased*
Stargazer take 1	*unreleased*

Stargazer take 2	*unreleased*
Stargazer take 3	*unreleased*
Stargazer take 4	*Rising Deluxe Edition*
A Light In The Black	*unreleased*
Still I'm Sad	*unreleased*
Drum Solo	*unreleased*

Pirate Sound, Los Angeles, California, 21st May 1976

Kill The King take 1	*unreleased*
Kill The King take 2	*unreleased*

These were recorded on a ninety minute Memorex tape, but it is unclear as to how long each run through lasts.

Pirate Sound, Los Angeles, California, 29th May 1976 ++

Rainbow Jam *	*unreleased*
Lazy intro	*unreleased*
Mistreated	*unreleased*
Chat / Jam	*unreleased*
Jam	*unreleased*
Chat	*unreleased*
Sixteenth Century Greensleeves	*unreleased*
Man On The Silver Mountain	*unreleased*
Keyboard Solo	*unreleased*
Blues Jam **	*unreleased*
Mistreated	*unreleased*
Jam	*unreleased*
Stargazer (partial)	*unreleased*

(Spread over two ninety minute tapes, but unclear as to how long the entire recording lasts).
Written on the tape box after 'Rainbow Jam' it says: "w/ John "Bonzo" Bonham (awesome)." After Man On The Silver Mountain it says: "(This is for u Bonzo ole kid) awesome." And after 'Blues Jam': "maybe Bonzo on drums (incredible)."

Pirate Sound, Los Angeles, California, May 1976

Kill The King	*unreleased*
Mistreated	*unreleased*
Sixteenth Century Greensleeves	*unreleased*
Catch The Rainbow	*unreleased*
Man On The Silver Mountain	*unreleased*
Stargazer	*unreleased*
A Light In The Black	*unreleased*
Drum Solo	*unreleased*
Still I'm Sad	*unreleased*

These recordings are rehearsals for the impending world tour and were made by sound engineer Robert Simon, Pirate Sound's proprietor, using overhead mics. It was during these that 'Kill The King' was worked out. Blackmore claims that they had tried rehearsing 'Tarot Woman' as the intended set opener, but he was not happy with the outcome, hence the reason for developing another song. The first recordings listed are likely to have all been done in one day, although rehearsals would have been for several days, so it is feasible that 'Tarot Woman' was rehearsed, but just not captured on tape. 'Do You Close Your Eyes' was developed the year before at rehearsals for the same purpose.
+ All of these recordings were unofficially released on a bootleg entitled *Tower Of Babel.*
* Led Zeppelin's John Bonham performs on 'Rainbow Jam'.
** Possibly features Bonham.
The last tape is a full dress rehearsal before the tour and logically was recorded after the first two rehearsals, so theoretically either 30th or 31st of the month, but this cannot be confirmed.
Simon: "Done right before the first live show. Excellent complete set. It was recorded from overhead mics placed above the rehearsal area on to cassette. The sound quality is excellent and well balanced as all can be heard."
++ All of the above information comes from the owner of the tapes who worked with Robert Simon and has them on cassettes. The date information that he provided is as written on the tape boxes. However, if Bonham does appear then the date must be incorrect. Although Led Zeppelin were in Los Angeles in May, Bonham, Plant and Page are documented as flying back to London on 26th with no evidence that Bonham returned by the 29th or indeed the following month.

Houston Music Hall Texas, USA, 10th July 1976 (Oyster records promotional film)

Man On The Silver Mountain	*Nightmoves, Live In Munich 1977 (re-issue)*
Stargazer	*Nightmoves, Live In Munich 1977 (re-issue)*
Light In The Black	*Nightmoves, Live In Munich 1977 (re-issue)*
Cozy Powell drum solo	*Nightmoves, Live In Munich 1977 (re-issue)*
Do You Close Your Eyes	*Nightmoves, Live In Munich 1977 (re-issue)*

All tracks are brief edits only. It is unknown if other songs from the concert were recorded. It's not unreasonable to suggest that everything was recorded from 'Man On The Silver Mountain' onwards, even if the full show wasn't. Searches for the complete film reels have so far come to naught and it is unlikely the rushes still exist.

Sporthalle, Cologne, Germany, 25th September 1976

Kill The King	*Live In Köln 1976*
Mistreated	*On Stage; Live In Köln 1976*
Sixteenth Century Greensleeves	*Live In Germany 76; Rainbow Family Album; Live In Köln 1976*
Catch The Rainbow	*Live In Köln 1976*
Man On The Silver Mountain	*Ritchie Blackmore Rock Profile Vol 2; Live In Köln 1976*
Stargazer	*Live In Germany 76; Live In Köln 1976*
Still I'm Sad	*Live In Germany 76; Live In Köln 1976*
Do You Close Your Eyes	*Live In Köln 1976*

The tapes for this show now reside at Abbey Road's archive.

Philipshalle, Düsseldorf, Germany, 27th September 1976

Kill The King	*Live In Düsseldorf 1976*
Mistreated	*Live In Düsseldorf 1976*
Sixteenth Century Greensleeves	*Live In Germany 76; Live In Düsseldorf 1976*
Catch The Rainbow	*Live In Düsseldorf 1976*
Man On The Silver Mountain	*Live In Düsseldorf 1976*
Stargazer	*Live In Düsseldorf 1976*
Still I'm Sad	*Live In Düsseldorf 1976*

The tapes for this show now reside at Abbey Road's archive.

Messezentrum Halle, Nuremberg, Germany, 28th September 1976

Kill The King	*Live In Nürnburg 1976*
Mistreated	*Live In Nürnburg 1976*
Sixteenth Century Greensleeves	*Live In Nürnburg 1976*
Catch The Rainbow	*Live In Nürnburg 1976*
Man On The Silver Mountain	*Live In Germany 76; Live In Nürnburg 1976*
Stargazer	*Live In Nürnburg 1976*
Still I'm Sad	*On Stage; Live In Nürnburg 1976*
Do You Close Your Eyes	*Live In Nürnburg 1976*

The tapes for this show now reside at Abbey Road's archive.

Circus Krone, Munich, Germany, 29th September 1976

Kill The King	*On Stage; Live In Germany 76; Rainbow Family Album*
Mistreated	*Live In Germany 76*
Sixteenth Century Greensleeves	*Ritchie Blackmore Rock Profile Vol 2*
Catch The Rainbow	*unreleased*
Man On The Silver Mountain	*unreleased*
Stargazer	*unreleased*
Still I'm Sad	*unreleased*
Do You Close Your Eyes	*Musikszene 1976, Live In Germany 1976*

The tapes for this show now reside at Abbey Road's archive. Of the four German shows recorded by Martin Birch, this one still remains unreleased in its entirety.

Koseinenkin Kaikan, Osaka, Japan, 8th December 1976

Kill The King	*unreleased*
Mistreated	*unreleased*
Sixteenth Century Greensleeves	*unreleased*
Catch The Rainbow	*unreleased*
Lazy	*unreleased*
Man On The Silver Mountain	*unreleased*

Stargazer	*unreleased*
Still I'm Sad	*unreleased*
Do You Close Your Eyes	*unreleased*

Koseinenkin Kaikan, Osaka, Japan, 9th December 1976

Kill The King	*unreleased*
Mistreated	*A Light In The Black 1975-84*
Sixteenth Century Greensleeves	*unreleased*
Catch The Rainbow*	*On Stage*
Purple Haze	*A Light In The Black 1975-84*
Lazy	*A Light In The Black 1975-84*
Man On The Silver Mountain	*A Light In The Black 1975-84*
Stargazer	*unreleased*
Still I'm Sad	*unreleased*

*Part released.

During his introduction to 'Sixteenth Century Greensleeves' Ronnie Dio dedicated it to Tommy Bolin.

Budokan, Tokyo, Japan, 16th December 1976 (Afternoon show)

Kill The King	*unreleased*
Mistreated	*unreleased*
Sixteenth Century Greensleeves	*unreleased*
Catch The Rainbow	*unreleased*
Man On The Silver Mountain	*On Stage*
A Light In The Black	*unreleased*
Still I'm Sad	*unreleased*

The only show recorded that included 'A Light In The Black'. Sadly the tapes have not been located.

Budokan, Tokyo, Japan, 16th December 1976 (Evening show)

Kill The King	*On Stage, On Stage Deluxe Version*
Mistreated	*On Stage Deluxe Version*
Sixteenth Century Greensleeves	*On Stage, On Stage Deluxe Version*
Catch The Rainbow	*On Stage, On Stage Deluxe Version*
Lazy	*On Stage Deluxe Version*
Man On The Silver Mountain	*On Stage Deluxe Version*
Blues	*On Stage, On Stage Deluxe Version*
Starstruck	*On Stage, On Stage Deluxe Version*
Stargazer	*unreleased*
Still I'm Sad	*unreleased*
Do You Close Your Eyes	*On Stage Deluxe Version*

Before Universal received the tapes to compile the *On Stage Deluxe Version*, they were in correspondence with Simon Robinson, who had previously been archiving them. He confirmed the following:

Having sorted through the archive the following Rainbow live material is all that has survived in the HEC vault:

8th December four reels

16th December four reels

+ one odd reel from 9th December

The reels do not state which of the two Tokyo shows the 16th is. Nor do we know if they are complete, although as there are four reels we hope so. All are at the studio currently being stabilised prior to archiving, as they are dodgy Ampex stock. We'll then be able to work out what's what.

Quite where the other reels ended up is a mystery to me.

As you suggested I think the best option here is to try and make a full show of alternate or unedited (if they were badly treated on *On Stage*) versions. I guess it's too much to hope 'A Light In The Black' is one of the tracks to have survived.

From Deep Purple to a totally new spectrum.
RITCHIE BLACKMORE'S
RAINBOW
Ritchie Blackmore. His guitar helped sell 14 million records in just one year.
Ritchie Blackmore. One of the founders and driving forces of the phenomenally successful group, Deep Purple.
Ritchie Blackmore's Rainbow. Because he decided to go in search of new colors. And found a totally new spectrum of sound.
Blackmore's superstar credentials and the advance word that precedes this album combine to make it one of the year's most eagerly anticipated releases for rock fans.
Rolling Stone, Crawdaddy, and the cover of Circus Magazine have already committed to Rainbow.
It's time for every store to stock and display this album. And keep their eye on the totally new spectrum on the horizon.
RITCHIE BLACKMORE'S
RAINBOW
POLYDOR
Ritchie Blackmore's
Rainbow
PD-6049
Polydor
Marketed by Polydor/Distributed by Phonodisc
Available in Canada through Polydor Ltd

Cash Box, 23/08/1975

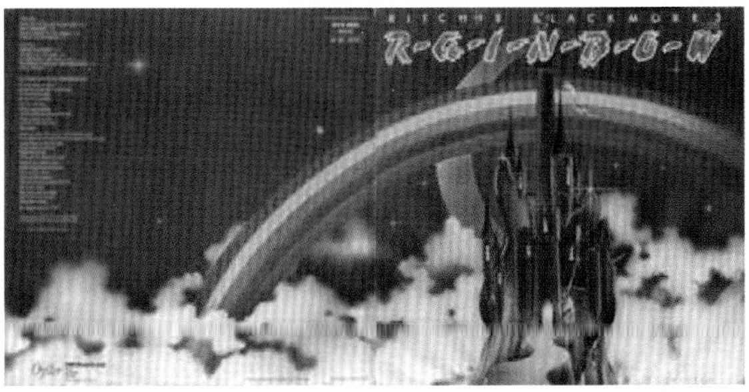

RITCHIE BLACKMORE'S RAINBOW album

charts	debut	peak	weeks	chart-runs & extra notes
UK (Music Week)	13/09/1975	11	8	13-11-33-36-34-58 (6 weeks from September 13th to October 18th 1975) Album reached no.11 on September 20th 1975. In Record Mirror LP reached no.11 too, but chart-run was slighty different. No.10 in NME. 8/08/1981: 91-99 (2 weeks)
USA (Billboard)	6/09/1975	30	15	79-64-54-44-37-35-31-30-64-88-91-109-107-103-192 (15 weeks from September 6th to December 13th 1975) Album reached no.30 on October 25th 1975. No.29 in Cash Box.
CANADA (RPM)	18/10/1975	83	3	91-83 14/02/1976: 96
DENMARK (Danmarks Radio Top 20)	10/09/1975	14	4	20-14-14-14 (4 weeks from September 10th to October 1st 1975) «Top 20» was the top twenty best-selling discs in Denmark. The "discs" refers to albums and singles both. Therefore, at one chart were listed a 45s and long-plays.
SWEDEN (Topplistan)	27/11/1975	24	4-bi-weeks	27/11/1975: 50 10/08/1976: 36 (Rainbow Rising no.48 in this time). 12/08/1977: 24-42 (2 bi-weeks)
JAPAN (Oricon)	21/10/1975	26	6	16,890 [LP] (sales numbers)
AUSTRALIA (Australian Music Report)	20/10/1975	55	12	
NEW ZEALAND (RIANZ)	21/11/1975	40	1	

UK: BPI award album by SILVER disc on November 1st 1975.

Ritchie Blackmore is proving that his departure from Deep Purple was not the artistic and financial disaster many predicted. Blackmore's "Rainbow" album, currently thirty-two with a bullet on the **Cash Box** album charts, sold 51,000 units the week of Oct. 4 and a thus far total of 257,982 units . . .

Cash Box 18/10/1975

Man On The Silver Mountain single

JAPAN (All Japan Pop 20)	21/12/1975	27	8	
AUSTRALIA (Australian Music Report)	1/03/1976	81	5	

charts	debut	peak	weeks	chart-runs & extra notes

RAINBOW RISING album

charts	debut	peak	weeks	chart-runs & extra notes
UK (Record Mirror)	5/06/1976	11	33	50-11-18-13-16-22-28-37-49-33-37-40-45-51-29-51-40-35-52-45-36-57 (22 weeks from June 5th to October 30th 1976) Album reached no.11 on June 12th 1976. No.15 in NME. In 1980 Rainbow Rising re-rising over charts! 23/02/1980: 72-56-63-62-53-64-64 (7 weeks from February 23rd to April 5th 1980; at this time band toured in UK and a new album Down To Earth and hit-single All Night Long were also in charts). 19/04/1980: 73 (1 more week) 8/08/1981: 75-86-62 (3 weeks from August 8th to August 22nd 1981) In total 33 weeks on charts.
USA (Billboard)	5/06/1976	48	18	128-90-78-66-56-48-48-86-85-81-79-77-97-95-93-103-178-179 (18 weeks from June 5th to October 2nd 1976) Album reached no.48 for 2 weeks on July 10th & 17th 1976. No.54 in Record World, no.76 in Cash Box.
CANADA (RPM)	19/06/1976	17	20	93-83-76-72-58-35-33-23-19-17-31-41-48-86-82-81-73-72-70-85 (20 weeks from June 19th to October 30th 1976) Album reached no.17 on August 21st 1976.
GERMANY (Der Musikmarkt)	15/07/1976	38	4 months	43-44-39-38 (from July 15th to October 15th 1976)
SWITZERLAND (Der Musikmarkt)	15/07/1976	13	6 half-months	21-20-13-20-22-25 (6 half-months from July 15th to October 1st 1976)
DENMARK (Danmarks Radio Top 20)	16/06/1976	17	4	16/06/1976: 18-20 4/08/1976: 17-17
SWEDEN (Topplistan)	22/06/1976	23	4-bi-weeks	27-23 (2 bi-weeks - June 22nd & July 6th - then between July 6th and August 10th chart wasn't compiled) 10/08/1976: 48 21/09/1976: 44 Album reached no.23 on July 6th 1976.
JAPAN (Oricon)	21/06/1976	12	13	34,360 [LP] (sales numbers)
AUSTRALIA (Australian Music Report)	12/07/1976	33	34	
NEW ZEALAND (RIANZ)	9/07/1976	36	3	36-40-38 (3 weeks from July 9th to 23rd 1976)
UK (Official Charts)	12/03/2011	163	1	Deluxe-Edition No.7 in UK Rock chart.

UK: BPI award album by SILVER disc on September 1st 1976 and by GOLD disc on October 3rd 1979.

Polydor Inks With Oyster

NEW YORK — Polydor Incorporated has signed a long term licensing agreement with Oyster Records for worldwide distribution and marketing. Oyster artists included in the initial agreement are Blackmore's Rainbow, whose just released "Rainbow Rising" album was the first under the new deal; Roger Glover, whose album is set for a release shortly and Ian Gillian, whose "Child In Time" album is slated for release early this month. Also included in the arrangement are the English recording group The Strawbs.

cash box 12/06/1976

charts	debut	peak	weeks	chart-runs & extra notes

Starstruck single

GERMANY (Der Musikmarkt Radio Chart)	15/09/1976	42	1 half-month	Airplay chart, not sales.
NETHERLANDS (Free 40 Top 10)	6/11/1976	1	5	Also airplay chart.

RAINBOW ON STAGE live album

UK (Record Mirror)	30/07/1977	7	10	16-7-10-13-23-30-36-54-50-55 (10 weeks from July 30th to October 1st 1977) Album reached no.7 on August 6th 1977. No.14 in NME.
USA (Billboard)	16/07/1977	65	9	108-96-85-75-69-65-77-107-175 (9 weeks from July 16th to September 10th 1977) Album reached no.65 on August 20th 1977. No.76 in Record World, no.86 in Cash Box.
GERMANY (Der Musikmarkt)	15/08/1977	28	5 half-months	39-28-33-33-40 (5 half-months from August 15th to October 15th 1977)
AUSTRIA (Der Musikmarkt)	15/09/1977	15	1 month	
SWITZERLAND (Der Musikmarkt)	1/08/1977	15	5 half-months	1/08/1977: 18 (then 1 half-month drop-off from charts) 1/09/1977: 15-24-25 (3 half-months from September 1st to October 1st 1977, then again 1 half-month off-charts) 1/11/1977: 19
NETHERLANDS (Nationale Hitparade)	6/08/1977	17	3	18-17-19 (3 weeks from August 6th to 20th 1977)
SWEDEN (Topplistan)	15/07/1977	25	4-bi-weeks	30-25-27 (3 bi-weeks from July 15th to August 12th 1977) 9/9/1977: 48
FINLAND (Suosikki)	Oct/1977	20	1 month	Sisältää hitin book given info that album no.21 (but this is the result of combining information from different sources, in Intro magazine no.23).
JAPAN (Oricon)	15/07/1977	6	13	39,810 [LP] (sales numbers)
AUSTRALIA (Australian Music Report)	15/08/1977	22	10	
NEW ZEALAND (RIANZ)	18/11/1977	29	1	

UK: BPI award album by SILVER disc on August 15th 1977.

Chart information compiled by Aleksey Kononow.

RITCHIE BLACKMORE'S
R-A-I-N-B-O-W
The sensational debut album
by the ex-lead guitarist of Deep Purple
RITCHIE BLACKMORE'S RAINBOW
Oyster Records
Marketed by EMI Records
Album OYA 2001
Cassette TC-OYA 2001
Cartidge 8X-OYA 2001

Oyster

Although Blackmore had left Deep Purple, he was still contracted to the organisation. So the story goes, Oyster Records was set up to appease Blackmore as he wanted to avoid association with Deep Purple where possible, and didn't want Rainbow to appear on Purple Records. However, it was more a case that the need for the new label was due to the complex system operated by Deep Purple (Overseas) Ltd. that effectively resulted in Oyster Records Ltd., a subsidiary of Purple Records Ltd. being created and incorporated on 24th April 1975, less than three weeks after Blackmore's last Deep Purple show.

Billboard magazine (14th June 1975) reported that Purple had gained a reputation as a heavy label, and Oyster was intended to bring in a bit of balance. *Music Week* clarified matters on the same date by revealing that Purple would be kept solely for Deep Purple's own records in future and that records by all other Purple label signings would come out on Oyster with the view of projecting the label to the industry with a different image.

It also reported that the design of the label was causing problems and if they weren't solved the label might be dropped. This little news story seems rather odd, which if I have read into it correctly suggests that the graphics department was struggling to get the desired visual effect – the inside and outside of an oyster shell on the a and b sides, possibly inspired by The Beatles' Apple label design. But to imply that the label would have been dropped because of that does seem somewhat strange. Surely a revised design could have simply been created?

As a subsidiary to Purple Records, Oyster Records Ltd. was distributed in Europe (and also Mexico, Australia and New Zealand) through EMI.

Oyster can't really be considered Rainbow's label, but it is worth including here because of the reason for its creation and that it was a relatively small and short-lived label that is not worthy of its own book.

The label's first releases were scheduled for Friday 15th August 1975 – Rainbow's debut album, plus two singles by different artists, which despite the sequential catalogue numbers were released in reverse order one week after the other.

For America, as had been the case with Purple Records, the matter was somewhat different. When Purple Records was launched in 1971, initially a deal was done in the States with Capitol Records, who pressed up three nifty promotional singles of three of the first acts on the label, all on purple vinyl in custom purple record bags, with custom purple Capitol labels. Deep Purple itself continued to be released on Warner Bros. By 1974 when Warner switched to the Burbank label design, Purple's releases also included the Purple Records logo on the label, albeit, horizontal.

However, concerning America, trouble was afoot following Ritchie's departure from Purple. In fact, whilst Deep Purple (Overseas) Ltd. was in the process of setting up both Oyster Records and an American record deal for Blackmore's new album, they hadn't even informed Warner Bros. that Blackmore had left the band! On discovering the news, Warner Bros. president Joe Smith wrote a rather irate letter to John Coletta, dated 29th May '75 outlining his embarrassment that he had not been informed of Blackmore's departure or that MGM artists Elf had also ceased to be. As detailed in the section on the first Rainbow album, Elf had recorded their third and final album, *Trying To Burn The Sun*, at the start of the year, but like *Ritchie Blackmore's Rainbow*, the album had yet to be released.

Initially no deal was done to license Oyster in America (or Canada and Japan), instead, the Rainbow album was licensed to Polydor for those territories.

As a business entity, Purple Records had never achieved any success outside of the band itself. In fact, in a letter to John Coletta in December 1975, accountant Bill Reid pointed out that Purple Records had still to make a profit. All its other releases had largely been ignored, despite large sums of money invested into them. Whilst the remit from day one, with the company slogan "the open ear", was to embrace an eclectic array of acts across numerous genres, for the other artists, being associated with one of the foremost heavy rock bands often meant that in general the media shunned them and most records sold in very small quantities.

Oyster was always destined to be a strange beast. John Coletta said at the time, that the remit was to switch those artists over to the new label; "Oyster Records provides the opportunity to altar that impression and so broaden our musical horizons," he explained.

With the debut album from Ritchie Blackmore imminent, the UK press release also said that Oyster

Oyster catch a Rainbow

THIS WEEK a new label, Oyster Records, is launched. Its managing director will be John Colletta, already managing director of Purple Records. Oyster will handle all future release from the Purple Organisation except Deep Purple who will record exclusively for Purple Records.

John Colletta said this week: "In the past artists, other than Deep Purple who had records released on Purple Records were often wrongly categorised by the media before their records were even listened to simply because they recorded for what was supposedly a predominantly heavy label. Oyster Records provides the opportunity to alter that impression and so broaden our musical horizons.

"Ritchie Blackmore's departure from Deep Purple provides Oyster with its first album. Ritchie Blackmore's Rainbow has its first LP released this week. The band comprises Blackmore and former members of ELF although former ELF bassist Craig Gruber who is featured on the LP has now been replaced in the group by Jimmy Bain from British band Harlot. In addition, on August 15, Oyster release a first single 'Strawberry Fields' the old Beatles classic given a new treatment by Natural Magic.

Tony Ashton's 'Resurrection Shuffle' follows as the next single on August 22, emphasising the diversity of musical styles that the new label will present. Future releases from Oyster will include albums from former Purple people Ian Gillan and Roger Glover.

TONY ASHTON: 'RESURECTION SHUFFLE' (OYSTER).
I'LL GIVE you a really interesting pun here — it's a pearl of a record on Oyster, right? A definite hit, there's no two ways about it I love this record. They've changed the artists' name 'cos it used to be Ashton, Gardner and Dyke, but no way can it fail. I've played it often at home believe it or not. Good for you Tony, keep doing it, please. Make another one like it. Love it to death.

POP

STARLINERS: Weekend Girl (Oyster OYR 104). 'How does it feel to be down at the disco on a Friday night/When the weekend comes and your lessons are over everything's alright?' . . . move over Rollers, here come a third-generation Liverpool band with a tune and a lyric precision-engineered for maximum sales appeal in the 10-14-year-old female market. The rest of us will cringe, but for the nymphets, it's bang on target. John Peel should keep a plentiful supply in his glovebox.

■ STARLINERS

would be releasing albums by Ian Gillan and Roger Glover amongst its roster. Hardly a broadening of musical horizons there, and at this juncture, logically keeping other former Purple members on the parent label was surely more commercially and artistically sensible? That said, kick-starting Oyster with a number of established names was potentially a financial right move for the new label even though it contradicted the suggestion that they wanted Oyster to be devoid of the "heavy" image.

As members of Deep Purple, Blackmore, Lord, Paice, Gillan and Glover had all been issued with shares amounting to one fifth of 26% of the equity of Purple Records Ltd. when it was created in 1971. As Oyster was now a division of Purple, Reid pointed out that it presented other problems. Part of the manufacturing and distribution deal with EMI Records specifically stated that it would apply to any other label set up by Purple — A totally reasonable contract clause that prevented another record label from escaping from the obligations to EMI under the Purple Records deal.

But this system presented problems when Glover and Gillan left the group. In the case of Glover, he was still employed as an A & R man for the label so he continued to benefit. Ian Gillan however had not only left the group but in effect the company and his share of equity was to be transferred to the remaining three members.

With Blackmore having now left Deep Purple, and his new project to be released on Oyster Records, Reid pointed out that whilst it was still perfectly reasonable for him to receive a share of Purple Records in respect of the albums that he had contributed to, it made no sense for him to benefit on forthcoming Purple releases on the parent label that he would not be making any contribution to. Coletta had already agreed that Blackmore would have one fifth of 26% of shares in Oyster Records Ltd.

This section of the book covers all the known Oyster releases, which means that Rainbow's 1975 North American and Japanese releases are not included but can be found elsewhere in the book.

Gillan band

IAN GILLAN, former Deep Purple vocalist, has announced his return from the motorbike showrooms to the rock stage with a hot-shot new band.

The working title which could well be changed (and maybe could do with it!) is Gillan's Shand Grenade.

The line-up is Johnny Gustafson (ex-Roxy, bass and vocals), Mark Nauseef (ex-Elf and Rainbow, percussions), Mike Norman (keyboards) and Ray Fenwick (lead guitar) with Gillan singing and writing most of the material.

The band are going into the studios in January to record an album for release to coincide with a projected March tour of the UK. They begin rehearsals for their live show in Paris at the end of January.

Meanwhile the existence of a 'Deep Purple Live In France' album has been confirmed. The suggestion that Richie Blackmore's refusal to help with overdubs was delaying its release was denied by Purple Music who say that there are no problems, it will be released but that "the time is not right."

Kokomo to

KOKOMO WILL full-scale UK tou though no dates confirmed. La augmented thei with three date venues.

IAN GILLAN'S BACK
YOU'D BETTER BELIEVE IT!
THE EX DEEP PURPLE VOCALIST
HAS FORMED HIS OWN BAND
AND RECORDED
A SUPERB DEBUT ALBUM
THE IAN GILLAN BAND
'CHILD IN TIME'
ON OYSTER
RECORDS AND TAPES
Oyster

Oyster (EMI distributed releases)

UK discography

Singles

OYR 101	22nd August 1975	**Tony Ashton**: Resurrection Shuffle / Ballad Of Mr Giver
OYR 102	15th August 1975	**Natural Magic**: Strawberry Fields Forever / Isolated Lady
OYR 103	10th October 1975	**Rainbow**: Man On The Silver Mountain / Snake Charmer
OYR 104	30th January 1976	**Starliners**: Weekend Girl / Kiss Me Once More
OYR 105	20th February 1976	**Reflections**: Whenever I'm Away From You / I Can Only Love You

Both the test pressing and the promotional copy of OYR 103 credits the record to Ritchie Blackmore, only the commercial release credits it to Ritchie Blackmore's Rainbow.

OYR101 is credited to Tony Ashton although the a-side is actually Ashton's song as performed by Ashton Gardner & Dyke. The b-side is from his joint collaboration *First Of The Big Bands* album with Jon Lord and is credited to both although the latter's name is spelt John. It was also released in a picture sleeve and was the only one of the five singles released in the UK that was.

'Natural Magic' [OYR 102] was a joint collaboration between Eddie Hardin and Roger Glover.

Very little is known about the short-lived band, The Starliners, but according to their bassist in a message on 45cat.com, OYR 104 was recorded in the Marquee Studios and the band stayed in the Inverness Court Hotel and rehearsed in Shepperton Studios and their P.R was Peter Frolick of Purple Records.

To the best of my knowledge, apart from OYR 103, the only other single to be issued outside of the UK was OYR 101 which was released in Portugal as 8E 006-96 933 MG. The b-side of that release is also credited solely to Tony Ashton, unlike the UK version.

A very rare white label test pressing and the demo copy of the debut Rainbow single, both of which credit it solely to Ritchie Blackmore, whereas the commercial release credits it to Ritchie Blackmore's Rainbow.

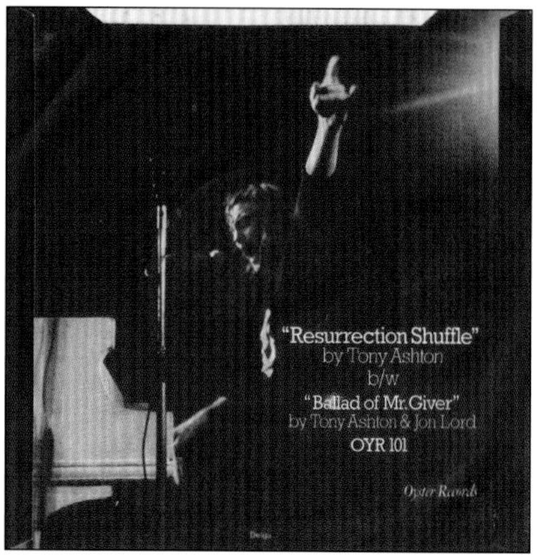

The Tony Ashton release was the only one of the 5 UK EMI distributed singles to be released in a picture sleeve.

A record store window display for the album. Those posters would be hard to find these days.

Album

OYA 2001	15th August 1975	**Rainbow**: Ritchie Blackmore's Rainbow
TC-OYA 2001	15th August 1975	**Rainbow**: Ritchie Blackmore's Rainbow (cassette)
8X-OYA 2001	15th August 1975	**Rainbow**: Ritchie Blackmore's Rainbow (8-track cartridge)

I have listed the cassette and 8-track catalogue numbers for this release. Although all the later Oyster albums (see further on) were released on cassette, the 8-track releases, which were always more popular in America, were soon phased out.

UK pressings of both the album and the single were pressed up for export to Denmark as well. Whilst the album had a completely different catalogue number (6C 062-96787), the single had the same, but unlike the UK version it was released with a picture sleeve, which was commonplace in mainland Europe. This particular release was probably only a small pressing of a few hundred and is one of the rarest versions of the single to be found today.

Ritchie's records

I HAVE bought about three albums by Ritchie Blackmore, all being Rainbow! I have had to take them all back, and they were bought from different shops. Has anyone else had any trouble on this Oyster label — many of my friends have. Could I please have an address to send off a complaint to, so that I can get a decent record? It is so disappointing, because this is truly an excellent album. — **Fay, London.**

SPEAKING as a self-confessed Ritchie Blackmore fanatic, I am obviously interested in collecting any recordings made in his pre Deep Purple days. Are there any such recordings available? — **Tony Shelley, Leicester.**

■ **First, the faulty records: when we spoke to Oyster they were very apologetic and said if you return your copy to them at 25 Newman Street, London W1, they will replace it for you.**

We have not been able to trace any recordings made by Ritchie Blackmore previous to his Deep Purple days, although he did a lot of work in Germany and there may be some with German groups. He has also recorded with Screaming Lord Sutch and Dave Berry, and if you write to Oyster at the above address they will be able to forward your letter to his agent to find out if there are any copies available of these early recordings.

Over the Rainbow

RECENTLY, I managed to scrape enough cash together to get Ritchie Blackmore's 'Rainbow' album. So, I rushed home and played it, and all went well until I got to side two, track two — 'Temple Of The King', when a fuzz came on, occuring on every revolution like a scratch.

So I exchanged the faulty record at the shop, which is rather out of the way, but very cheap, and they exchanged it. But I then discovered that the replacement also had the same fault.

The next day I had to go off on holiday and came back a week and a half later to find that I couldn't comply with the shop's return conditions. The record had to be back within a week if I were to get a refund. — **Stewart Cameron, Edinburgh.**

■ **No shop is entitled to come out with return conditions like the "one week" restriction which you mention. If an album is faulty when you buy it, you have every right to return it and exchange it for another record or ask for a refund. I think that it is reasonable to return a record within two weeks of purchase. Try taking it back to the shop again — if you have no luck wrap it up and parcel it off to the Customer Liaison Officer, Phonodisc Sales Ltd, Clyde Works, Grove Road, Romford, Essex. They will carry out a test and report on your dodgy album and send you a new copy.**

EMI appeared to have some pressing issues with Blackmore's album if the press coverage is anything to go by.

Non-UK releases

This is where things start to get a bit strange but also fascinating for collectors. Throughout the majority of Europe the album was released with the same basic catalogue number of 96 787. As was EMI's convention, each European country's catalogue number had a unique prefix; 1C was Germany, 2C, France etc followed by either 062 or 064. Sweden however used the UK catalogue number.

It's further afield where unusual variations occurred. New Zealand used the UK catalogue number but the initial release used the Purple Records label. To this day I have yet to ascertain as to why this would have been the case. The rear sleeve clearly indicates that it is on Oyster. Given the apparent problems they had with the label's design, I can only surmise that the artwork hadn't reached New Zealand in time to go to press, so the Purple label was used instead. A New Zealand pressing with the correct Oyster label also exists, which gives credence to my suggestion, but it's unlikely that this mystery will ever be unravelled.

Israel also used the OYA2001 catalogue number but also with the Purple Records logo, albeit a totally different design than elsewhere.

Venezuela went one step further and did actually release it as a bona fide Purple Records release, complete with a conventional Venezuelan Purple Records catalogue number.

'Man On The Silver Mountain' / 'Snake Charmer' was the standard single release in most territories. Along with the album, here are the other known releases of both:

The rare UK pressed release specifically for Denmark.

Brazillian release.

Israeli release: Black or red, it's Purple, but it's still also Oyster according to the catalogue numbers.

Both New Zealand releases. It is unclear how many were made with the Purple label but it's very rare nevertheless. Also note that the A-side with the Oyster label actually uses the design that should be for the b-side.

Overseas Discography – Country by country

Album

Ritchie Blackmore's Rainbow:
1C 062-96 787, Germany
2C 062-96 787, France
3C 064-96787, Italy
4 C 064-96787, Belgium
5C 062-96787, Netherlands
6C 062-96787, Denmark (see page 206)
OYA 2001, Sweden
8E 064-96787, Portugal
J 064-96.787, Spain
2J064-96787, Greece
LSOY 73023, Yugoslavia (released via the State label Jugoton)
OYA 2001, Israel
OYL-42001, Brazil
SLEM 628, Mexico
PLPS-4011, Venezuela
OYA 2001, New Zealand
OYA-2001, Australia

French release

Singles

Man On The Silver Mountain / Snake Charmer:
1 C 006-97 061, Germany
2C 010-97061, France
4C 006-97061, Belgium
5C 006-97061, Netherlands
8E 006-97061 F, Portugal
1 J 006-97061, Spain
OYR 103, Denmark (see page 206)
SOY 88876, OYR 103, Yugoslavia (released via the State label Jugoton)
OYR-11006, Australia (Released 27th January 1976)
EMI also released this single in Guatemala, sometime between 1978-83 on a standard EMI label design, with the catalogue number of EMI 4178.

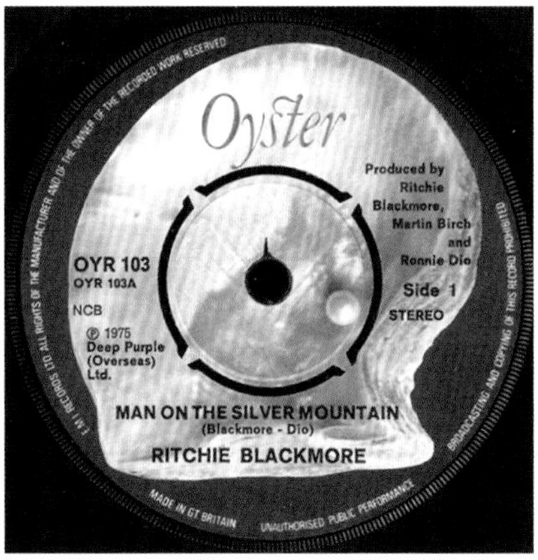

The very rare UK pressed Danish release in a picture sleeve. The label credits it to Ritchie Blackmore. Given that the album had been released two months prior, and that the sleeve (probably printed in Denmark) credit it as Ritchie Blackmore's Rainbow, it is odd that the label was printed that way.

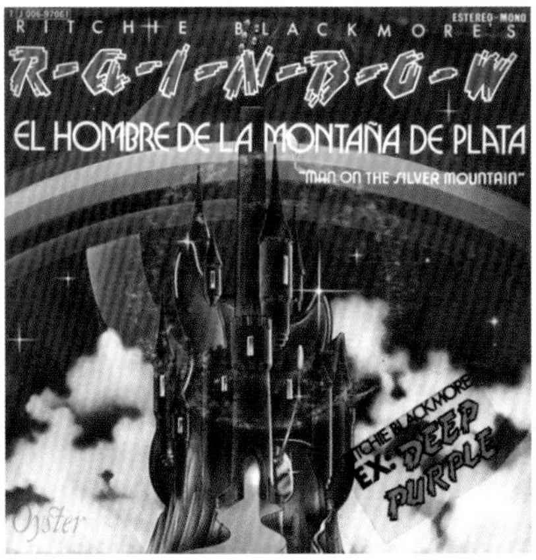

Spanish cover

3C 006-97224 1975 Still I'm Sad / Temple Of The King

This coupling was unique to Italy.

OYR 099 1975 Temple Of The King / Snake Charmer

4PUR 9005 1975 Temple Of The King / Snake Charmer

Once again New Zealand used the Purple label with an Oyster catalogue number but it was also issued in a Purple Records bag. As with the album, it was a bona fide Purple Records release in Venezuela.

Oyster
polydor
MARKETED BY POLYDOR INCORPORATED
STRAWBS
Thames

Oyster
STRAWBS
polydor

Oyster
IAN GILLAN BAND
polydor

Oyster (Polydor distributed releases)

On 1st April 1976, a three year worldwide deal was struck whereby Deep Purple (Overseas) Ltd. licensed all future Oyster label recordings to Polydor to market and distribute. Rainbow had initially signed with Polydor for America but now an agreement was in place to supply albums, not only from Rainbow, but also Ian Gillan, Roger Glover and interestingly Deep Purple, plus Strawbs in exchange for hefty advances, all under the Oyster imprint. In the case of each artist it's worth mentioning that the contract specified required constituents. In the case of Rainbow, both Blackmore and Dio; in the case of Deep Purple both Lord and Paice, and in the case of Strawbs, Dave Cousins.

The latter — often mistakenly referred to as The Strawbs had previously scored a big UK hit in 1973 with 'Part Of The Union'. Written by band members Richard Hudson and John Ford, they left shortly after its release and had their own success as simply Hudson and Ford ('Pick Up The Pieces' and later as The Monks with 'Nice Legs Shame About The Face'). Strawbs continued with Dave Cousins at the helm and Chas Cronk and Rod Coombes replacing the departed duo and as a band with some considerable stature were a fine addition to the label.

Roger Glover — who had become an A & R man for Purple Records following his departure from Purple — had played bass on Dave Cousins' 1972 solo album *Two Weeks Last Summer* and may well have been the conduit for signing the band. Interestingly, in March 1975, when interviewed by Pete Makowski for *Sounds* about the music he was listening to, Blackmore replied, "I've been a bit narrow minded really. I listen to a few groups, I listen to Paul Rodgers singing, I think Robin Trower came out with a few new things, I also listen to the Strawbs a lot. They're a much better band than I thought they were. The *Hero And Heroine* album was brilliant, it's a pity that wasn't a hit." Was it just coincidence that Strawbs ended up on Oyster?

The Oyster deal struck between Deep Purple (Overseas) Ltd. and Polydor promised to supply at least one album per year for three years for all the label's signings. Rainbow's advance amounted to $200,000 per album with lesser amounts for the other artists. The advance for Deep Purple was $175,000 per album because USA, Canada and Japan were excluded as Warner Bros. still had the band under contract for those territories, with a potential $400,000 for all territories once Purple were free from their obligation with Warner Bros.

Of course, Purple had effectively ceased to be after the last performance in March, although no announcements were made until July. However, Polydor did end up getting the spin off band Paice Ashton Lord, albeit minus USA, Canada and Japan where Warner Bros. still retained the rights.

It is peculiar that Oyster was supposedly set up partly so that some of the Purple Records artists could be transferred to it in order to hopefully give them a greater chance of exposure without being associated with a label of heavy rock, yet in effect Oyster had now become the home for all Purple members solo work. As you will see in the discography, aside from those in the contract, recordings by Coverdale and Lord were also released on Oyster, albeit in specific territories only, as some of them were not part of the agreement with Polydor and were often licensed to various different labels around the world.

In reality, however, it all proved to be somewhat academic. In January '78, just twenty months on, an agreement was made between Deep Purple (Overseas) Ltd. and Polydor to cease the label. The former had supplied insufficient recordings to allow Polydor to recoup the monies paid. Ian Gillan broke away from Purple's management and in doing so signed a new deal with Chris Blackwell's Island label.

From herein, Rainbow's third album appeared on a standard Polydor label. The earlier Rainbow albums, as well as Paice Ashton Lord's *Malice In Wonderland* were re-issued at later dates with new catalogue numbers but still used the Oyster branding even though the label had technically ceased.

Roger Glover's *Elements* — which was earmarked for Oyster — was released worldwide on Polydor whilst Strawbs switched to Arista. The separation between Polydor and Oyster was mirrored by a split between Purple's managers Tony Edwards and John Coletta. Whilst they still had to do business together under the banner of the numerous companies that they both had stakes in, their relationship had become strained. Coletta had set up Seabreeze Productions and managed David Coverdale, whereas Tony Edwards created the label Safari, which aside from releasing Glenn Hughes' debut solo album, also put out re-issues from Elf, Roger Glover and Jon Lord. Edwards later set up another label, Connoisseur Collection. It released several albums from the Purple family, including previously unreleased live albums from both Purple and Rainbow.

One final oddity was a 1980 release in New Zealand by Australian Joe Dolce. There was a standard Polydor release of his awful 'Shaddup You Face' that was a number one hit in Britain the following year, but some were pressed up with Oyster on the label which could possibly have been initially used in error.

Gillan: not Deep enough

IAN GILLAN BAND: 'Child In Time' (Oyster 249 0136) ***

MAYBE THE storming excellence of one-time Purple stablemate Ritchie Blackmore's Rainbow's second album has prejudiced by ability to enjoy this, Ian Gillan's debut solo LP, I don't know. But after listening to 'Child In Time' a few times, the word that springs most readily to mind is 'disappointing'.

After he left Deep Purple in 1973, vocalist Ian Gillan had no intention of returning to the rock music business. He felt 'totally drained' and went about pursuing more conventional business interests. But, ultimately, the pull proved to be too strong and after a few attempts at recording a pure solo LP, Gillan began to assemble a group of musicians around him with the objective of recording a more band-orientated album, 'Child In Time' being the end result.

Today, the Ian Gillan Band comprises, besides Gillan himself, guitarist Ray Fenwick (ex-Spencer Davis), bassist John Gustafson (one-time Roxy Music), Mark Nauseef (ex-Velvet Underground and Elf) on drums and Colin Towns, keyboards.

Impressive enough credentials, but the album, produced by Roger Glover, really fails to get off the ground. In the accompanying biography Gillan lays claim to the fact that his voice has improved over the years, but there's little evidence of it here. Certainly, in the context of this rather more laid back and tasteful band, his vocals are better-paced and impeccably phrased, but the world-renowned silver-throated Gillan scream is not in as much evidence as, I suspect, more listeners would want.

This is typified on the title track itself, 'Child In Time', which pales drastically when compared to the versions on Purple's 'In Rock' and 'Made In Japan' albums. Atmospheric enough, it nonetheless fails to build in intensity and certainly possesses none of the manic drive that steams out of the grooves of the 'In Rock' version.

That said, there's still plenty here to satisfy the long-frustrated Purple fan — especially the opening track, 'Lay Me Down', which is in the fine 'Fireball' and 'Strange Kind of Woman' tradition. But, generally, the songs have little shape or definite form and fade unceremoniously when they end.

The final result, I think, is rather akin to Bad Company — good enough, but failing to approach the heights of Free's musical ability and originality. With the Gillan Band, you'll probably spin this album, think 'Mmmm . . . OK', and then dive straight for your copy of 'In Rock' to see how it used to be done. — **Geoff Barton.**

pic by Steve Emberton

GILLAN: disappointing

album and he may well be the next most famous name in rock after the Rolling Stones but I've never heard a whisper of him before. And it transpires that he provides 40 minutes worth listening to intently from start to finish including a few really attractive items that persuaded me to put it in my posterity pile rather than the chuckouts.

It's the words that make him different. This is an American dole queue: 'some of them got sheepskins and PHDs/It's a sorry situation that you can't avoid/When you're over educated and unemployed.' There's a comic song about a father and daughter team who bump off lodgers to steal their cars, and a couple of touching love songs, 'Old Fashioned (straight romantic) and 'That's What Friends Are For' (bitter-sweet irony about a guy trapped in love with a girl who's his 'best friend' and doesn't fancy him).

A couple of the tracks are clever without a lot to say or any true shafts of wit (like 'Banana Republics') but mostly he's very enjoyable in an area with Nilsson, Randy Newman and Harry Chapin and its perameters.

Though the music isn't remarkable Goodman's guitar, Jeff Gutcheon's piano and various fiddlers often make it sparkle. — **Phil Sutcliffe.**

Think . . . Feel' replete with

OYSTER RECORDS have signed a three-year distribution and marketing deal with Polydor. Among the first albums from Oyster are Ritchie Blackmore's 'Rainbow Rising', the Ian Gillan Band's first album, 'Child In Time', Roger Glover's follow-up to 'The Butterfly Ball', and a new Strawbs album. The Strawbs album is the first of a three-record deal recently signed and the album is currently being finished at the Manor Studios.

Ritchie Blackmore's Rainbow album is released at last this week. This new LP is being distributed by Polydor, not EMI, so we lose out on that beautiful pastel-coloured Oyster record label. Its substitute is a boring ol' customised red Polydor logo. The music is GREAT, however . . .

ROGER GLOVER is now rehearsing for an album which he will be recording in Germany next month. Meanwhile, 'Love Is All' from the Butterfly Ball, which features Roger, is being released as a single next weekend by Oyster.

Gillan spring tour

IAN GILLAN's band is being launched with an extensive tour of France this month and is expected to play Britain in late spring.

They have dropped their working title of 'Shand Grenade' and as the plain Ian Gillan band open in Toulouse on April 14 with 13 gigs following inside two weeks.

They also have an album called 'Child In Time' expected to be released in the UK in May on the Oyster label (shared by Ritchie Blackmore's Rainbow).

The band's line-up is Ray Fenwick (ex-Spencer Davis, guitar), John Gustaffson (ex-Roxy and Big Three, bass), Mickey Lee Soule (ex-Elf, keyboards), Mark Nauseef (ex-Velvet Underground and Elf, percussion).

UK discography

All UK releases are listed in order of catalogue number (not release dates). Accurate release dates are given based on contemporary information, not retro data such as the notoriously unreliable Wikipedia! However, even contemporary data can be contradictory. Oyster's own *Rising* press release says June although it came out in May.

Singles

2066 699	13th August 1976	**Great**: Oh Wot A Big One / G.W.R
2066 705	30th July 1976	**Strawbs**: I Only Want My Love To Grow In You / (Wasting My Time) Thinking Of You
2066 744	29th October 1976	**Strawbs**: Charmer / Beside The Rio Grande
2066 818	20th May 1977	**Strawbs**: Back In The Old Routine / Burning For Me
2066 845	26th August 1977	**Rainbow:** Live - Kill The King / Man On The Silver Mountain / Mistreated
2066 846	19th August 1977	**Strawbs**: Keep On Trying / Simple Visions
POSP 274	10th July 1981	**Rainbow:** Live - Kill The King / Man On The Silver Mountain / Mistreated

As you can see, the OY prefix numbering system was not used for the UK or indeed the rest of Europe. Polydor just stuck with their regular numbering system. In fact, the Oyster font was also used in a secondary way on some single releases, and all the Strawbs releases also came in standard Polydor record bags, giving the impression that Oyster was merely an afterthought.

Aside from Strawbs, Great was one that came to Deep Purple (Overseas) Ltd. through their connections with British Lion Films, one of the many businesses that the Purple management team had a vested interest in. The two tracks composed by Jonathan Hodge are from the 1975, twenty-eight-minute Oscar winning animation film about Isambard Kingdom Brunel, distributed by British Lion. The single is a DP (O) Ltd. production and definitely the most obscure release on the label.

A press report in May '76 suggested that a Roger Glover single from *The Butterfly Ball* was scheduled for release but it never materialised. The re-issue of Rainbow's 'Live' EP after the label was defunct, still included the Oyster imprint, hence why it is included.

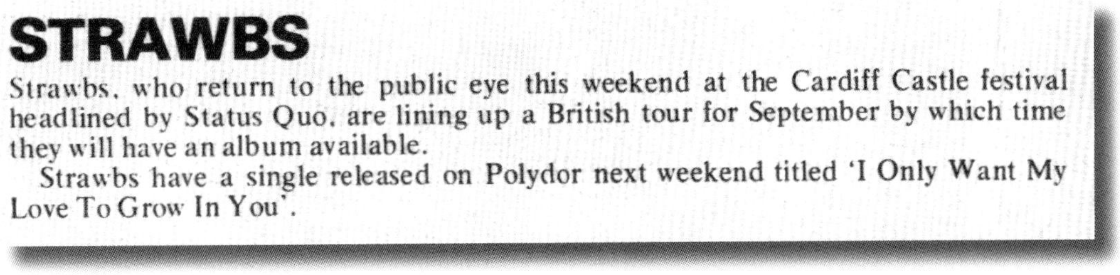

STRAWBS

Strawbs, who return to the public eye this weekend at the Cardiff Castle festival headlined by Status Quo, are lining up a British tour for September by which time they will have an album available.

Strawbs have a single released on Polydor next weekend titled 'I Only Want My Love To Grow In You'.

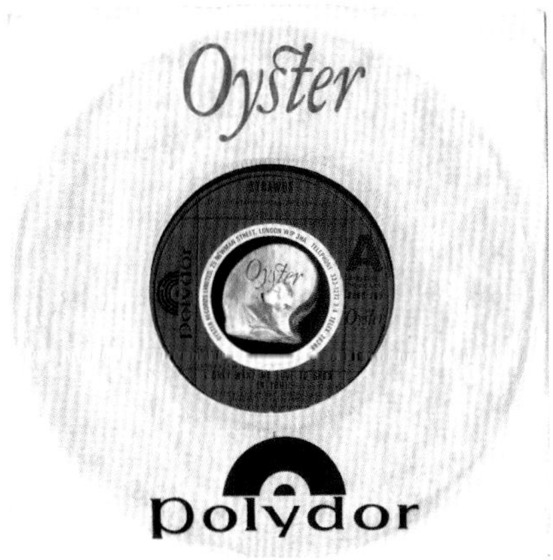

This is a promo copy of the first Strawbs release with its own Oyster bag and an Oyster sticker.

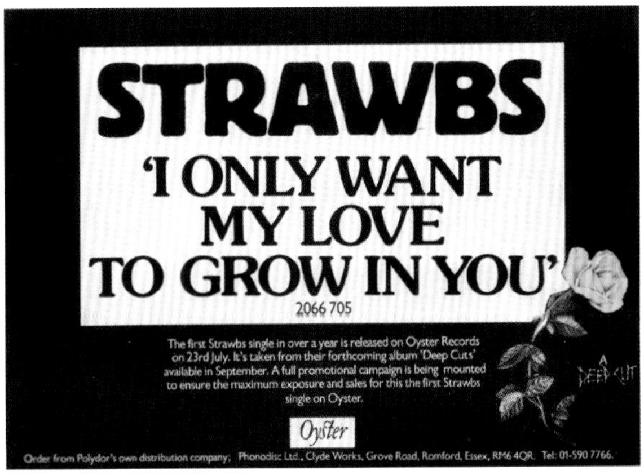

Albums

2490 136	July 1976	**Ian Gillan Band**: Child In Time
2490 137	21st May 1976	**Rainbow**: Rising
2490 141	1976	**Rainbow**: Ritchie Blackmore's Rainbow
2391 234	1976	**Strawbs**: Deep Cuts
2391 269	1977	**Paice Ashton Lord**: Malice In Wonderland
2391 287	July 1977	**Strawbs**: Burning For You
ACBR 261	1976	**Ian Gillan Band**: Child In Time (Club edition)
ACBR 262	1976	**Rainbow**: Rising (Club edition)
2657 016	July 1977	**Rainbow**: On Stage
2683 078	September 1978	**Rainbow**: Ritchie Blackmore's Rainbow / Rising
2482 485	1978	**Paice Ashton Lord:** Malice In Wonderland *special price edition*
2490 137	1978	**Rainbow**: Rising *special price edition*
SPELP 35	August 1983	**Rainbow**: Rising

The Club edition releases refer to the Audio Club of Britain (later known as Britannia Music Club) which was a mail-order music club in the UK in the 1970s. It was a membership club that once joining, you committed to purchasing a certain number of records per year. The enticement was being able to buy some extremely cheap records at the introduction to the club. These releases were supplied with Audio Club's own unique catalogue numbers always starting with ACB, which they then used to entice club membership.

With the rights having now gone to Polydor, the first album was re-issued not long after *Rising*. Like Rainbow's Live EP re-issue, the special price editions, the double re-issue of *Ritchie Blackmore's Rainbow* and *Rising* and the 1983 re-issue of *Rising* were all released after the label had ceased but still used the Oyster imprint. In fact, the double re-issue - although assigned a different catalogue number - actually just used stock of both standard Oyster versions of the albums.

The most obscure Oyster release and aside from Rainbow's EP, the only one to be released in a picture sleeve.

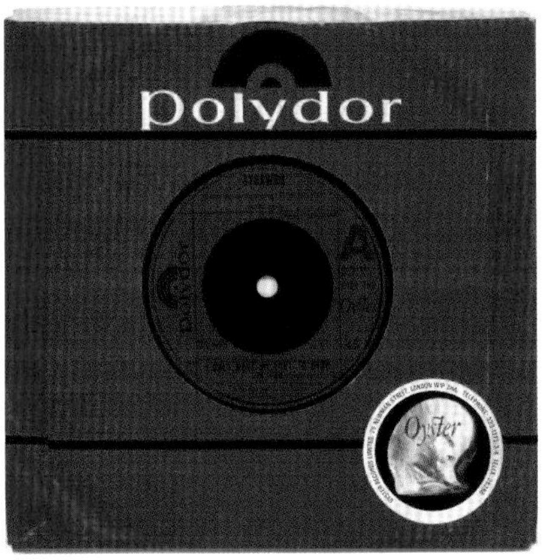

Another promo copy sent out from the Deep Purple offices in Newman Street, London, with the promo sticker, but with a standard Polydor bag.
All the UK releases also had these rather uninspiring injection moulded label designs, with Oyster far less prominent than Polydor.

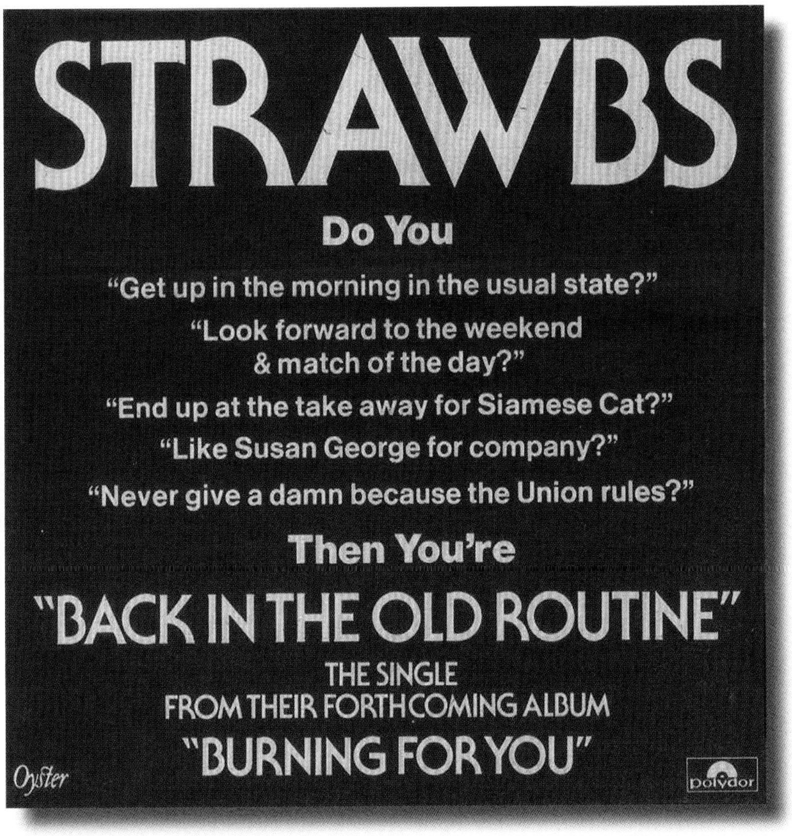

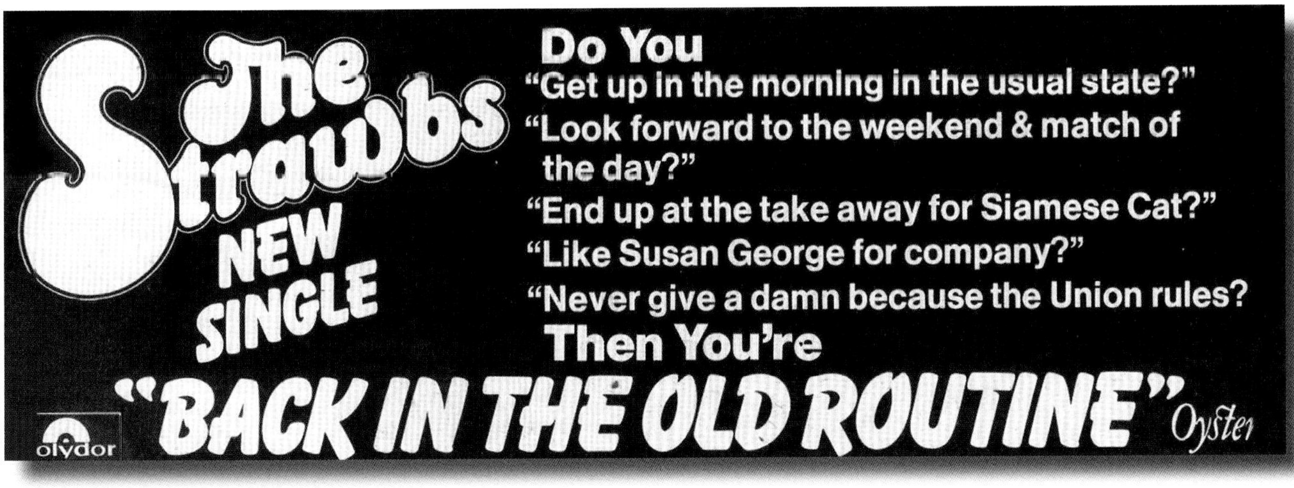

STRAWBS
BURNING FOR YOU
ALBUM · CASSETTE
Oyster
polydor

STRAWBS
Their New Album - Available Now!
polydor

Oyster Polydor releases by territory

This is the list of releases in the major territories, including those that contained unique releases.

USA Discography

Singles

OY 701	1976	**Blackmore's Rainbow**: Starstruck / Run With The Wolf
OY 702	1976	**Strawbs**: I Only Want My Love To Grow In You / (Wasting My Time) Thinking Of You
OY 703	1976	**Ian Gillan Band**: Down The Road / Lay Me Down
OY 704	16th August 1976	**Strawbs**: So Close And Yet So Far Away / A Soldier's Tale
OY 705	1976	**Strawbs**: Heartbreaker (Long Version) / Heartbreaker (Short Version) *promo only*
OY 705	1976	**Strawbs**: Heartbreaker / Burning For Me

Rainbow's only single released in America on Oyster, was also planned for UK release but never materialised. Here are three different versions. Major record companies in the States used several different pressing plants across the country and clearly each one laid out the label information in their own way.

Promo and commercial versions of the Ian Gillan Band's only Oyster US single release.

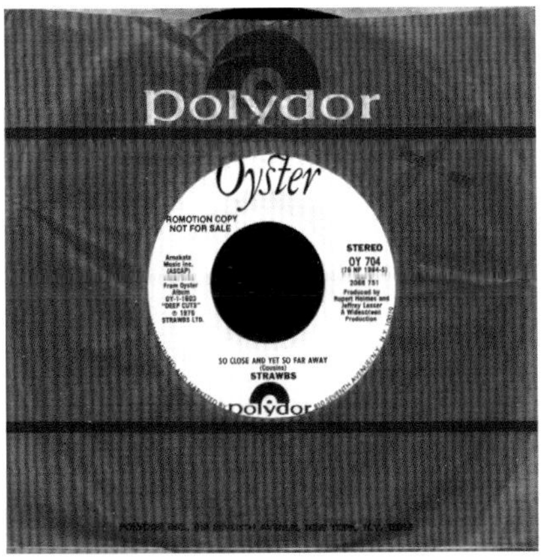

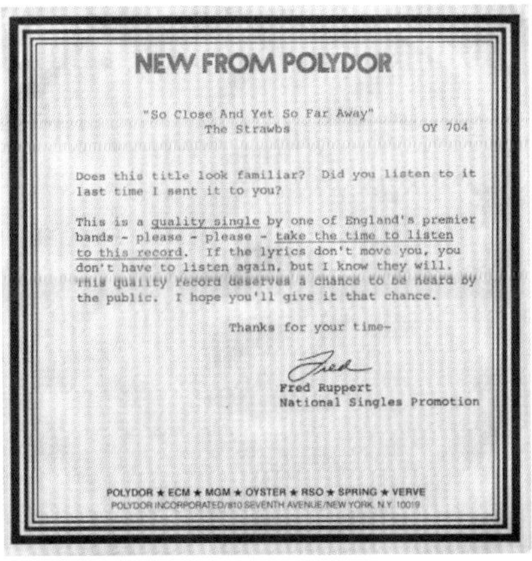

NEW FROM POLYDOR

"So Close And Yet So Far Away"
The Strawbs OY 704

Does this title look familiar? Did you listen to it last time I sent it to you?

This is a quality single by one of England's premier bands - please - please - take the time to listen to this record. If the lyrics don't move you, you don't have to listen again, but I know they will. This quality record deserves a chance to be heard by the public. I hope you'll give it that chance.

Thanks for your time-

Fred Ruppert
National Singles Promotion

POLYDOR ★ ECM ★ MGM ★ OYSTER ★ RSO ★ SPRING ★ VERVE
POLYDOR INCORPORATED/810 SEVENTH AVENUE/NEW YORK, N.Y. 10019

Another example of Polydor's randomness with the Oyster catalogue. Two promo copies of 'I Only Want My Love To Grow In You', one issued in an Oyster sleeve, the other in a Polydor sleeve with the release date stamped on it. This was also the last promo released in the States that was a mono / stereo coupling. This was the standard way of pressing up promos sent out to radio stations with some broadcasting in stereo on FM, others in mono on AM.

STRAWBS
DEEP CUTS
Their new album. Their unique sound. Watch for their extended tour!
A Widescreen Production
STRAWBS
OY-1-1603
8T-1-1603
CT-1-1603
Marketed by Polydor Incorporated, 810 Seventh Avenue, New York, N.Y. 10019
A Polygram Company, Distributed by Phonodisc, Inc.
Oyster
Where you raise your standard of listening.
Polydor

In the Strawbs' 10-year existence we have seen them change from bluegrass to progressive rock to chartbound contenders. We witnessed the band becoming a launching pad for such superstars as Rick Wakeman, Sandy Denny, Richard Hudson and John Ford. But the band has always remained the Strawbs, singular and unique.

The present and most successful Strawbs line-up is Dave Cousins on guitar and vocals, Dave Lambert on lead guitar, bassist Chas Cronk and drummer Rod Coombes. The Strawbs now also has two semi-permanent member keyboard men, Robert Kirby and John Mealing.

Strawbs' music has varied in accordance with its personnel, but it has always been under the guidance of the group's founder and creative force Dave Cousins. "Deep Cuts" is a slight change in direction as for the first time Dave Cousins and Chas Cronk are writing together. The result is a fresher and more light-hearted album.

"Deep Cuts is among the best of the Strawbs albums," says Cousins. "It's the most consistent, flowing all the way through. I'd say it's the greatest leap forward for the Strawbs, taking us out of FM and into AM. There are no songs to commit suicide by."

According to Cousins, "Deep Cuts" was completely written within a week. "The songs just kept pouring out. They've been building up for some time. At one point I wrote six in 24 hours."

But problems arose once the band started recording in January. "This album took the longest time ever for us to record," he reflects. "We were locked in the old Strawbs period. It was too much Strawbs revisited. We wanted something new."

With the help of Chas Cronk and producer/artist Rupert Holmes ("He's one of the most talented musicians I've come across. He told me if he ever played in a group it would be a group like the Strawbs"), a new Strawbs sound was created. After six months in the studio, "Deep Cuts" emerged as a memorable tenth [illegible] of the Strawbs' new era.

Cousins' enthusiasm for the new album shows as he gives deep quotes on some of the deep cuts.

I ONLY WANT MY LOVE TO GROW IN YOU: "Am yes, the single. We have high hopes for this one. It's about my current lady friend, the same one for which I wrote 'Grace Darling' and 'Lemon Pie' from the 'Ghosts' album."

TURN ME ROUND: "A religious epic inspired by watching John Denver performing 'The Eagle and the Hawk' at the Palladium. The last verse is perhaps the most vivid and graphic I've ever written. It's about creating a painting in a studio and that verse came just like a painting, in an outburst of passion. It just flashed on the paper like vivid visual colors."

HARD, HARD WINTER: "This one was written in Regina, Canada, which is probably the most boring place in the world. We were all feeling very quiet and depressed; it was the beginning of our last tour, the long, long American tour from which we all came back quite exhausted."

MY FRIEND PETER: "The tax situation in Britain is so incredibly bad. Peter, a friend of mine in West Country where I live, actually gone bankrupt, butchered by the taxmen. They can enter your house day or night without a warrant. The song is about the impossibility of the whole situation. I wanted to do it in a Thirties vamp style, but Rupert wanted it more modern. That's the way we did it."

THE SOLDIER'S TALE: "It deals with the retreat of Bonnie Prince Charles from the Battle of Culloden, which marked the defeat of the Scots at the hands of the British. They ceased to be a monarchy. The idea came about 18 months ago while I was in Scotland."

SIMPLE VISIONS: "A break up in my personal life. I was blind but now I see. The revelation that came when I put my head on the block. I don't want to get too specific about this one."

I'M WASTING MY TIME (THINKING OF YOU): "I was just about to wrap it up but Rupert suggested we add another verse at the end. We were sitting around in the studio drinking this awful wine. I added the last verse: 'Getting high drinking Algerian wine' which is very realistic. But the song is me reflecting on my lady friend, Lemon Pie."

BESIDE THE RIO GRANDE: "The first cowboy version of the [illegible], written in Albuquerque."

In store for the Strawbs is a U.S. tour starting in October '76, while Dave Cousins plans on seeing his book of poetry "Search Me" being published very shortly.

Ten years later and the Strawbs are better than ever.

STRAWBS

Oyster Polydor

Ten years have come and gone. Groups have splintered and dissolved, falling by the wayside to become footnotes in rock 'n' roll encyclopedias. Longevity by itself has proven to be an essential element in measuring a group's importance and popularity.

The magical music of the Strawbs has always held a special place in the hearts of many. Cult followings evolved into mass acceptance. This mass of fans will not let their band die. It is for this reason the Strawbs are the most established folk/rock band from Britain, cherished in all four corners of the globe.

STRAWBS DISCOGRAPHY

DEEP CUTS—1976
NOMADNESS—1975
GHOSTS—1975
HERO AND HEROINE—1974
BURSTING AT THE SEAMS—1973
TWO WEEKS LAST AUGUST—1972
GRAVE NEW WORLD—1972
FROM THE WITCHWOOD—1971
JUST A COLLECTION OF ANTIQUES AND CURIOS—1970
DRAGONFLY—1969 (released only in England)
STRAWBS—1968 (released only in England)
STRAWBS—1967 (released only in England)

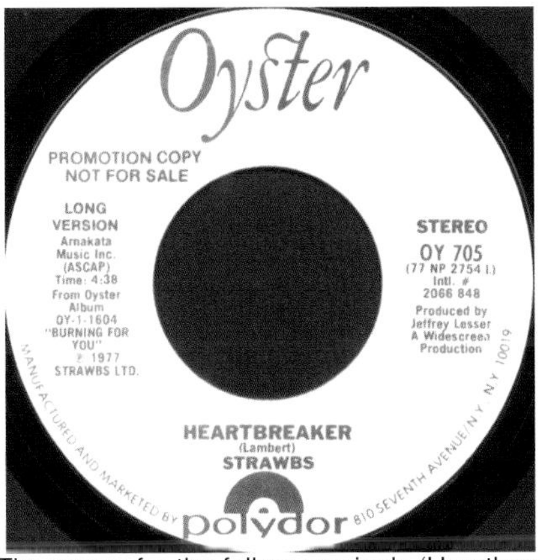

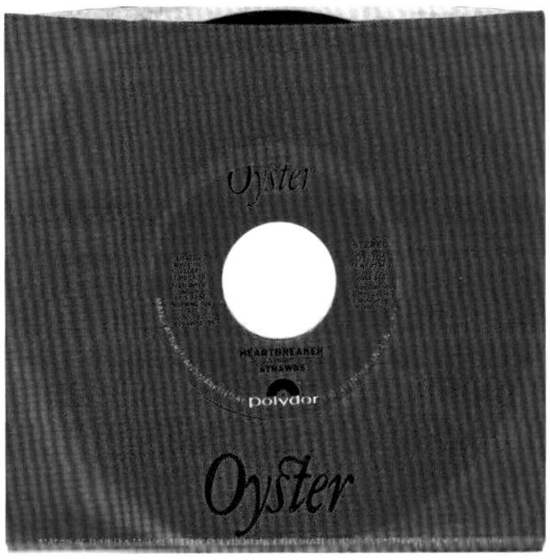

The promo for the follow up single 'Heartbreaker' contained full and edited versions of the track. The commercial release was the edited version, with 'Burning For Me' on the B-side.

Albums

OY-1-1601	May 1976	**Rainbow**: Rising
OY-1-1602	July 1976	**Ian Gillan Band**: Child In Time
OY-1-1603	October 1976	**Strawbs**: Deep Cuts
OY-1-1604	July 1977	**Strawbs**: Burning For You
OY-2-1801	July 1977	**Rainbow**: On Stage

Unlike the UK, Polydor in the States used a numbering system unique to the label.

Germany Discography

Singles

2066 705	1976	**Strawbs**: I Only Want My Love To Grow In You / (Wasting My Time) Thinking Of You
2066 709	1976	**Blackmore's Rainbow**: Starstruck / Run With The Wolf

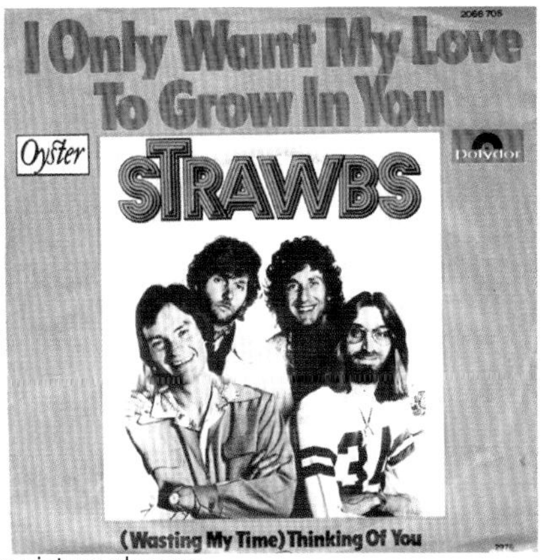

Both German single releases came in attractive picture sleeves.

Albums

2391 224	May 1976	**Rainbow**: Rising
2391 232	July 1976	**Ian Gillan Band**: Child In Time
2391 233	1976	]**Roy Buchanan:** ⊠A Street Called Straight
2391 234	October 1976	**Strawbs**: Deep Cuts
2391 272	May 1977	**David Coverdale**: Whitesnake
2417 313	1977	**Paice Ashton Lord**: Malice In Wonderland
2808 010	1977	**Rainbow**: On Stage (Special Edited Versions) *promo only*
2675 142	July 1977	**Rainbow**: On Stage

The Roy Buchanan release was on Polydor throughout Europe but in Germany some copies included the Oyster imprint. Coverdale's debut album was only released on Oyster in Germany and Japan. My research indicated that the seconds Strawbs album was not released in Germany although there was a version with German copyright text around the label which is thought to have been made for Norway.
The first Rainbow album was re-issued twice with different catalogue numbers but are on standard Polydor labels with no mention of Oyster. Likewise a six-track 33 1/3 7" promotional single featuring two Paice Ashton Lord tracks, alongside two each from Atlanta Rhythm Section and The Steve Gibbons Band was released by Polydor with no Oyster reference.

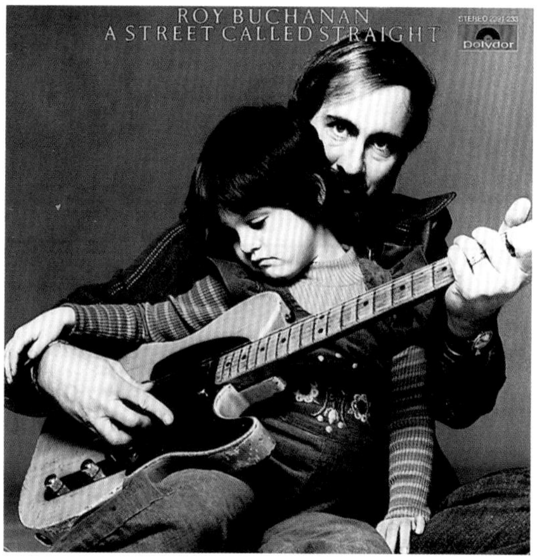

The American guitarist Roy Buchanan's album was released on Polydor throughout Europe. It's unclear as to why some German copies included the Oyster imprint. It could have simply been a pressing plant error.

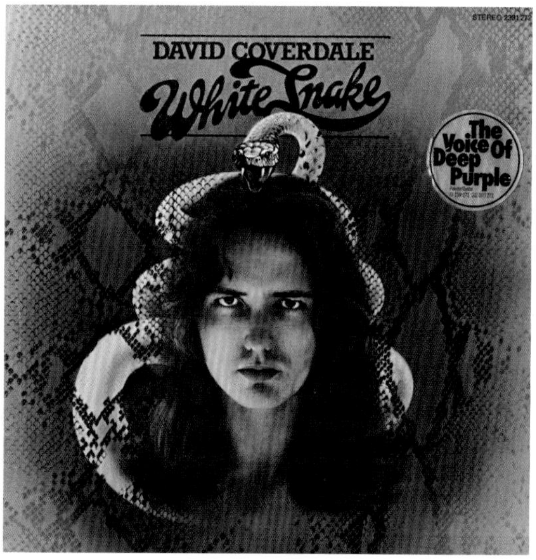

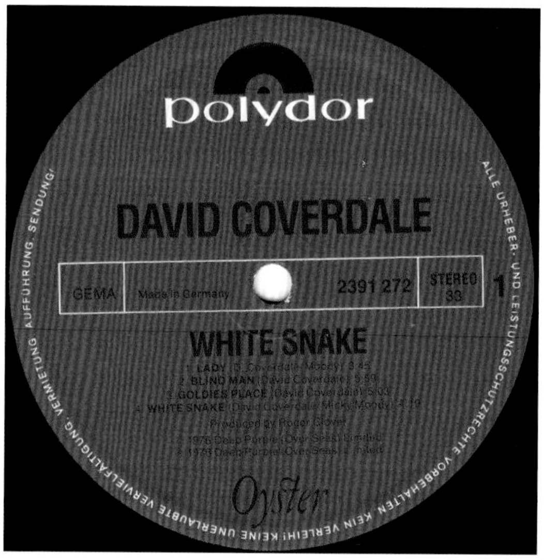

David Coverdale's debut solo album was released on Purple in the UK but elsewhere it appeared on a multitude of different labels. Somehow Oyster did a deal for it for Germany however.

France Discography

Singles

2066 679	1976	**Ian Gillan**: You Make Me Feel So Good / Shame
2066 705	November 1976	**Strawbs:** I Only Want My Love To Grow In You / (Wasting My Time) Thinking Of You

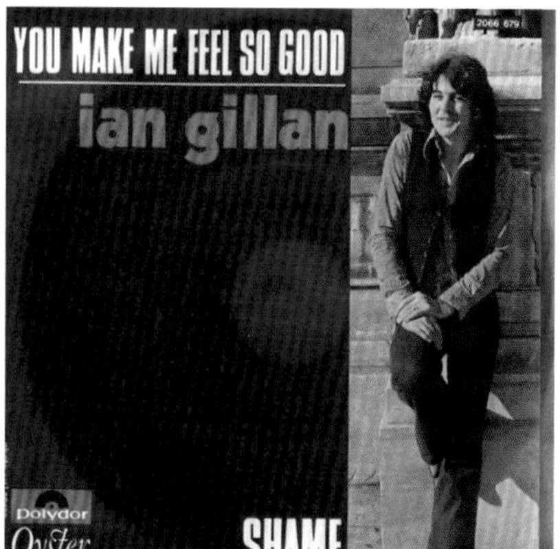

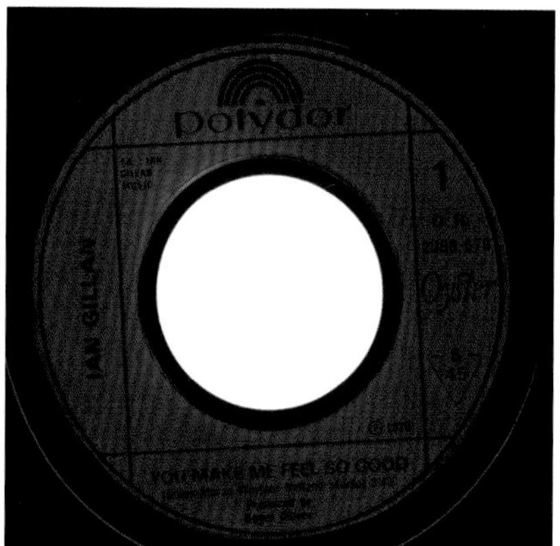

This single was only released in France and Spain and credits it to Ian Gillan solely.

Albums

2391 224	May 1976	**Rainbow**: Rising
2490 136	July 1976	**Ian Gillan Band**: Child In Time
2391 269	1977	**Paice Ashton Lord**: Malice In Wonderland
2391 287	July 1977	**Strawbs**: Burning For You
2675 142	July 1977	**Rainbow**: On Stage

Research suggests *Deep Cuts* was not released in France which seems particularly odd given that they released a single from the album. *Malice In Wonderland* was issued in a gatefold sleeve. Italy was the only other country to release it that way.

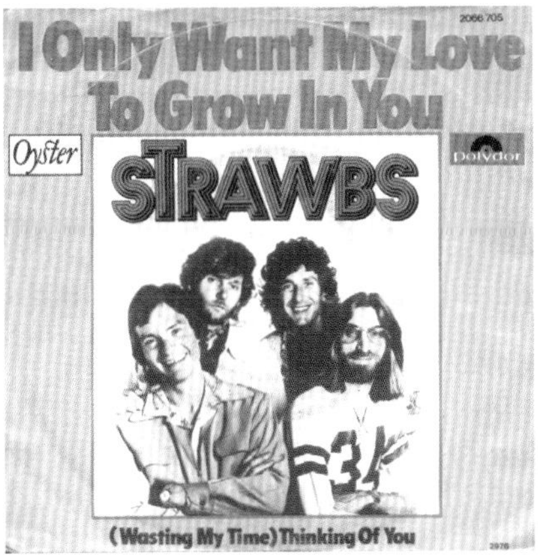

Elsewhere in Europe each country presented the releases differently. In Belgium they included the Oyster imprint on the sleeve but not on the label, whereas in the Netherlands, Oyster was as prominent as could be.

Japan Discography

Singles

FR-145	June 1976	**Rainbow**: Tarot Woman (promo only flexi disc included with *Rising* promo release))
DWQ 6010	September 1976	**Blackmore's Rainbow**: Starstruck / Run With The Wolf
DWQ 6016	November 1976	**Strawbs**: I Only Want My Love To Grow In You / (Wasting My Time) Thinking Of You
DWQ 6038	1977	**David Coverdale**: Whitesnake / Hole In The Sky

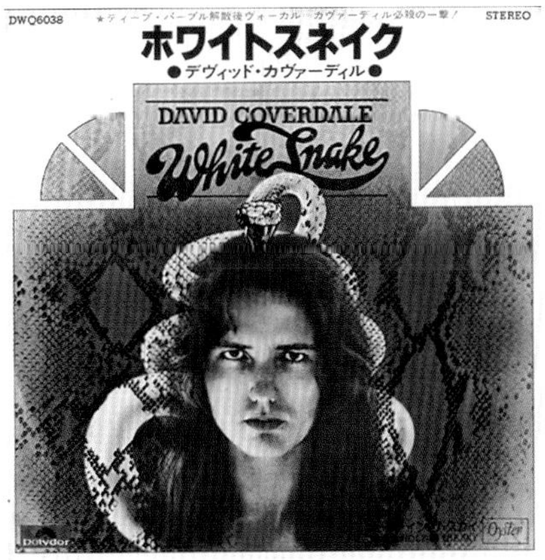

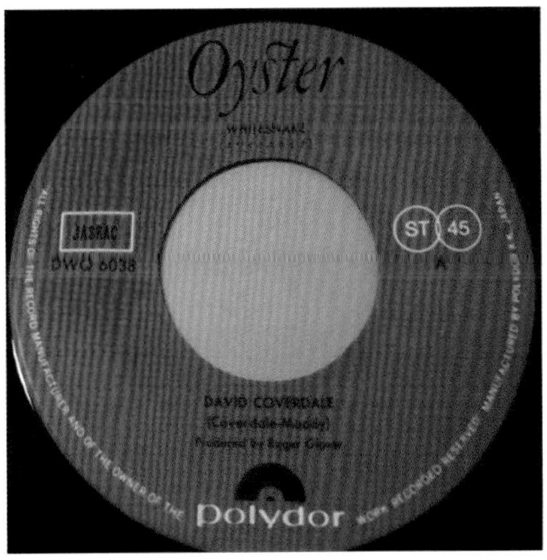

All three Japanese single releases came in unique sleeve designs. The Coverdale coupling was also released in France but not on Oyster.

Albums

MWF 1004	1976	**Rainbow**: Rising
MWF 1005	1976	**Ian Gillan Band**: Child In Time
MWF 1015	1976	**Strawbs**: Deep Cuts
MWF 1017	1976	**Jon Lord**: Sarabande
MWF 1027	1977	**David Coverdale**: Whitesnake
MWF 1034	1977	**Strawbs**: Burning For You
MWZ 8103/04	1977	**Rainbow**: On Stage
MPX 4024	1980	**Rainbow**: Rising
MPX 4025	1980	**Ian Gillan Band**: Child In Time

The first 50,000 of *Rising* came with a poster and a wider obi strip that explains the fact.
See the Rising section of the book for more information

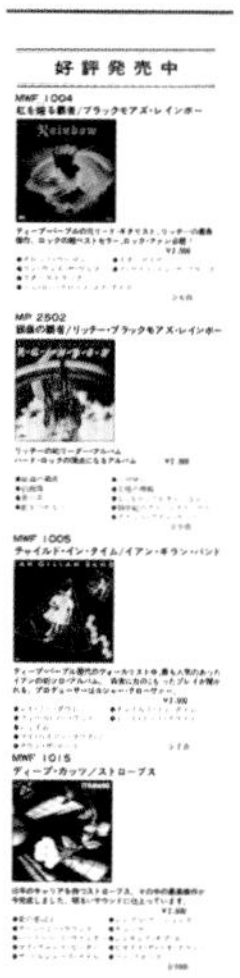

Jon Lord's *Sarabande* album was only released on Oyster in Japan. It was released on Purple in the UK and much of Europe and was not even released in America.

New Zealand Discography

Singles

2066 709	1976	**Blackmore's Rainbow**: Starstruck / Run With The Wolf
2066 705	1976	**Strawbs**: I Only Want My Love To Grow In You / (Wasting My Time) Thinking Of You
2066 818	1977	**Strawbs**: Back In The Old Routine / Burning For Me
POLY 98	1980	**Joe Dolce Music Theatre**: Shaddup You Face / Ain't In No Hurry

Just three singles released in New Zealand during the label's existence including 'Starstruck' but then Polydor randomly used the Oyster branding for Joe Dolce's 1980 release! More than likely in error, a version with the same catalogue number was also released with a standard Polydor label, but it remains a mystery to this day!

New Zealand singles came in Polygram bags that have a certain similarity with the Purple Records logo.

Long after the label had ceased to be, this bizarre release was put out

Albums

2391 224	1976	**Rainbow**: Rising
2391 232	1976	**Ian Gillan Band**: Child In Time
2391 234	1976	**Strawbs**: Deep Cuts
2391 269	1977	**Paice Ashton Lord**: Malice In Wonderland
2391 287	1977	**Strawbs**: Burning For You
2672 038	1977	**Rainbow**: On Stage

Two versions of *Rising* exist, one with no mention of Oyster but using the same catalogue number. This could possibly be a later re-issue but clearly New Zealand had a habit of pressing duplicate releases with different labels.

As this instore display mobile shows, with the move to Polydor, Oyster's roster increased to include several Purple spin-off acts, including Paice Ashton Lord but despite the investment the returns were not forthcoming.

Oyster Productions

EMI – EMS-80351 1975 Michael Des Barres, Silverhead – Live At The Rainbow London

Silverhead had previously released two studio albums on Purple Records. Despite being recorded in 1973, this Japan only release is credited as an Oyster production. It was recorded using the Manor Studios mobile at the band's show as support to Nazareth and produced by Roger Glover under the name R. David (his first initial and middle name).

Reflections

As part of the Oyster story, I thought I would mention Reflections. Very little has been documented about this band, which, from 1980 spawned Rainbow's backing vocalists, Dee Beale and Lin Robinson. The six releases listed below is – to the best of my knowledge – their complete output, over a four-year span. They were signed to Purple Records where they released their first two singles: The second one was produced by Roger Glover under his often-used name R. David. He also composed the b-side 'Little Star'. Glover's song could be construed as somewhat prophetic with the opening lyrics, "I've watched every rainbow fade away."

The following year, Reflections switched to the newly formed Oyster Records, although it had no effect on their fortunes. After Oyster was transferred to Polydor, the band switched to EMI but the first release was credited as an Oyster Records Production produced by Purple Records.

The last two singles had no Oyster/Purple credits but the b-side of the last release, 'Midnight Lady' was co-written by Lin Robinson and fellow band member Kemp. Because of the Oyster and Rainbow connections, I have decided to include the full Reflections discography here as a final wrap up of all things connected to Oyster Records.

Reflections, UK Singles Discography

Purple, PUR 124	1st November 1974	Love And Affection / No More
Purple, PUR 127	16th May 1975	Moon Power / Little Star
Oyster, OYR 105	20th February 1976	88Whenever I'm Away From You / I Can Only Love You
EMI, EMI 2476	18th June 1976	I'll Always Be In Love With You / Too Good To Be Forgotten
EMI, EMI 2733	6th Jan 1978	Something Good's Gonna Happen / Do It To Me
EMI, EMI 2778	14th Apr 1978	Rockin' Good Way (To Mess Around And Fall In Love) / Midnight Lady